SIZE MATTERS NOT

WARWICK DAVIS
(The Author)

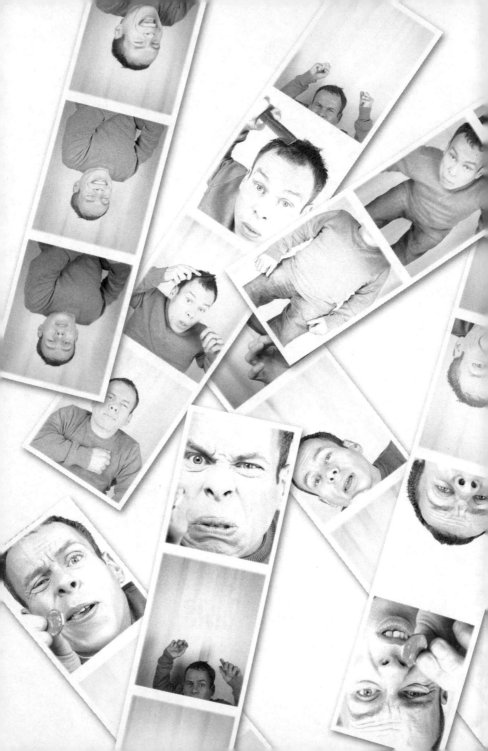

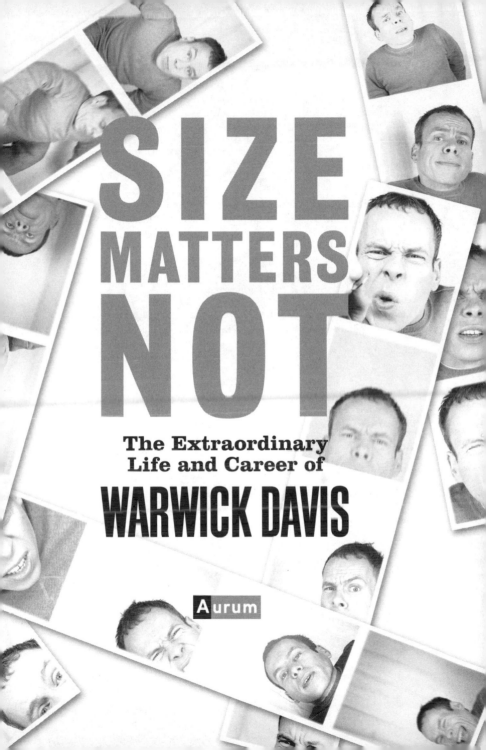

CONTENTS

DEDICATION

Mum and Dad – You gave me life

Nana Davis – You started it all

George Lucas – For all the opportunities

Sammy, Annabelle, Harrison, Lloyd and Baby George –
You make me feel 10ft tall

Love and magic … always x

FOREWORD

He was just a little guy when I first met him nearly three decades ago. But even at the age of eleven, and standing just two feet eleven inches tall, I could tell at our first meeting that Warwick Davis was not only agile, but full of life and spunk. Something about him cried out that he was a very special person, and in the years since as I've gotten to know Warwick as an actor and as a human being, I'm happy that my first instinct was correct.

It was his grandmother who heard that the *Star Wars* folks were holding auditions for people under four feet tall for *Return of the Jedi* — but it was Warwick who had the gumption and self-confidence to think that he could get a part. When I saw him in his tiny Ewok costume, and got to know him better, I started giving him more and more things to do. What struck me was how energetic he was, how enthusiastic — and very, very intelligent. When he got those extra pieces of business in the film, he did them really well, made them his own, and they looked great on camera. He may have started out as an extra, but he turned into a much more central character, Wicket W. Warrick, Ewok hero. He repeated that role in two made-for-television movies.

When Ron Howard and I decided to do *Willow*, it was really the experience of working with Warwick that gave me the confidence that we could do a film with not just a few dozen little people, but with a few hundred. I told Ron that Warwick was a very talented actor and could actually play the lead in a movie. After Ron talked to him and did a few screen tests, he agreed. Warwick worked very hard and turned in a great performance. He was all of seventeen.

I've done a number of movies with little people and have gotten to know some of them quite well. I've been asked why I've used little people as heroes. Perhaps part of it, deep down, is the fact that throughout high school I was always the shortest one in the class, so perhaps I instinctively took on the fantasy life of a little person who overcomes all obstacles. And part of it is my real-world desire to point the spotlight on the struggles of society's downtrodden, whether they be 'different' physically, mentally, ethnically or even financially.

Warwick has already led an extraordinary life: actor, director, businessman and devoted husband and father. He has undergone tremendous physical and other challenges and has become an even stronger force of nature by overcoming them. As I've gotten to know Warwick over the years, there has been one defining quality that has always shone through: he's a really good person. He's smart, sensitive and thoughtful. He's very talented, as his long list of notable movie and television credits will attest. He's also fun to be around. And Warwick has gone – and continues to go – in many different and interesting directions, all of which have helped him accomplish a great number of goals. This book recounts just the first forty years of what I'm sure is going to continue to be an amazing life. In my book, for all that he has done and for his innate decency and integrity, he's a true hero.

George Lucas, Skywalker Ranch 2009

Prologue

Expecting Someone Taller

3 February 1970

My dad had been sitting with no little anxiety in the expectant fathers' waiting room when he saw the doctor marching down the long corridor towards him. The doctor stopped at the doorway and studied my father for a moment or two.

'Mr Davis,' he said seriously, 'would you please stand up?'

My father rose unsteadily.

'Hmmm,' the doctor continued in a thoughtful and slightly puzzled tone, a tone that suggested all was not as it should be. He frowned and looked my father up and down. 'Walk to the door and back.'

'Excuse me?' Dad was understandably perplexed. He had been expecting the doctor to enter the room and say something along the lines of: 'Congratulations, you're the father of a healthy boy/girl,' and he would in return hand the doctor a cigar.

But in those days every single doctor was male and studied at the Gene Hunt Macho-Man School of Medicine, where any leanings towards sensitivity, consideration and empathy guaranteed you a Fail and a foot in the backside.

This was 1970, the year of cheesecloth and satin, when men were men and wore sideburns, perms, Brut and gold medallions and did not, under any circumstances – unless they were wearing a white coat – witness childbirth.

'Walk to the door and back,' the doctor repeated impatiently, as if this was expected of all new fathers.

My dad did as he was told.

'You're not unusually short, are you?' the doctor asked.

'Er . . .'

The doctor turned and started to leave the room.

'Excuse me!' my dad called after him. The doctor froze, leaning on the half-open door.

'Is it a boy or a girl?'

The doctor looked back at him for a moment and tilted his head as if deep in thought. 'I've forgotten.' The door swung closed behind him.

At that moment the dinner trolley rattled past. Dad saw a healthy king-sized cockroach crawling happily out from under one of the plastic plates and swore that no child of his would ever be born in that hospital again.

It was touch and go for a while. The doctors didn't know I was going to be born little and I had far too much anaesthetic in my system (Mum had a Caesarean). Although I won this first round I was soon battling against pneumonia and was rushed by ambulance to Queen Mary's specialist children's hospital, my anxious parents following right behind.

'Don't worry,' the doctors told my parents once they'd arrived, 'we gave him the last rites in the ambulance.'

Yes, they really knew how to break bad news in those days.

Despite their gloomy predictions, and despite having to spend the first two months of my life in hospital, I fought my way into the world. Eventually the doctors sat down with my mum and dad. This time they had a little bit more to say.

'Your son will be wheelchair-bound and dead by his teens, if he survives these first few months.'

This, as it turned out, was completely, utterly and entirely incorrect.

Chapter One

E Eetee, Eetee Chiutatal Bok Ootu Ootu Chuu-ock[1]

'Mum, who's George Lucas?'

Practising my 'come hither' look.

Ready for Little Chint Primary.

A mini-motortrike would soon follow.

Sports day: Thanks to my waddle, the egg-and-spoon race became the 'pick-up-the-egg-and-spoon' race.

Me, Mum and my younger sister, Kim.

Me, Kim and Dad.

Just your average family — although I'm first to admit that the dog rodeo was a touch unusual.

Was I really that small or is that just tall grass?

'What would be the dream thing you'd most like to do?' Mum asked. I considered carefully. 'Think about it, Warwick, anything you want. The *most* fantastic thing you could *possibly* imagine.'

I was eleven years old and Mum was picking me up from school. Suddenly I had it. Of course! It was obvious. 'Drive a go-kart!' I exclaimed.

Mum looked at me in the rear-view mirror. 'Come on, Warwick, what do you love more than anything else?' Hmm . . . tricky. What could possibly be better than driving a go-kart?

I'd come a long way since Mum and Dad had brought me home from hospital. I'd grown from strength to strength – although not in height. But what I lacked in inches I made up for in explosive energy. I was a handful, albeit a small one.

While my size has of course played a huge part in my life,[2] it has never been an excuse. Indeed it came to be one of my greatest assets (alongside my charm, wit and intellect, of course).

My size, however, had given my parents plenty to worry about for the first few years of my life, medically speaking at least. When I was a baby, my head was out of proportion to the rest of my body, and for a time the doctors were concerned that it might

---

[1] Ewokese for 'A Long Time Ago in a Village Far, Far Away', although the literal translation is: 'A While Ago in a Tree Hut Across the Valley'.

[2] Brace yourselves: this book is pun-heavy, most of them unintentional.

become too heavy for my neck, but thankfully my body gradually caught up.

My legs proved to be more problematic. I'd been born with talipes (club foot) which meant both my feet were turned inwards and I stood on my ankles as I walked.

I had to wear splints every night to try to straighten them, but this had limited succes so I went for a major operation to correct this when I was two years old. The surgeons cut the back of my legs from my ankle to my knee, undid all the tendons in my legs like the shoelaces in a knee-length boot, then re-tied them again so I could put my feet flat on the ground.

While I was in hospital, I was photographed several times – the doctors said they'd never seen anything like me before. I hated it; it made me feel like an exhibit in a freak show. My parents didn't like it either but they felt they had to go along with the men in white coats and imagined this would help the doctors advance their knowledge. Granddad, 'Poppa', tried to comfort me by calling me his 'little champ'.

Although I came home with plasters on both my legs and walked like a stick man for six weeks, I refused to let them hold me back. I climbed everywhere I possibly could and took particular delight in giving my parents palpitations by balancing on chairs and tables.

It was while I was in hospital that the doctors told Mum and Dad that I had achondroplasia, the most common genetic cause of dwarfism.[3] To some extent, it was reassuring for them to know what it was that had made me small. My parents found this time

---

[3] As it turned out, the doctors were wrong yet again and it would be many years before I would discover that I had a far more unusual and complex one-in-a-million condition (lucky me).

in my childhood especially difficult but they resolved that they would make sure I lived just like any other child would. The only concessions to my short stature at home were a lowered light switch in my bedroom and my very own sink.

My dad was an insurance man who worked at Lloyd's in the City of London, following in the footsteps of his father. He was proud of what he did but felt the pressure of the City and the long commute from our home in Tadworth, Surrey. Although it was all he knew, he had secret fantasies of becoming a lumberjack. His chance came when the insurance market went haywire in the long recession of the late 1970s. He bought the finest chainsaw available, a chequered shirt, marched out to the woods and started cutting down trees. After a while, people started to pay him.

My father has a wicked sense of humour; I think this may have influenced some of his many successful money-making schemes, one of which involved selling land to the Americans. He bought a small field and sold it off by the square foot so that Americans could own a piece of England (he'd post them the certificate of ownership as proof).

His scheme has since been repeated, with some people even selling portions of the Moon. I don't know quite how that's possible but anyone who bought a square foot of land from my father actually still owns that piece of land.

Our household was firmly conservative. No elbows were allowed on the dining table, where we always ate dinner, and we had to finish whatever was put on our plates. Kim, my stubborn sister, once spent four hours shepherding a dozen or so peas around her plate after discussions about the edibility of peas got totally out of control.

There was only one exception to this rule and it applied to my father. We had an in-and-out gravel drive, of which he was extremely proud. We lived in Lovelands Lane, a cul-de-sac, and it was one of those roads that appeared – to time-short drivers anyway – as if it might possibly be a shortcut to a nearby A-road.

Every so often a car would zip up our little cul-de-sac, discover they were driving towards a dead end, realise that my father's through-drive would save them from the inconvenience of stopping to make a three-point turn, and so drive straight through and round, spinning their wheels and scattering Dad's precious gravel before zooming off back towards the main road, usually even faster in an effort to make up for lost time.

Invariably, this would happen at suppertime. It had an extraordinary effect on my father. He would sit bolt upright in his chair, as if zapped by a cattle prod. He'd then throw down his cutlery and napkin and leap up, knocking his chair over. By the time it hit the ground he was outside, sprinting towards his Jaguar, leaping over the bonnet in a single jump before diving in on the driver's side. The ignition was instantly followed by the engine's roar as the Jag flew out of the drive (throwing yet more gravel towards the house). Seconds later Dad would be grinding through the gears, screaming down Lovelands Lane in hot pursuit of the trespasser.

Mum would sigh stoically. Kim would smile (she'd no longer have to eat all her peas). I, on the other hand, would mutter 'kaggernash!', a swear word of my own invention, created so I could 'curse' within earshot of my parents. I used it on this occasion because it was my job to sweep the gravel back to perfection. Fortunately, I had come up with a cunning plan that made the job easier, even a little fun. I owned a Honda ATC 70. I tied a garden rake to the back of the tiny motorbike and drove up and down until the gravel was as smooth as a Japanese garden.

Hours after the dinner plates had been cleared away, my father would return, driving sedately and smiling strangely. He never spoke about the outcome of his pursuit. We didn't know whether he had caught up with the trespassing driver, or what had transpired between them if he had.

I half-expected the police to roll up one day (hopefully they wouldn't skid to a halt in the drive) and arrest Dad on suspicion of mass murder, finally linking him to all the shallow graves and burned-out frames of Cortinas, Capris, Escorts and Fiestas that littered the countryside surrounding the pleasant village of Lower Kingswood, Surrey.

Mum, meanwhile, was mainly kept busy with Kim, my average-sized, younger sister and me, although she also worked as a secretary and personal assistant. I was a real handful, a tightly wound ball of rubberised energy that bounced around the house and garden at giddying speeds. If I wasn't swinging from lampshades (at two-foot-six I was the perfect height to play Cheetah, Tarzan's monkey, and relished the role a little too much), I was charging my bike through stacks of cardboard boxes, copying *The Dukes of Hazzard*.

My parents were wonderful and devoted lots of time to Kim and me but, of course, this didn't mean they were perfect. My earliest memories tend to be of a traumatic nature. One of the very first is of my mother and father walking with me in the countryside, each of them holding one of my hands as they swung me back and forth, much to my screaming delight.

For reasons that to this day remain unclear, Mum and Dad both decided to let me go when I was at the zenith of one such arc. I sailed like a tiny screaming football into a forest of stinging nettles. To me this forest was just like the kind you find in *Lord of the Rings*,[4] full of giant walking trees and plants that entwined themselves

---

[4] No, I wasn't in *Lord of the Rings*, I'm too short for a Hobbit.

about one's limbs. I fought my way out of the undergrowth (overgrowth in my case), a furious screaming red mass of mump-like blisters. Mum was mortified while Dad maintained an 'It'll toughen him up' approach to parenting.

My very earliest memory was no less traumatic. I was crawling around the lounge floor when I found a pin and decided what better way to treat such a find than as food, and swallowed it. It pierced my tonsil. I screamed the house down and twenty minutes later, after a brief stop in the operating theatre, a surgeon waved the pin under my mortified parents' noses and told them, 'He could have died from this, you know.'

My parents really wanted to send me to a 'normal' (as opposed to a 'special') school. In the mid-70s, being little was seen as psychiatric as well as physical.

All too often, little people were put up for adoption by parents who'd had the bejeezus scared out of them by ill-informed doctors with little scientific and absolutely no social knowledge. Invariably, these children struggled to find a home.

As the time neared for me to start school, Mum and Dad visited the headmaster of Little Chinthurst, an excellent local primary. They were really worried that he might view me as being 'disabled', or that I was simply too small to fit in.

Dad was so concerned that even though he was wearing a suit when he got back from work for the interview, he changed into a fresh one. He really wanted to give the best possible impression. My parents didn't mention I was smaller than average until right at the end of the interview.

'Oh, really?' the headmaster asked, 'that's interesting because we've just had another little chap leave.'

Mum and Dad were pleasantly gobsmacked. Sure enough, one of the coat hooks in the cloakroom was lower than all the others.

Of course, at school I was indeed entirely 'normal', just a tad smaller than my classmates. Although kids can be cruel, none of them ever saw me as being particularly different, although there was one unusual exception: Pedro, a Puerto Rican boy who had a bad case of lollypopguildophobia.[5] The first time he caught sight of me his eyes saucered. He yelled, '*Extraterrestre!*' and ran screaming straight out of the school gate. Poor Pedro was so traumatised at the prospect of seeing me on a daily basis that he was forced to abandon the school.

I never thought about the fact that once they were five years old my classmates were already taller than I would ever be. There was no eureka moment; nobody sat me down and told me I wasn't going to grow up to be my father's height. I didn't know what it was to be tall and was used to being small, so I just felt, well – normal. I was unusual in that I had an enormous amount of energy with a personality to boot. When I realised that I was getting left behind height wise, I simply turned up the volume.

Having said this, we had a weekly woodwork lesson where we were supposed to choose something we would make for our end of term project. While most of my classmates made toy boats, boxes and stools I decided that it would be appropriate to hack together a pair of stilts.

I had absolutely no desire to use them or to be taller at this stage and, as unbelievable as this might sound, I did not realise for one second what the connection was. Throughout my early life I suffered from the rather naive trait of missing the blindingly obvious.

---

[5] An irrational fear of little people. Lollypopguildophobia would also send people with hippopotomonstrosesquippedaliophobia (fear of long words) into convulsions.

In this case, I just thought a pair of stilts would be easy to make. Boy, was I wrong. The hammer and chisel did not sit easily in my hands and the results were . . . curious. For some reason, we were supposed to show our finished pieces to the headmaster. His study was just like Dumbledore's: there was the leather sofa, the softly ticking clocks, the shelves lined with leather-bound books. He looked at me and frowned.

Before him were two wonky sticks of unequal length. In fact, if the brief had been to make two pieces of wood look as unlike stilts as possible, then I would have won first prize.

'And, er . . . what have you made, Warwick?'

'Stilts, sir.'

'I see, ahem, yes, stilts,' and then he had a sudden choking fit and quickly ushered me out of the room.

The headmaster was a decent enough guy who obviously loved his job. He once summoned my class to his study in groups of three or four at a time. Rather conspiratorially, he beckoned us inside. 'Look at what I've got here,' he said, and pointed at an oversize calculator on his desk. 'The ZX 81. This is the *future*.' He raised his eyebrows significantly. Whatever he was trying to communicate went straight over my head. 'And I've got the RAM pack,' he added grandly. I blinked blankly back at him.

Little Chint, as the junior section of school was known, was packed full of bizarre teachers. The science teacher had suffered from polio as a child and wasn't much taller than me. She walked up and down the classroom as she lectured us; her limp was so large that she would disappear and reappear behind the laboratory benches as she went.

The headmaster had an obsession with Cliff Richard. In assembly he'd play us modern religious sermons recorded by the Peter Pan of Pop, none of which ever seemed to make any sense.

Mr Miller, the Latin teacher, was known as 'Windy Miller' for reasons too obvious to go into here and was ironically cursed with an enormous nose, while Mr Scully (a.k.a. 'Yellowbeard') liked to nip out every five minutes for a cigarette. He'd hide behind the school wall but we could tell when he was on his way back to the classroom because the cloud of smoke that always accompanied him started to move. Then there was the teacher, whose name escapes me, who would whirl around and throw a piece of chalk at anyone who was mucking about while his back was turned. We thought he had psychic abilities but in reality he could see us all in the reflection of his glasses as he wrote on the board (he let us into his secret on our last day).

Sports day proved to be difficult. I sway a bit when I walk and so the egg-and-spoon race turned into a pick-up-the-egg-and-spoon race and when the teacher shouted 'GO!' at the start of the sack race, I pulled up the sack and disappeared inside. As for the obstacle course (essentially a couple of upside-down benches and a few hoops), well, I might as well have been trying to get into the SAS.

Unusually, I loved school dinners. They did a great mashed potato, a wonderful meat pie and fantastic rice pudding with jam. The only thing I couldn't handle was cabbage. The problem was, we were supposed to eat everything on our plates before we could leave. To get round this, I'd pop the cabbage in my pocket and then spend a few minutes out in the playground surreptitiously scattering cabbage pieces in the style of *The Great Escape* tunnellers getting rid of the soil they'd dug out.

The only incident of bullying I ever suffered was pretty mild, as it goes. As my classmates began to overtake me height-wise, there came a time where two of my best friends, Paul and Richard, started to use my height for their own amusement. They managed to lock me in a classroom simply by closing the door behind them, knowing that I wasn't able to reach the handle to open it.

I returned home in a miserable mood. Dad asked me what was wrong and I explained. He just nodded and didn't say too much at the time. Behind the scenes, however, he came up with a cunning plan.

As they were my 'best friends', Dad had Paul and Richard's phone numbers and so he called their homes and asked to speak to them personally.

'Warwick's been telling me that he's been having a bit of trouble at school and that two of the kids locked him in the classroom today,' he told them. 'He doesn't want to tell me who did this, however. As you're his best friend I'm asking you to keep an eye out for him and to let me know the next time this happens, so I know exactly who's behind it.'

I never had another day's trouble from Richard or Paul and normal relations were resumed.

My routine at the end of each school day was to get changed out of my uniform, hang it up (I was also an obsessive-compulsive child), make a cup of tea and then switch on the TV to catch my favourite shows.

I never missed an episode of *Scooby Doo*, broadcast once a week at 4.30 p.m. Back then, if you missed it, you missed it. There were no video recorders (except for some extremely expensive top-loaders with huge buttons and dials), no Sky Plus, just three channels to choose from and that was it.

Then there was *Take Hart* with Tony Hart. (My mum's claim to fame was that she once acted in a famous road safety advert for Brittax with Tony. She put on her seatbelt while Tony did the talking.) Another favourite was *Rentaghost*, a long-running children's TV series about a bunch of ghosts trying to set up their own business. This would later become a major source of inspiration for my own filmmaking.

Once the news came on at 5.40 p.m., I switched over to BBC2 for the *Laurel and Hardy* re-runs. These were a huge influence on my own physical comedy. They are simply timeless and now my own kids have got into them; their favourite episode is 'Brats', made in 1930, where Stan and Oliver look after themselves as kids. This relied upon some quite sophisticated special effects work and an awful amount of physical pain, something I would come to experience myself, also in the name of comedy.

When he was home Dad's word was final on what we watched and that meant sport or *Last of the Summer Wine*. He enjoyed wrestling, which was broadcast live on ITV on Saturday afternoons. It was beamed from some dodgy town hall from locations across the UK I'd never heard of before. It was nothing like the slick American shows you see today. The blokes were as fat as Sumo wrestlers and were covered in hair, prison tattoos and Brylcreem. The air was blue with fag smoke exhaled by a flat-cap-wearing audience.

The fact that these hugely fat men would beat each other up straight after Saturday kids' TV never seemed to trouble anyone. I can remember the big bout of the time would be between Big Daddy (good guy) with a record-breaking 64-inch chest and the amazing 48-stone Giant Haystacks (bad guy) – he looked like a man who had been bottle-fed scrumpy since birth. As far as I could tell, it pretty much came down to two blokes charging at each other using their bellies as battering rams.

Dad also enjoyed snooker and the Derby, but what took precedence over all else was Wimbledon. Then, this being such a special occasion, the television would be connected to an extension, taken outside and we would watch it in the garden. Dad also did this for the Grand Prix, which was the only time the TV was allowed on during lunch or dinner, when it would be turned round to face the table so my dad could see it while he ate.

As blindingly obvious as it may seem my first film memory really was of *Star Wars*, which came out when I was seven years old. The excitement it caused reached insane levels. The local cinema was literally surrounded by a queue.

Just as my friend and I finally completed the circuit and stepped up to the ticket booth, as if on cue they did that classic thing of flipping the sign round in our faces – CINEMA FULL. Then a man emerged and, with an air of great importance, strung the magical velvet rope between two short steel poles, thereby preventing entry into the building. Being British, we would never dare to challenge the authority of the velvet rope, but we weren't afraid of a queue either and so we stayed put until the next showing. We were the first in and therefore able to choose the best seats.

We left the cinema in a daze and, after I got home, I spoke to my mum at about a hundred miles an hour trying to explain the plot as she applied her make-up, ready to go out. From that day on, my friends and I talked about *Star Wars* constantly.

It should therefore have been at the forefront of my mind when my mum repeated her question. 'Come on, Warwick,' Mum said earnestly, 'what do you love more than anything else?' There was nothing I liked more than the idea of driving a go-kart, so I shrugged my shoulders. Mum sighed, then smiled brightly. 'How would you like to be in *Star Wars*?'

Chapter Two
An Ewok is Born

Nana Davis (who got me my big break), me and Mum
on the day of the *Return of the Jedi* cast screening.
Behind us Dad is holding up my Darth Vader action
figure carrying case, given to me by Mark Hamill.

On my way to Elstree to film *Return of the Jedi*.

Mrs. Susan Davis,
Robyns Cottage,
Lovelands Lane,
Lower Kingswood,
Surrey.

March 2nd 1982

Dear Mrs. Davis,

Please find enclosed Warwick's Contract for the
location shooting. This will only be valid if
we obtain the necessary permits for the boys to
work in the U.S.A.

Please would you sign the Contract, and return
the copy to us, keeping the original for
yourself. Thank you.

Yours sincerely,

DOUGLAS TWIDDY,
Production Supervisor.

P.S. To confirm our telephone conversation, please could you
let me have:
1) A letter from both you and your husband, and signed by
you both, permitting me to apply for the licence for
Warwick to work abroad.
2) A letter from Warwick's Headmaster agreeing to Warwick's
going away, and listing his grades.
3) A Doctor's Certificate certifying that Warwick is fit to
travel.

Thank you.

CHAPTER III PRODUCTIONS LIMITED

DIRECTORS: ROBERT GREBER (U.S.A.), HOWARD KAZANJIAN (U.S.A.), R.M.F. FLETCHER, MALCOLM FARRER-BROWN, ROBERT WATTS
REGISTERED OFFICE: 6, BROAD STREET PLACE, LONDON, EC2M 7JT REGISTERED IN ENGLAND, NO 1379915

My sister and I making friends with Mark Hamil (aka Luke Skywalker).

Another toy for the *Star Wars* collection — except this one was based on me!

The dads with two Ewok sons, me and Nicky Read.
Courtesy of Lucasfilm Ltd.

A 'heads-off' moment. Note the costumes hanging behind me. After a few weeks of filming they had a unique aroma.

David Tomblin directs me in *Return of the Ewok* as Nicky Read looks on.
Courtesy of Lucasfilm Ltd.

It was all thanks to my Nan.

Nan could easily have been the inspiration for Professor Minerva McGonagall. My parents were very social; they were always going to Saturday evening dinner parties or some kind of dinner and dance, which meant that my sister and I were placed in the loving care of Nana Davis.

She lived in a huge and ancient magical mansion in the small Surrey town of Banstead. The windows were latticed with lead, and beams hundreds of years old crossed the ceilings. The fireplace roared while the wind howled down the chimney and we'd sit in what was probably the cosiest lounge in England, eating Nan's salad sandwiches (once you added lots of salad cream they were fine) and watching TV game-shows all night long: *Play Your Cards Right*, *Game For a Laugh*, *Family Fortunes*, the *Generation Game* and so on. Every now and again we played board games or cards.

Nan was totally obsessed with the weather and she passed this obsession on to me. There always seemed to be something weird happening at her house. No sooner were we through the door than she'd be telling me in a suitably atmospheric voice as she waggled her fingers descriptively, 'Just had some ball lightning here the other day, I was on the stairs just here and right outside the lead window there was a huge, dancing ball of light.'

For some reason there were always really, really bad storms at Nan's house, it was as if she were Thora, the Goddess of Thunder and Lightning.

To make things even more interesting, her house was also full of ghosts and ghouls. Not the *Rentaghost* kind but proper horrors – the beheaded, drowned and buried alive sort.

'I saw the Green Lady the other day,' she'd say, tucking my sister and me up in bed, 'she walks the secret passage between here and the church,[6] she's been ringing those bells again.'

These were the old servant's bells; the masters of the house could call them from any room in the house, so if you rang the lounge bell, the bell under the sign marked 'lounge' would ring in the servants' quarters.

Guess where we slept? I looked up at the bells in horror and trembled as Nan continued.

'She moaned at me something horrible the other night, she did. She's not at rest, you know. Gives me the chills.'

Then with a cheery 'Goodnight', spoken as if she'd just been talking about the price of cheese with the milkman, Nan switched off the light and shut the door with a solid 'clunk'. I lay there staring at the bells, waiting for one of them to ring.

Any midnight trip to the bathroom was fraught with terror. I'd wait until the last possible moment before sprinting down the huge hallway, which seemed to me to be about the length and height of Westminster Cathedral, in what was a dramatic race against time.

Nan had been listening to the radio when a call went out for little people to appear in the new *Star Wars* film. She was unsure about telling Mum and Dad as I was still only eleven and she was worried it might be exploitative.

---

[6] There actually *was* a secret passage from the cupboard under the stairs to the nearby fifteenth-century church.

She thought it over for a couple of days and when Dad visited she'd actually decided against mentioning it. It was only when he came back into the house after he'd forgotten something that she decided it was fate and told him. Once Dad heard the words 'Star Wars' he knew I'd want to do it. Also, by that point Mum had started sending me to drama classes in an attempt to channel my extrovert energy.

Mum called them straight away. 'I'm sorry,' the production assistant said, 'but we've been overwhelmed with calls, we've got all we need.'

Mum hung up. A few minutes later the phone rang again. It was the production assistant.

'How tall is your son?'

'Two feet eleven inches.'

'Could you bring him in?'

It was a wise move to have kept this secret from me until the last moment. My overexcitement at the prospect of being in a *Star Wars* movie would have been catastrophic for the Davis household. I nearly exploded with excitement as we drove there and talked incessantly the whole way.

Suddenly I was at Elstree Studios, auditioning for *Revenge of the Jedi,* as it was called then. Production assistant Patricia Carr was impressed by my lack of height; even for a little person I was short at two-foot-eleven.

'Well, George said we needed some little, little people to play Ewok children,' Patricia said, 'and I think you'll do just fine.'

My face lit up to sunbeam proportions.

'Right then, you'd better head down to the wardrobe department and they'll take your measurements for your costume.'

I led the way at a steady sprint, determined to reach wardrobe before anyone changed their mind. My face was a picture of wonder. Elstree was like Hogwarts, a huge, ever-changing, mysterious new world full of unexpected wonders. I hurried along the long white labyrinthine corridors desperate to see what lay in wait around the next corner. Everywhere people rushed about the building. I hoped to catch a glimpse of a Stormtrooper or Chewbacca strolling past, but was disappointed to encounter just one rather average-looking humanoid after another.

Wardrobe, as it turned out, was a misleading term for what most people my height would more accurately describe as a Torture Factory. My costume 'fitting' actually involved the making of a full-sized body and head cast, which would be used as a mannequin by the costume makers. This is not an experience for the faint-hearted, especially when it comes to taking a mould of the head.

Mum left me to it and went off to get a cup of tea. When she returned I heard a muffled scream, followed by 'What have you done to my son?!'

I was stretched out, bound from head to foot in a bright white, full-body plaster cast. I'd been wrapped in clingfilm and covered in Vaseline before the plaster cast had been slapped on. Unlike my fellow little actors, I'd actually been enjoying the experience, although the challenge of staying still while everything set was extremely trying.

Every now and again, Mum would shout, 'Are you OK in there, Warwick?' but because of the algenate (a milkshake-like substance more commonly used by dentists to make casts for dentures) over my ears I could barely hear or move my mouth and would reply with 'Hummpff?'

One person was specifically employed to keep my nostrils – the only part of my head that was uncovered – clear from the runny gloop (sneezes or allergies can be lethal). Some people find the whole process unbearable; it's not something for claustrophobes or asthmatics.

But while the older, more experienced creature actors shuddered at the thought of being turned into a human Twix, for me this was the most exciting moment of my life to date. Once the mixture had been moulded on, it was reinforced with plaster bandages. When these were all dry, they were pulled off and I looked, fascinated, into an inverse copy of myself.

'Cool!'

'That's the first time anyone's actually enjoyed the experience,' said make-up artist Nick Dudman.

Before we started filming we were invited to go and see *The Empire Strikes Back* (the second film in the trilogy) at a special screening at Elstree Studios. I hadn't yet seen it and was surprised and fascinated by how dark it was; I was dismayed to see that it ended on such a grim note.

Good job I'd be on hand to sort it all out for the grand finale.

My first day's filming was amazing. Up to that point I'd never met another little person in my entire life. When you're young and as short as I am, you tend to feel as if you're the only little person in the world. It was therefore a real magical moment for me when I walked into a studio to find forty people of similar proportions staring back at me. There was one other eleven-year-old, Nicky Read, who was just a couple of months older, and we became friends straight away. In fact, we all pretty much got on from the first moment, young and old, male and female. We all bonded over being short. Peter Burroughs, one of the older men there, would eventually become my father-in-law, poor fellow.

We were there to work with the choreographer on our fitness and 'Ewok movement'. We had to learn to behave like primitive but feisty and furry forest dwellers. Soon all forty of us, dressed in tracksuits, were running round the studio growling at each other and anyone unlucky enough to stick their head round the door to see what was going on.

On the day I was due to pick up my costume and try it on for the first time, I could hardly contain myself. Most older actors looked at their Ewok costumes with utter dread. They saw the thick layer of foam, the full-body fur suit and shuddered, knowing that a long, hot, sweaty and difficult few weeks lay ahead of them. All I could think about was that I was going to be fighting Stormtroopers all day long.

'Bring it on!'

It was beautifully made and only took five minutes to put on. I was one of the lucky ones because my costume actually fitted really well and was among the most convincing. Some of the older, less fortunate Ewok actors looked like teddy bears. Teddy bears who had been run through cement mixers before being pounded repeatedly with cricket bats.

The heat in the costumes was truly extraordinary; Kenny Baker, who also played R2-D2, described wearing an Ewok suit as 'like being poached'. Fortunately, you, dear reader, can only imagine quite how interesting the aroma in the Ewok dressing room was after six weeks of filming and no washing. I, however, still have those pungent memories.

Filming began in January 1982, one of the coldest English winters on record. Heavy snow had fallen several times throughout December and January. Temperatures dropped to a record-breaking minus-25 degrees Celsius. We filmed on a set inside Elstree but our dressing rooms were trailers parked outside. Once the cry of 'Heads off!' had been given and it was time for a break, forty Ewoks and one seven-foot Wookie emerged from the building without their heads and walked towards the trailers. It was so hot inside the suits that little clouds of steam followed us as we walked. It was very refreshing for about thirty seconds before the cold really started to bite.

Nearly all the Ewok Village scenes were shot at Elstree and there were some significant Ewok-related problems during quite a few of them. For example:

> Han Solo: I'm sure Luke wasn't on that thing when it blew.
> Princess Leia: He wasn't. I can feel it.
> Han Solo: You love him,
> [*pause*]
> Han Solo: don't you?
> Princess Leia: Yes.
> Han Solo: All right, I understand. Fine. When he comes back,
>   I won't get in the way.
> Princess Leia: Oh, Han, it's not like that at all.
> [*whispering*]
> Princess Leia: He's my—
> Random Ewok [*rolling past screaming*]: Aaaaargh!
> George Lucas: CUT!

As far as forest-dwelling creatures went, the Ewoks were incredibly unstable. One of the main problems proved to be their orange eyes. As heat built up inside the head they steamed up, so none of us could see where we were going. Even a special anti-mist spray proved ineffective. In an attempt to get round this, we didn't wear our heads during rehearsals and I memorised how many steps I needed to take for any one scene and roughly where each tree stump or branch was.

The Ewoks' rallying cry was 'Heads on!' followed by a grumble of discontent from everyone (except me). An army of dressers would fasten our heads and we'd cross two of our three Ewok fingers, hoping that we'd still be standing by the time it was all over.

Typically, at the end of any scene half a dozen Ewoks would be rolling around on the ground, having tripped up or fallen over something or someone, or having run into one another. Luckily I was able to get up on my own. When some of the more rotund Ewoks fell it was almost impossible for them to get up – or stop rolling. I had visions of some unlucky fellow carrying on down Elstree High Street still rolling strong on his way to the A1. Between filming normal-sized 'Ewok collectors' were dispatched to set them upright ahead of the next take.

Falling over and rolling about on Endor was all well and good until we shot the scenes in the Ewok village, which was thirty feet above the ground.

This was done to give it on-screen depth and the 'village' set was created by mounting dozens of fake polystyrene trees on a mass of scaffolding that filled the entire stage (real tree branches were attached to help them look real). It was surrounded by a cyclorama, a painting of the Endor forest to provide background. It was very 'Rolf Harris', in that it was hard to tell what it was until you were far enough away. Little bridges connected all the Ewok huts – which, as I've already mentioned, were *thirty feet above the ground*.

To make things even more interesting, the Ewoks had lots of campfires, so the special effects team burned lots and lots of incense to create a thick smoky haze, just to make sure we really, really couldn't see a damn thing. The Ewok body count should have shot through the roof but the perilous combination of the height and the smoke actually had the effect of making us concentrate very, very hard on where we put our feet so, against the odds, we managed to stay upright.

While no Ewoks were harmed in the making of this movie, the same cannot be said for humans. There is a scene where Chewie, Han, Luke, C-3PO and R2-D2 are walking through the forests of Endor and a hungry Chewie spies some meat hanging in a tree. Before Luke can say 'Chewie – no!' the hungry Wookie takes the bait and our heroes are caught in a classic jungle trap, scooped up in a net.

In reality, this net was held by a bloke driving a JCB. Several million dollars' worth of acting talent were entirely at his mercy so one can only imagine the thoughts that must have whizzed through his brain when the rope snapped and the cast dropped to the ground. Fortunately, no one was seriously hurt.

At the end of each take, my fellow Ewoks would collapse in sweaty relief. David Tomblin, the first assistant director (Spielberg's favourite AD and George's right-hand man) who was running the Ewok scenes would then typically say: 'Can we go again or do you need a break?'

While the older Ewok actors groaned and begged for thirty minutes' rest I hopped up and down, eager to prove I was feeling fine and pleaded: 'Please can we keep killing Stormtroopers?' I had been told to throw a rock at a Stormtrooper and I wanted to make damn sure it was going to hit him – right between the eyes.

'Well, if he can do it,' David said, 'and he's only eleven, then you guys can too!'

I was christened the 'ever-ready Ewok'.

As soon as our first break on our first day finally came, I dashed to the trailer, leapt out of my costume and put on my roller skates. I skated past the Ewok stage and into the next building and there, looking just like the scene in the Mos Eisley spaceport in *Episode IV*, was a huge stage with the full-size *Millennium Falcon*.

I think I said something like 'Woooooow' as I rolled past to the next stage where I suddenly found myself skating round the Emperor's throne room. This was quickly followed by Yoda's hut and the Degobah swamp (not the best place for roller skating), before I ended my tour at Jabba the Hut's palace.

Now this was really magical.

Unlike my older counterparts, I didn't realise there were rules – written and unwritten – that governed one's on-set behaviour. You didn't talk to or touch the stars, something I managed to do frequently.

Spying a certain Mr Skywalker in his new all-black Jedi costume I tugged on his sleeve: 'Excuse me. Can I see your light sabre?' The young Jedi was very gracious about it.

Robert Watts, a delightful, avuncular and much-respected producer on *Jedi* took a bit of a shine to me and brought me to the attention of David Tomblin. David was a great character, a genuinely lovely man with immense experience and knowledge; he'd worked as Assistant Director to Stanley Kubrick and on such notable films as *Never Say Never Again*, *Gandhi*, *Superman* – the list was endless. He was also the mastermind behind the cult TV series *The Prisoner*.

When he was interviewed for a Channel 4 documentary, *Six Into One: The Prisoner File* in 1984, he recalled: 'I have just worked on a George Lucas film called *Return of the Jedi* and, to get permission to work in the States, I had to write down every film that I had been on. I got to 478 and then decided that was probably enough to convince them that I had a reasonable amount of experience.'

One of David's responsibilities in *Jedi* was 'Ewok distribution', and he couldn't help but notice my tireless enthusiasm. He liked the fact I didn't understand films, that I didn't know the rules and wandered around during shoots chatting to the stars just like a curious Ewok would. These days, kids are a lot better informed about how movies are made, but in 1981 I didn't have a clue, and neither did anyone else my age.

I took what little I'd learned about improvisation from acting school, added some of our family's pet dog's behaviour and my Ewok character emerged to explore the Moon of Endor.

In one scene the Ewoks encounter R2-D2 and C-3PO and decide that the golden robot is a god.[7] I thought that R2-D2 would look so extraordinary to a young Ewok, who had after all seen nothing but plants and trees his whole young life, that he would want to check the robot out, so I wandered over and started poking and peering at him (I always assumed R2 was a he).

The older actors, meanwhile, would play by the rules; they would do what they were told, which was much better for such a complicated film. These days it rarely happens; an actor might approach a director with an idea and if they're lucky they'll get the chance to rehearse it, but out of politeness rather than any urge to actually put it on film.

The advantage I had was that I just did it 'live' so to speak, so it was captured on film and they could see straight away that it worked. This moment caught director Richard Marquand's eye and he built a whole scene around me investigating R2-D2.

I was on my way.

---

[7] Anthony Daniels, who played C-3PO, likes to be treated as a god in real life. I once did a *Star Wars* show at Disney with Anthony where he got the whole audience to bow down to him as if they were Ewoks. He was also wearing a metallic-gold jacket; this would have been like me going on wearing a fur coat.

Chapter Three
Just Me and Princess Leia

May 12th 1983.

Hi Warwick,

Thanks for your letter to George. He has seen
it and will be writing to you but at the
moment he is extremely busy because "Jedi"
is about to be released. He did ask us to let
you know that you look great in the film.
Enclosed in the two parcels (I hope they both
arrive together!) are some Jedi T-shirts, toys
etc.
At the moment we do not have a complete set
of all the new Jedi toys but these are the ones
we do have. When we get more in we will be
sending them to you.

Hope everything is going well for you and your
family.

Best regards,

IAN BRYCE

WARWICK DAVIS

"WICKET"

If you wrote me a fan letter in 1983, this is what you would have received – had you included an SAE.

Chillin' between takes.

A heads-off moment with my sister, Kim.

With weightlifting champ
Dave Prowse, aka Darth Vader.

Shooting *Return of the Ewok* at
Chelsea FC. 'When the ball lands
here, you grab it!'

The ever-ready Ewok –
I'd roller-skate my way round
Elstree in between filming;
I saw many strange and
wonderful things as a result.

Filming *Return of the Ewok*. He was a
real cabbie who couldn't act.

Princess Leia introduces
me to her fellow rebels.

Courtesy of Lucasfilm Ltd.

Just me and Princess Leia — I was asked to perform this
scene after fellow Ewok actor, Kenny Baker, fell ill. The
bright spot to the left is the result of a Biker Scout missing
us with his blaster.

Courtesy of Lucasfilm Ltd.

At the wrap party – I managed to miss most of it by falling asleep. Thanks for not waking me Carrie!

Carrie Fisher and I getting cosy on Jabba the Hutt's tail.
Courtesy of Lucasfilm Ltd.

A few days later, David Tomblin took me to one side and said, 'How would you like a speaking role in your own Ewok adventure, Warwick?'

Once he'd got his hearing back, David continued.

'Well, I've got an idea for a short featurette called *Return of the Ewok* which we might use to promote *Jedi*. George likes the idea and has given me permission to use the entire set and cast, whatever I want. And I want you to star.'

The resulting twenty-three-minute film was never finished or officially released and has since become part of *Star Wars* folklore; the original 16mm print was lost and only six VHS copies still exist. I have one of them, which I've since converted to DVD. It has occasionally been shown at conventions and it's a film *Stars Wars* fans always talk about.

I still have the original script and looking at it now I can see it was completely bonkers – in a good way. David told me that these crazy ideas had come to him in the middle of the night and he'd scribbled them down in a frenzy until the whole concept was complete.

The plot (such as it is) is that I (as Warwick, in human form) have left home to seek my fortune. After a stint as Chelsea goal-keeper (this was filmed at Stamford Bridge on match day), I decide to become an actor.

To cut a long story short, I end up backstage on the set of *Jedi*. Viewing the film after all this time I can't believe the state of the dressing rooms. These were the stars of the film and they had these tiny, draughty boxes with a chair, a shoddy plywood desk and quite possibly the most depressing 1970s paisley curtains ever made. The dodgy furniture must have been especially hard to bear for former bespoke carpenter Harrison Ford; he was making a portico for Francis Ford Coppola when George gave him the break of a lifetime and offered him the part of Han Solo.

In the film, I meet Han who then takes me to Mark's dressing room where he's also in costume. Sadly, neither of them know about Ewoks or where they live. 'Let's ask Carrie,' Mark says . . . and sure enough, we do.

And WHOAH! Cue wolf whistles and a sudden increase in advance bookings for *Jedi*. Carrie is in *the* gold bikini, with very little left to the imagination.

Carrie had apparently complained about her costumes in *Star Wars* and *The Empire Strikes Back*, saying they were so long and shapeless that no one could tell she was a woman. So she asked George Lucas if she could wear something 'womanly'. Bearing in mind that, in George Lucas's words, 'there is no underwear in space', the costume designers did remarkably well to come up with a matching metal bikini, which revealed that Carrie was – absotively posilutely – a woman.

The problem was the metal didn't always follow Carrie's body, so there were numerous 'wardrobe malfunctions' during which certain parts of her anatomy made unexpected appearances – I didn't see it, but it happened in the scene where she strangles Jabba the Hutt, for example. For the action sequences a rubber version was made so Carrie could leap about without fear of embarrassment.

Anyway, back to *Return of the Ewok*. Carrie turns this way and that and then looks down and bends forward to talk to me.

I got a little wobbly at this point. I wasn't sure why exactly – I was just on the cusp of adolescence so wasn't able to fully appreciate the loveliness of Carrie's outfit. But I did notice that the eyes of my costume steamed up a little quicker.

David had asked Mum and Dad to appear in this promo film (they were supposed to have flown on a space cruiser to pick me up from Endor at the end of my adventures) and they dressed up in their Sunday best for the occasion. When they arrived on set, David said, 'I want you to walk through those brambles, nettles, across that mud, then through that ditch towards Warwick who's coming down the hill towards you.'

Being English and overly polite they failed to point out to David that they had dressed in their Sunday best, wearing heels and brogues, and that the last thing they were able or willing to do was fight their way up the swampiest, brambliest hill in the world. But struggle they did (for several takes) – and then walked back down again afterwards. You can clearly see that Dad was desperately trying not to slip as he gingerly fought his way down the one-in-four hill.

Their dialogue was added in later.

Mum: Oh, Warwick, there you are.

Dad: Where on Earth have you been?

Me: I've been in a movie, which reminds me could I have my pocket money? I need to pay my agent ten per cent.

Mum: You won't be getting any pocket money for a very long time. Do you realise how much it costs to hire a rocket these days?

Me: We could always get a lift back in the *Millennium Falcon*.

Dad: Don't be ridiculous. Stop these fantasies immediately. Who's that little green man?

Yoda: May the Force be with you ... Dad.

It was completely nuts but hilarious.

One day on set producer Robert Watts asked me to sit in front of a white screen while I was photographed in and out of costume.

'What's this for?' I asked.

'Warwick, how would you like to go to America?'

The picture was for a passport photo; six Ewok actors had been chosen to fly to America to film the final phase of *Revenge of the Jedi*. We would be joining forty or so American little people who were also playing Ewoks. This was done for the sake of continuity, so that the audience would recognise key characters within the two distinct groups of Ewoks and they would appear to be part of the same tribe.

The sail barge scene in the Tatooine desert (where Luke rescues a recently defrosted Han Solo and Princess Leia kills Jabba the Hut) and the Endor exteriors were the only scenes shot in the USA. In those good old days the British Film Industry was in rude health and the UK had a wealth of technicians who were able to make great movies for less money than Hollywood.

To me this was utterly mind-blowing. I'd been filming with my screen heroes for five weeks, with no school to speak of, and now I was going to get on a plane for the first time in my life, and fly to Disneyland (that's what I thought America was) to fight Stormtroopers for eight weeks.

I flew with Mum, Dad and my sister, along with five other families, including Nicky's. The plane seemed to me to be as big as the Albert Hall. This was still a time when transatlantic travel was the preserve of the rich and famous, so the plane was almost empty.

The in-flight entertainment was decidedly ropey – they tried to project a 16mm film onto a screen in the middle of the cabin but the film kept falling off the spool every time we hit a spot of turbulence. So Nicky and I played hide and seek for about five hours, never running out of hiding places.

And then suddenly, there I was, in California, standing under redwood trees about a hundred metres tall, where I was introduced to Ray, our schoolteacher.

'Hang on a minute,' I said. 'Schoolteacher? Nobody told me about this.'

The law said I was only allowed to work for four hours a day as an actor but I had to do six hours of schooling. I was ready to cry 'Mutiny!' But that was before I got to know Ray.

Ray didn't look like your average teacher. He had long blond hair, wore Ray-Bans and was tanned a golden brown. Imagine a younger Owen Wilson but with a slightly less impressive nose.

The first thing he taught us was how to hatch and raise chickens and to identify poisonous plants. There was not so much as a sniff of algebra.

'What are you gonna need algebra for?' Ray asked with a smile. 'Now, who wants to know how to start a fire without using matches?'

Where did they find this guy? I loved Ray and school became almost as much fun as fighting Stormtroopers. One moment I was out battling the Empire alongside Princess Leia and Luke Skywalker, and the next I was running back to the Portakabin desperate to check that George the chicken was still happily eating his daily seed ration.

The cast and crew immediately made me feel like a member of the Lucasfilm family. I think they warmed to me in part because I had no inhibitions. I still had absolutely no idea how I ought to behave on a movie set. I was just a little kid having fun and I didn't quite realise just how important or significant the people around me were. Including the man himself.

It was David Tomblin who plucked me from out of the crowd and brought me to the attention of George Lucas.

'Warwick, this is George Lucas,' David said. If David had told me that George played a Stormtrooper, then I would've been impressed, but all I could tell at that point was that George was a man with big hair, glasses and a beard.

'Oh, right,' I said without any enthusiasm whatsoever.

Thus started a lifelong friendship.

There was much falling over of Ewoks in the redwood forest set. The undergrowth was always dealing us funny little surprises; even the Stormtroopers were having trouble staying erect.

A few days later, a slightly worried-looking David approached me: 'Warwick, we've got a bit of a problem,' he said. 'Kenny Baker's been taken ill with food poisoning and he had a big scene to shoot today. George would like you to take over Kenny's role as Wicket.'

'No problem!'

'This one's really important, Warwick, you'll be filming a five-minute scene with Carrie Fisher.'

I ran around in circles in excitement, waving my spear in my own Ewok dance of victory.

Kenny was consigned to the background and became Paploo but, bless him, he never felt any ill will towards me. 'I'm just happy to be able to spend a bit more time out of the sweatsuit,' he said graciously. Besides, he still had the great chase scene where Paploo steals a Biker Scout's speeder.

My big scene took place after Leia crashes her speeder bike while being chased by Biker Scouts. Wicket finds her unconscious and together the Princess and the Ewok take out two Biker Scouts before heading off to find Han and Luke.

I would be the first Ewok the audience would see and so, as the ambassador for my racea, so to speak, I wanted to make a good impression. I would certainly set the Ewok tone for the rest of the film. I had no time to prepare but I'd been playing an Ewok for weeks, so I just did what I thought an Ewok would do naturally with Princess Leia. When she appeared on set, Carrie immediately showed her concern for me.

'Are you OK in there, Warwick?' she said. 'It must be so hot.' She reached down behind a log and pulled out a carton of chocolate milk with a long straw and fed me cookies in between takes.

She was everything an eleven-year-old Ewok could possibly wish for. By this time Carrie was already battling drink and drug addiction. But if there was a bottle of vodka with a straw hidden behind another branch, I didn't see it. She was so caring towards me. Whenever there was a pause, she asked if I needed anything. 'Could I have another one of those cookies?' became my standard reply.

From that day forth I became Wicket and was pushed to the front of the Ewok tribe.

I kept improvising like mad.

There was another scene where, purring like a cat, I hug Han Solo's leg while C-3PO tells us stories around the campfire. The look of surprise and then resignation on Harrison's face wasn't acted.

As for Jedi Skywalker, he was elevated to supreme emperor best-friend status when he asked, 'Say, Warwick, do you collect *Star Wars* toys?'

'Of course!' I replied, 'I love them.'

In these innocent days, *Star Wars* toys were the only movie merchandise that existed in any significant quantity. George Lucas had craftily waived his up-front fee as director for the original film and negotiated ownership of the licensing rights. A relieved studio, thinking *Star Wars* would be a flop, gratefully accepted. This decision earned George hundreds of millions of dollars, as he directly profited from all the licensed games, toys and collectibles created for the franchise.

Mark asked me if there were any toys missing from my *Star Wars* collection. 'Oh yes,' I said, and I wrote out an enormous list covering two sides of A4 which detailed exactly which toys I didn't have and handed it over with a hopeful grin. The very next day Mark appeared on set laden down with dozens of boxes and bags and presented me with the entire collection, the whole lot. What a guy!

'Just swing the bolas around your head, Warwick,' David urged, 'just like a lasso.' That was the limit of my weapons training for the final battle scenes on Endor. David wanted to capture a funny scene – after all, nothing's funnier than when something ridiculous happens in the heat of a deadly epic battle. How would Stan Laurel have played this, I wondered?

Bolas are a throwing weapon made up of a short length of rope with two rocks tied to either end. The original idea was to get them round the legs of your prey but, humans being humans, they've also been adapted for use on enemy soldiers. The Ewoks used bolas to great effect by throwing them round the necks of Stormtroopers and knocking them out with the rocks.

In the film we see one Ewok after another taking down several Stormtroopers with the bolas – until you get to young Wicket, who entangles himself in the deadly weapon and is hit in the head by his own bolas.

When the rocks hit me, my head made the same noise as a coconut being hit with a bat. I then did a pretty good impression of Stan Laurel being walloped on the head by Oliver Hardy with a mallet in *Way Out West*: a slight pirouette before falling with great speed towards the ground. To my surprise, there had been a communication breakdown between the various props people – the crash mat that was supposed to be below me had been tidied away, no doubt trying to prevent Ewok trip-ups – so I hit the floor hard (thankfully the foam padding of my Wicket costume absorbed the worst of the impact).

That was my first lesson in the pain involved in physical comedy. I now take great pleasure in re-enacting that scene at *Star Wars* conventions (with the original bolas and a cushion) and it always goes down a storm.

Maybe it was the air or the fact that we were no longer at home, but moving the production to the US seemed to turn everyone into practical jokers. My favourite incident was a dastardly plan hatched by the entire Ewok cast. We donned our costumes and bombarded the canteen with water bombs, just as the stars and crew were having lunch. God knows what they thought as they saw forty Ewoks charging them with water-filled balloons,

'Ah, Ah!' we said smugly, wagging our fingers forbiddingly, as some enterprising crew members prepared to launch their retaliation in the form of jam doughnuts. 'We're in costume!' They couldn't attack without ruining our costumes and thereby the rest of the day's filming.

On another occasion we sent the Ewok bus up to the set with a note saying that the Ewoks had had enough and were on their way to the airport (which for some people was only a half-joke). Production assistant Ian Bryce, who received the note, flew into such a panic as a result that he leapt into a car and headed off at top speed to the airport to try and talk us out of going. Fortunately, he got a flat tyre just after he left and when our bus pulled up a second time, we were all wearing T-shirts that read *Revenge of the Ewok*.

I didn't realise but as the only kid on the set apart from Nicky, I was a kind of moral guardian. All the other actors were on their best behaviour whenever I showed up; booze was put away, cigarettes were stubbed out, swearing and dirty jokes were halted mid-flow, and so on.

The whole *Jedi* experience was great; I had no idea that this was a defining time in my life; at the time it felt like I'd won an amazing competition. As we finished filming the last Ewok scene and the cry 'Heads off!' echoed through the redwood forest for the final time, one Ewok actor said with some passion, 'Well, thank God that's over!' While many of my fellow Ewok actors were truly grateful that their costumed torture had finally come to an end, I moped about miserably. I did not relish the idea of leaving this galaxy of adventure for a life of normaldom.

To mark the end of principal photography, the producers organised a wrap party for all cast and crew. I managed to miss most of this by falling asleep. There's a picture of me out cold on a chair during the Ewok wrap party with Carrie Fisher behind me, her finger over her mouth, going 'Shhhh!'

The day after the wrap party I said my goodbyes to everyone, from George the chicken to George the Jedi Master, from Ray the wise surfer dude, to Carrie, Mark and Harrison, from Nicky to Kenny, not forgetting Sal and Phil – two little people who became my friends and both married very tall girls who happened to be twins.[8]

I was leaving so many friends and it was utterly heartbreaking. Still, at least we arrived back in the UK just in time for the school summer holidays. I was glum but grudgingly glad to be back home when Dad said the magic words: 'Warwick, how would you like a holiday in the caravan?'

---

[8] They divorced. Both of them.

Episode VI $^{1/2}$
RETURN OF THE EWOK

In search of his destiny, twelve-year-old Warwick Davis goes to his local job centre...

Pondering the destinies on offer...

Hmmm... Why not?

I'm certain I could have out-lifted him pound for pound.

Well, things could hardly get any worse for Chelsea...

The smell of Deep Heat leaves me dizzy.

Moments later I find myself sprawled in the back of the net with the ball.

This is more like it! *Star Wars*, my favourite film!

Mark Hamill, who (for the purposes of this promotional film) has been fighting Darth Vader inside my local cinema, pops out to say 'hello'.

If I want a job in *Star Wars* then
I need an agent.

Unfortunately, the only person
I can find is Maxwell Mercury
(aka Roy Kinnear).

'I can play small parts.'

Max: 'How about Boba Fett?'

More like Baby Fett!

'I know,' says Max, 'you can play
an Ewok!'

Ewok costumes only come in one size.

I set off to the film studios
to find Endor.

'Keep the change cabbie!'

Me: *'I'm looking for Endor, where the
Ewoks live. Nice curtains, by the way.'*

Harrison: *'Let's ask Mark.'*

*'You remind me of Chewie when he
was a kid.'*

'Ewok? What's an Ewok?'

'Errr... Hi Carrie... We forgot what we came for.'

'Try stage eight. Maybe Endor's there. May the Force be with you.'

'Can you show me the way to stage eight?'

'Ask Frank Oz – he's got a hand in everything.'

'Crikey! Darth Vader!'

'I am fluent in over six million forms of communication...'

'And you'll make a very nice lampstand,' says producer Robert Watts.

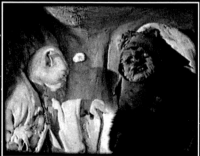

'Your Galactic Ticket to Endor I have.'

'Sorry, no Ewoks.'

I ditch the costume.

'Hmmm... Weren't you in
Time Bandits?'

'Are you an astronaut? Can I get a
lift in your rocket to Endor?'

One short flight later and I catch up
with the gang, only to find the forest
swarming with Imperial Troops.

Harrison: 'What's that Ewok up to?'

I have a cunning plan...

'This should do the trick.'

'Take that Vader!'

Harrison: 'Thanks kid, you did a great job.'

My parents arrive to take me home. For some reason they're wearing their Sunday best – hardly ideal for the forests of Endor.

'Nice suit Dad.'

The Davis family loved caravanning – Dad was probably the only man in the UK who towed his with an E-type Jag.

A rare sunny day in a field next to a pub.

This is more like it. If you weren't careful during the night, you could end up frozen to the condensation on the window.

Chapter Four

The Caravan of Courage

The first caravan we owned was called a Monza. It sounds exciting, as if it were something sleek and luxurious, like a Grand Prix driver's mobile dressing room. In reality it was a shed on wheels. The condensation that covered the inside of the single-glazed windows would turn into ice on a cold morning.

Water was pumped into the sink using a foot pedal, causing the Monza to sway rudely from side to side; simply washing up would leave Mum exhausted. About the quality and weight of a good piece of tinder, the caravan was lit by gas. It wasn't as if we couldn't afford something better – my dad was well off, he had a good job and even used his silver E-type Jaguar to tow the box on wheels.

The four of us somehow managed to bed down fairly comfortably each night. However, I had to be careful I didn't roll over onto the window in my sleep otherwise I'd wake up frozen to the glass.

Despite this we loved it and we loved caravanning. We'd been going on holidays to Cornwall, Wales and Devon for as long as I could remember. After the Jag, we had an ancient but loyal Ford Cortina estate. Dad would take advantage of this by leaving very early in the morning. He'd pack everything else before folding down the back seats, lifting us out of our beds, still sleeping, and carrying us along with our bedclothes into the estate part of the car. He'd close the hatch very quietly and my parents then enjoyed a peaceful early morning drive without choruses of 'Are we there yet?' or 'I'm bored!' or 'Can

we stop at the Little Chef.[9] Can we, can we, can we, can we, can we?'
Instead my sister and I would wake up in some strange new land,
discovering we were indeed already 'there', wherever 'there' was.

'There' was usually in a field next to a pub where I'd have something in a basket (something that looked and tasted a little bit like
chicken) and a Britvic orange. Even to me, the Britvic bottles
were tiny, but I did love a Britvic. As long as I had that and a packet
of Salt'n'Shake crisps I was happy.

We'd cycle our bikes round the caravan site while Mum and
Dad sunbathed. I loved bikes. My first was a little silver model that
had clearly been constructed for a much younger rider, but it
suited my purposes to a T. I could reach the pedals and, to me at
least, it felt like the fastest thing in the world.

I usually found myself quite frustrated that we'd come all this
way and now all Mum and Dad wanted to do was sit there and do
nothing. Nothing whatsoever. 'Don't you want to do *something*?'
I'd ask. '*Anything*?' Now I'm a parent myself, I know where they
were coming from, just how precious and restorative the act of
doing nothing, just sitting and looking at the view, can be.

In the evenings we'd play board games, especially Monopoly,
usually while listening to Radio Two. Very often this would be
inside the caravan because it was raining outside. It was a very
simple way of holidaying and if that sounds a little depressing to
read now, it wasn't at all. I loved every single moment.

It scares me just how much 'stuff' there is to keep today's
generation busy on holiday, such as PlayStations, DVDs, satellite
TV, mobile phones. None of these things existed in our Monza
almost thirty years ago. There was just the four of us, a deck of
cards, Radio Two and the rain.

---

[9] 'So where is he then?' I once demanded of a waitress.

We mainly stuck to England although I do recall seeing an awful lot of ruined Welsh castles during one especially damp and misty trip. We also once bravely journeyed to Scotland, where we spent two days in the freezing rain before quickly heading south again as fast as the Monza would allow. We never returned.

Dad wasn't so keen on crowds on holiday so we avoided busy beaches. When he selected a caravan site he didn't look to see if it had the kid-friendly things such as a playground or a nearby fair, horse rides and so on. The important thing for him was that it was adjacent to a pub. Country pubs often used to have a field next door that they'd let out to caravanners, guaranteeing them a steady trade of fatigued parents and overexcitable children. Dad would then be able to enjoy the luxury of a leisurely lunch in a pub before swaying back to the caravan for a good long afternoon's stare at the scenery.

It wasn't long after we returned from another caravanning holiday in 1983 that the newly renamed *Return of the Jedi* (George felt this new title was more in keeping with Jedi philosophy) was ready to be shown, and on the Sunday before the world premiere we went to the cast and crew screening at the Marble Arch Odeon, London.

Goose bumps rose as the main titles rolled and I watched in utter fascination and amazement as the images began to appear. Elstree was utterly convincing as Endor, a thousand times better than I thought possible. Endor and the Ewok Village looked a lot darker than I remembered (we had been filming under very strong studio lights) and this darkness made it all look so much more realistic.

I noticed that a lot of scenes had been cut – there was one where I found and fired a Stormtrooper's blaster that hadn't made it, but I was delighted to see the bolas scene and even more delighted by the roar of laughter that erupted from the audience when I took a tumble. It had been worth the pain. I was also amazed to hear Wicket speaking in an alien language – I hadn't heard it until then.[10] And no one ever called the Ewoks 'Ewoks' in the film. Han Solo called them 'furballs' a few times. But no one referred to them as 'Ewoks'. No one had an explanation as to why; it just turned out that way.

Before I knew it the credits were rolling – and then there it was:

Wicket: WARWICK DAVIS.

Very cool.

The film was a huge success, critically (although some reviewers thought the Ewok victory over the Empire stretched credibility somewhat. Credibility? Come on, this is *Star Wars*, people!) and financially – it grossed over $250 million from a $32 million budget.

Meanwhile, school loomed like the Death Star over the end of the summer holidays. I was thirteen and due to start my secondary education at the City of London Freeman's School in Surrey. It was big in every sense of the word. The distance between classrooms could be over a mile (at least that's how it seemed to me) and the textbooks, when stacked in a pile, towered over my head. I couldn't carry them so I got a trolley and I sprinted the vast distance between lessons, my cart bumping behind me as I went.

The first day was a blur. There were plenty of curious stares and some surprised looks when a voice said loudly from knee height,

---

[10] Apparently, Ewokese was inspired by the dialect spoken by a remote Central Chinese tribe. Having said that, some fans have noticed that one of the songs sung by the Ewoks sounds like: '*Det luktar flingor här*', which is Swedish for 'It smells of cereal here'. I must admit that some of the Ewok costumes did smell a little like stale Rice Krispies.

'Excuse me! Coming through here!' but everyone was very pleasant and I was never bullied once.

Word gradually leaked out that I'd been in *Jedi* and I received a certain degree of attention as a result. When you're my height it's strangely hard to hide, so the best way for me to cope was to embrace my fellow pupils' curiosity. If there was one thing I'd learned from *Jedi*, apart from Ewokese, it was to be myself. As Ray my surfer dude teacher had said: 'People will like you for who you are, Warwick. There's no need for acting in the real world.' I made loads of great friends at secondary school, many of whom I'm still in touch with now.

As well as friends I also attracted my very own stalker: Daniel. He was already over six feet tall, skinny as a rake, into heavy metal, with long, long fair hair and always, always clad in black (imagine a young Stephen Merchant, but with longer, stragglier hair). He was also obsessed with *Star Wars* and with Princess Leia in particular. To say he had a HUGE crush on Carrie Fisher was an understatement.

'Awight there?'

'Hello,' I replied cautiously. Daniel looked so extraordinary to me I didn't know what to make of him.

'So . . . er,' he said.

'Yes?' I asked impatiently. 'Look, I've got chemistry to get to,' I added, tugging on my trolley. It was a good march across the playing field to get there on time and the chemistry book weighed a flipping ton.

'*You've touched her!*'

'Er . . .' I said, starting to walk quickly away.

'*Star Wars!*' Daniel added desperately. 'You were in it, right?'

'Yes.'

'You acted with Prin– . . . I mean Carrie Fisher?'

'Yes.'

Daniel sighed, a gormless half-smile on his face. 'What was she like?'

'Very nice.'

Daniel followed me wherever I went. I found him incredibly annoying but he persisted, constantly talking about nothing but *Star Wars*. We were truly the oddest couple, the shortest and tallest thirteen-year-olds in all of Surrey, the tall one always trailing the cross-looking short one at a safe distance, yelling the odd question.

Most of my time was spent trying to avoid him. It should have been easy to spot Daniel coming a mile off, but he'd always suddenly appear next to me as if by magic and say something like: 'So, the scene where Leia's got her hair down and they're telling stories round the campfire. Why didn't you wrap your arms round *her* leg? What made you choose Harrison Ford?'

He was always there, wherever I turned, and he talked incessantly and rapidly, without pause for breath, asking questions like: 'Is there a man inside C-3PO and why is he so slow? You'd think they'd make him more mobile, talking of which, how did R2-D2 cope with the surface of Endor?' He'd wind me up by asking, 'Are you sure you weren't in *Time Bandits*?'[11] a question that has since come to haunt me wherever I go.

He also forced me to listen to heavy metal in an effort to get me to appreciate its finer nuances. 'See, he's using a double bass drum kit with two pedals so he can churn out a hundred and fifty beats per minute.' All I could hear was the never-ending sound of a washing machine full of spanners on spin.

I was into Michael Jackson and had just heard 'Billie Jean' for the first time. I had it on a cassette kept in my huge Walkman. The first time I heard it, I didn't realise it was Michael, but the opening

---

[11] No, I wasn't.

beat blew me away. Like thousands of other teens, I'd religiously tune into Radio One's Top 40 with Bruno Brookes every Sunday, trying like thousands of other kids all over the country to hit play and record just at the right moment, before Bruno opened his gob and spoke over the music. I was a creature of habit and would even prepare myself for the experience every week by having a bath before the show.

My parents also influenced my musical taste at the time. The long holiday journeys to pubs with fields were often scored by the sound of The Carpenters, Fleetwood Mac and Neil Diamond playing on the 8-track.

I enjoyed school. I was outspoken, larger-than-life[12] and through some decent voice projection I was able to make sure I was heard everywhere I went. The one thing I dreaded though, was sport. By default I was the last person to be picked for any team.

The school refused to accept any of my excuses. I still can't understand why they thought that I, at three feet, would enjoy cross-country running. I mean, what *were* they expecting? I couldn't believe they wanted me to do the long jump as well. My 'leap' didn't even take me as far as the sand pit. Still, at least they didn't make me try the high jump.

I did once score a goal. Someone booted the ball at me and it bounced off my head and into the back of the net. The sports master was so excited that I didn't have the heart to disappoint him, so I pretended it was all planned.

For some reason, despite my extensive Wicket experience,[13] the school decided cricket was 'too dangerous' but they still found a way to torture me by making me keep score. I sat in a damp little

---

[12] I know, I know.
[13] Sorry, I couldn't resist.

hut with a tiny flap window, which was too high, so I'd have to spend the entire match on my toes struggling to change the adjustable flaps that showed the score to the outside world. It didn't help that the scoring system made no sense to me whatsoever.

The one sport I excelled in was badminton; I was all over the court in a Tasmanian Devil-style whirl and could get under almost any shot. I was also the perfect height to hit a smash just over the net at full stretch. Also, I could do more chin-ups than any other person in the school – although I had to be careful I wasn't left hanging anywhere I couldn't get down from again.

Academically, I was an average student, quite good at French, maths and English. The only play we did at school was *Oliver Twist* and shockingly I wasn't in it. Instead I was given responsibility for the lighting – and it was horrible. I hated it. I wanted to be in front of the lights not behind them.

In desperation to find a useful channel for my ridiculous energy and huge personality, Mum had packed me off to Saturday drama school when I was eight. The Laine Theatre Arts School in Epsom has a pretty good reputation; they've churned out more than their share of West End performers over the years.[14] I took to acting immediately, although Mrs Reynolds my drama teacher, who was distinguished by her extravagant moustache, was extremely serious and did her level best to remove as much of the fun from proceedings as possible.

I was also the only boy there. Every now and then another boy would show up for a few Saturdays but they always seemed to me . . . well . . . very effeminate.

Somehow, Daniel found out I went to drama school.

---

[14] Their names escape me. You'll just have to take my word for it.

'Can I come?' he asked.

I considered it and realised I would actually be grateful for the male company. I also relished the idea of what Mrs Reynolds would make of Daniel.

'There are lots of girls there,' I said.

Daniel's face became a picture of delight. 'Excellent!'

While my own curiosity was just starting to emerge, Daniel already displayed an extremely advanced interest in the opposite sex.

Mrs Reynold's moustache twitched when she saw Daniel. I could see she was thinking 'That boy's trouble', and she was right.

We behaved just as we did at school: I played the straight man to Daniel's idiot. Easy. Daniel loved it and we started performing our own comedy skits, which continually pushed the boundaries of *bad* taste and *in*decency. Once, in front of our class of girls, mainly posh ballerina types, all very nice and proper, we performed a short piece featuring two professors meeting in a coffee bar, both about to give a talk at a science conference. It was all puns and no plot, something along the lines of:

Professor Gasm: Good day, Professor Org.

Professor Org: Ah! Professor Gasm. Wonderful to see you again.

The professors shake hands happily.

Professor Gasm: I don't know why, but seeing you, well it
   makes me feel complete again.

Professor Org: I know just what you mean. Do you come
   here often?

Professor Gasm: Frequently, more than is good for my health,
   I fear.

Professor Org: Coffee?

Professor Gasm: Don't mind if I do.

Professor Org: Cream?

Professor Gasm: Oh, yes please, one can never have too much.

And on it went.

I'm not sure the sensitive Mrs Reynolds ever really recovered from the two professors; she was more appreciative of the girls who did complex studies about motion and modern interpretations of Middle Age plays.

Fortunately, it did go down rather better with our female classmates who, surprisingly to us, laughed along quite merrily, and it was this very response that saved us from being booted out. It also inspired us to do lots of other daft things, like re-enacting scenes from the *Twilight Zone* movie for our O levels, and overdubbing the *Star Wars* movies with silly voices and giving the films a very different plot.

Although extrovert, I could still be pretty awkward in some social situations and would often run out of things to say. Daniel, on the other hand, was just brilliantly social and he always broke the ice, even if it was with a window-rattling fart.

He was also very lucky with the ladies. While most teenage boys stared awkwardly from across the classroom, Daniel adopted the fearless approach of asking out girls he liked immediately.

I had no success whatsoever. I couldn't understand it – I mean, what's not to love? I was a good-looking movie star, if I say so myself . . . just a little bit below average in height. No different from Tom Cruise. But the teenage ladies at school wanted to fit in with all their friends and so they dated tall people. The height thing was hugely important to them. While most girls were more than happy to be my friend, none were prepared to go that extra mile (or two feet) and become a girlfriend.

Daniel, however, was never short of a girlfriend. It was a complete mystery to me; he was lanky, had disgusting habits, listened to awful music and had ridiculously long hair (by this time I was sporting a particularly fine and fashionable mullet).

There was one occasion where we both fancied the same girl. Blinded by a combination of her beauty and my own hormones, I resorted to dastardly methods to sabotage Daniel's advances. I wrote a letter explaining why Daniel didn't like her and couldn't go out with her and that I, on the other hand, would be delighted to take her out. At the last moment, I couldn't bring myself to slip it into her desk, so I ripped the letter up and threw it into an empty locker.

It was around this time that Daniel said, 'Do you realise we've just had a conversation without either of us mentioning *Star Wars* once?'

Bloody hell, I thought, we've only gone and become friends!

Chapter Five

Return of the Ewok

I made a special guest appearance at George Lucas's four-year-old daughter's birthday party. The kids got a tad overexcited and almost fed me to death.

Just a note...

Dear Wicket,
    Thank-you so much for coming to my birthday party. All the children loved you.
    I love my Hello Kitty bank. I am saving lots of money
    Thank you again Wicket. I can't wait until I see you again
                Yor friend
Love
Amanda
Lucas

A 'thank you' note to Wicket from Amanda Lucas.

'**W**ake up, Warwick!'

It was my sister. What the hell was she doing, in my bedroom and waking me up? 'Go away!'

'Someone's throwing stones at the house!'

'What?' I sat up. Sure enough, I could hear what sounded to me like gravel being thrown at the window. Except the sound wasn't quite right. It sounded more like popping. I ran to the window and looked out. Smoke was everywhere.

'The house is on fire!'

At that moment Mum and Dad burst into the room.

'Stay calm,' Dad said. 'It's in the garage, not in the house, but we have to get out now.'

We quickly played the game of 'If your house was burning down what would you grab?' I tried to gather all the important stuff that shouldn't go up in smoke. But by the time I got outside I realised with no little horror that I'd forgotten Jabba the Gerbil.

On his way out, Dad ran his palm over the living room wall that adjoined the garage. 'Ow!' He whipped his hand away, shaking it. If the door from the utility room to the garage had been open we would have lost the house.

All thoughts of the gerbil were quickly put to one side as I realised that my most prized possession was in that garage. 'My motorbike!'

While my sister was into horses, I was into horsepower and was now the very proud owner of a Yamaha PeeWee 50 motorbike, which – as the name implies – was tiny. I used to fly around the field that adjoined our house impersonating Evel Knievel and would spend hours collecting and arranging cardboard boxes to crash through.

I used to love *Kick Start*, the TV motorbike talent show. Contestants riding trials bikes would attempt to complete an obstacle course against the clock. My favourite part was when they rode over a VW Beetle and I tried to replicate that and as many of the other stunts they did as possible, such as riding in and out of ditches, bunny hops and pulling wheelies.

The fire brigade rolled up just in time to save the house and extinguished the fire without too much difficulty. It turned out that Dad had left the car battery charger on and it was this that had caught fire.

One of the firemen took us round to inspect the damage. He explained how lucky we were that the main house hadn't caught fire. There was a slight buckle in the ceiling. The fireman pointed to it and said, 'That steel girder must have been heated to over three thousand degrees, it's expanded into the adjoining wall and is now poking into your utility room.'

By then I was looking down at my bike in horror. All the plastic parts had melted into a smoking puddle on the garage floor, leaving a tiny metal skeleton behind.

Dad shared my look of horror but for different reasons. The fire had reached the paint cupboard, which was full of pots that dad had collected over a lifetime of DIY; every colour imaginable had lined those shelves. But they had exploded in the heat and had turned his car (a vintage Sunbeam) into Joseph's Technicolor Dream Car.

Miraculously, both vehicles worked fine when we turned their respective ignitions a few days later. They really knew how to build things to last in those days. Luckily, it was possible to order replacement parts for my motorbike and, although Dad looked like a wild rainbow hippy for a few weeks, he eventually had the car resprayed.

One day, while I was recreating *Kick Start* on my newly stuck-together bike, Mum, obviously terribly excited about something, called me inside.

'Lucasfilm want you to play Wicket again!'

My face lit up. 'No way!'

I know some *Star Wars* fans don't like them, but the public response to the Ewoks was overwhelmingly positive, so George Lucas had decided to produce a TV special with me reprising the role of Wicket. It would mean eight weeks in San Francisco filming near the Skywalker Ranch.

This was my first lead role but I took it in my stride. I knew the character inside out by then and I was bursting with enthusiasm. In the film Wicket had learned English and was able to communicate with the human stars, a pair of space kids. I was delighted to see that Ewok suit technology had improved somewhat – the mouth could actually move this time, although it was a little stiff, a bit like the *Monty Python* mouths in the Terry Gilliam animations.

Another new development was that I could now move the Ewok eyes using a wrist mechanism, which was weird at first but I soon got so used to it that I started to move my wrists in anticipation of where I was going to look – even when I was out of costume.

The main problem hadn't yet been dealt with, however; the eyes would still mist up within seconds. So, once again, I had to memorise the set layout and use the glare of the studio lights to judge whether I should turn left, right or keep going straight ahead.

The suit was a lot heavier as well and I fell over a great many times. Luckily it was so thick I never hurt myself, but it was also much harder to stop myself rolling down a hill once I'd started.

To my dismay surfer dude Ray had been replaced by the Snow Queen-esque Mrs Ramsay. She was a woman's woman and was pretty scary. She held an unshakeable faith in education over every other one of life's pursuits and was an obsessively strict time-keeper who held no fear of film directors. She once marched onto the set while the cameras were rolling and commanded: 'Warwick Davis, put down that spear immediately, modern political history awaits you!'

'Please, just one more take!'

'Absolutely not,' she'd say, tapping her watch with barely contained fury. 'Lessons should have started ten minutes ago.'

The one exception that did halt Mrs Ramsay in her tracks was the sudden appearance of the King of Pop. Apparently Michael Jackson was a big fan of the Ewoks and had dropped by to see us in the fur, so to speak. This was 1984, two years after *Thriller* and his legendary world tour. Jackson was at the absolute height of his godlike fame.

'Hi,' he said. 'Can I have my picture taken with you?'

My reply probably sounded like Ewokese but I gave the distinct impression that this would be more than OK. He put his arm round me, leaned in and 'snap', the moment was over.

'Well, it was lovely meeting you, I gotta run, I'm going to the White House now, I'm late for my meeting with President Reagan.'

And he was gone.

It was then that I realised I'd forgotten to remove my head.

'Oh no! No one will ever know it was me!'

Tony Cox and Debbie Carrington played my Ewok brother and

sister. They'd both been Ewoks in *Jedi* and have since gone on to have incredibly successful acting careers of their own. Tony was actually a stunt Ewok in *Jedi*, and acted as a double for Kenny in the scene where Paploo was struggling to keep a grip on the speeder bike he'd just stolen. To get the shot the crew positioned the bike so it was vertical and filmed Tony dangling from the handlebars with the camera tilted to match the on-screen perspective. Tony was also the fabulously brilliant little limo driver in *Me, Myself and Irene* and has been in dozens of Hollywood films, while Debbie has appeared in *Bones*, *Dexter*, *Nip/Tuck*, *Boston Legal*, *ER* and many more famous TV dramas.

We stayed in a Holiday Inn in Marin County, very near the Golden Gate Bridge. I leapt out of bed every morning and greeted the day with a twenty-step sprint and dive into the swimming pool, which was just outside our door.

When the film, called *Caravan of Courage*, aired it broke US TV records. It was so successful that George decided to show it in cinemas in Europe. I was invited to the special media screening in Leicester Square, so I took my nan. She loved it and appreciated the fact that I hadn't forgotten who started it all.

During filming it happened to be George Lucas's daughter's birthday. Amanda was four years old and she loved the Ewoks, none more so than Wicket. She was one of the reasons the Ewok movies were made. George saw that she and her friends couldn't get enough of the little furballs.

George appeared on set one day and asked me to come to Amanda's party in costume at his house and be Wicket for the day. 'Sure!' I said, 'that'd be cool!'

I arrived at George's fabulously enormous house just as all the kids were playing in the pool. They screamed when they saw me. 'Let's see if Wicket wants to go swimming!' one girl with pink cheeks and pigtails said.

I was under strict instructions not to ruin things by talking (at this stage Ewoks didn't speak English, neither did they sound like fourteen-year-old boys), so I backed away quickly, even though I was sorely tempted to risk drowning. It was a hundred degrees and I was melting inside that costume.

As soon as the chance presented itself, I dashed back inside for a brief 'heads off' moment before returning again in my highly flammable costume carrying the cake complete with four burning candles. Everyone sang 'Happy Birthday' and I cut a slice for the birthday girl. She then generously decided to share her cake with me. Of course, my costume wouldn't allow me to bite and eat but that didn't prevent the little girl from shoving the cake straight through the costume's mouth hole. Suddenly all of the little angels wanted to feed the Ewok and so they rammed cake into my mouth until my Ewok head was full and I started to suffocate. Fortunately the parents rescued me – 'Wicket's feeling a bit tired and full now, children, time for his nap' – and carried me away as I started to cough urgently. When they took the head off about a kilo of cake slopped onto George's lounge carpet.

The Battle for Endor quickly followed the success of *Caravan of Courage*. The plot involved a grumpy old spaceman and Wicket becoming friends. I was chuffed to bits to be Wicket once more; it was becoming a yearly treat and this time I was allowed to bring Daniel.

Daniel and I had an amazing time. To us, back in 1985, America really was the greatest country in the world by far. It was still a world of dreams and its image – among young people – had yet to be tarnished. It was the land that had everything your heart could possibly desire, from frozen yoghurt to Disneyland, with a Dunkin'

Donuts and a McDonald's on every street (most English towns didn't have McDonald's back then). But most of all it was the land of movies and back then you could see new films ages, sometimes years before they came out in the UK, conferring upon us substantial bragging rights for months after we returned home.

'Oh, we saw that when we were in America, didn't we, Warwick?'

And then I'd torture them by saying, 'Yeah, it was brilliant, you have to see it.'

While we were in the States, Mum got another call from Elstree, this time from Jim Henson Productions.

'Do you think Warwick would like to be a goblin?' they asked. 'We're making a movie called *Labyrinth* with David Bowie and we need experienced little people.'

Chapter Six

Starman in My Caravan

My father-in law, Peter Burroughs with David Bowie on the set of *Labyrinth*. I was probably in my caravan when this was taken.

Sam with the Goblin King.

*B*attle for Endor and *Labyrinth* were being made at the same time but with a little clever synchronisation of diaries, made easier by the fact that George Lucas was Executive Producer on each of the movies, I was all set to appear in both. My role in *Labyrinth* was more in the background and, thanks to animatronics, I was able to play two goblins called Bumpot and WW2. The film starred David Bowie, was directed by Jim Henson, puppeteered by Frank Oz and written by Terry Jones. You couldn't get any better than that. My life cast was made at Jim Henson's Creature Shop in leafy Downshire Hill (which ran off Willow Road!) in Hampstead, North London.

Jim's studio wasn't as big as I'd imagined and was both warehouse and workshop. It was packed floor to ceiling with Muppets, all sorts of weird creature creations and casts of famous people's bits and pieces. Powerful odours of glue, clay and fibreglass fought for supremacy. It may have been me but the glue seemed to be winning – the puppet makers all walked around in a happy, dreamy daze.

Jim Henson used to live right opposite the studio. So afterwards, covered in Vaseline and goodness knows what else, I was sent to have a shower in his house. He wasn't there at the time, so I had the place to myself. Like the studio, it was packed full of Muppets. Kermit sat on a window ledge in the bathroom while Beaker and Gonzo the Great propped each other up on a chair in the hall and a collection of Miss Piggy's wigs were piled on a hallway shelf.

It was brilliant but kind of freaky, I half-expected the characters to spring into life and start singing the theme song to *The Muppet Show*. I even protected my modesty by turning Kermit's head away from me while I was in the shower.

The life cast done,[15] it was time to begin filming. *Labyrinth* was shot at Elstree, on one of the stages used in *Jedi*. Now it's all gone and a Tesco stands in its place (some would say that's another empire to be fearful of). The Ewok Village set once stood right where the fish counter is today.

Although I wasn't in any scenes with David Bowie and his spectacular trousers,[16] I did manage to get a brief audience with the Goblin King and David was completely delightful. He seemed to be really enjoying making the film and was always in good spirits.

I was in the general goblin melee along with many other little people. The cast of *Labyrinth* contained many former Ewoks, including my good friend Peter Burroughs and his daughter Sam. Peter was also a stunt goblin. In one scene he had to swing over a castle wall. He was counted in on three, co-ordinated by the stunt director. Unfortunately, his assistant had steered a gaggle of goblins directly into his arc and despite desperate if confusing screams of 'Duck!' and 'Heads up!' Peter scattered them all like bowling pins.

I was into radio-controlled cars in those days and would amuse myself between scenes by racing my latest snazzy model around Elstree. I thought I was very cool and believed my wizardry with the remote control was something quite magnificent to behold. I even had dreams of turning pro and getting sponsorship. (When

---

[15] Henson kept my life cast in his house as an ornament. It's still out there somewhere. Come to think of it, there are bits of me everywhere.
[16] They left *nothing* to the imagination.

Sam saw me doing this for the first time, she sighed, 'What a spoiled little brat.')

A lot of the film involved my fellow goblins and me being chased by radio-controlled rocks of all sizes. They ranged from about five feet across to the size of a pebble. A guy with the controller would get them to roll using a powerful motor and steered them using an internal gimbal. They were a little unreliable, though, and their inertia would sometimes get the better of them so I'd still be running for my life long after Henson yelled 'Cut!'

While many were mechanised, there were also plenty of rubber boulders that were simply rolled downhill towards us. Sometimes, in an effort to make the rocks look as if they were chasing us, we were fastened to them with thin cables – but we often became entangled and would land flat on our faces before the giant stone rolled over us.

Jim had problems when the rocks were meant to chase me uphill and into my house. After some thought and experimenting with my video camera, I came up with the bright idea of running backwards with the rocks rolling downhill after me. 'Reverse the film and voila!' I said.

It worked and I was convinced I was a cinematic genius in the making.

There were quite a few accidents during the filming of *Labyrinth*. My animatronic head was made of fibreglass and metal and I had a moving beak attached to my chin. In one scene I had to run across an alleyway while being chased by goblins that were riding weird ostrich Muppets in the style of Bernie Clifton (in that the ostrich legs actually belonged to the 'riders').

There were six of these riding goblins that charged through all at once. I couldn't see them coming and take after take I ended up flat on my back as they took me straight out. It was like being inside a bell being repeatedly struck with a metal bar – and it always seemed to be the biggest bloke who managed to hit me.

Kenny Baker had it even worse. He was standing next to the castle wall when a cannonball was fired at it. The cannonball was of course magical and goblin-like – it had arms and legs. It was supposed to explode when it hit the building and it certainly did that. A huge cascade of sparks fell onto an unwitting, highly flammable Kenny, who promptly erupted into flames. For some seconds he just stood there, in that blissfully unaware state people go into when their hair is on fire, after which – when most of their hair has burned away – they innocently ask, 'What's that smell? It smells just like . . .'

Just as the flames of recognition flickered across Kenny's face, a stagehand came sprinting from the side and slapped him to the floor with an almighty forehand to his enflamed head. The flames were extinguished in seconds but poor Kenny was left with a severe case of sudden-onset baldness and temporary double vision.

The Davis family home was far, far way from Elstree and the hotel we were offered as accommodation had less charm than a real life Farty Owls (a.k.a. Fawlty Towers). For some reason, as soon as you stepped into your room, the temperature dropped to something close to freezing.

Then Dad had an epiphany.

'Well, we've just bought a bigger and better caravan, why don't we stay in that?'

It was true – in a rare fit of extravagance Dad had bought a caravan with double-glazing, cold running water and so much space it had an echo. He parked it just twenty feet from the stage door that led to the Goblin City. Suddenly I had a bigger and better dressing room than David Bowie – and it was closer to the stage.

All I had to do was wake up and wander into work.

Unfortunately, Dad made my life more difficult by staying with me for the entire five weeks of filming and inviting everyone to 'his place' for a drink. I struggled to sleep as the little actors Jack Purvis[17] and Kenny Baker traded showbiz stories with Dad.

With filming completed a wrap party was organised. Oddly enough, I met one of my childhood heroes – Miss Popov from *Rentaghost* – at the party, which was held on the Goblin City set. By then she was playing Audrey in *Coronation Street* but she still very kindly did Miss Popov's accent and touched her nose for me (this was how one disappeared in *Rentaghost*).

Kenny and Jack had formed a group called the Mini-Tones and they performed a cabaret atop the castle wall. It was a crazy place to have a party. This was the mid-1980s and everybody was dressed in white, the set was filthy and it wasn't long before everyone looked as if they'd just been down a coal mine.

Finally, after eight weeks spent running around the huge stage being chased by radio-controlled rocks and admiring (from afar) Peter's gorgeous daughter, the film was done and it was back to school.

---

[17] Jack Purvis was one of the few cast members who'd been in all three *Star Wars* films – as a Jawa, an Ewok, a Dustbin Droid and Chief Ugnaught. Jack also played a key role as Wally in Terry Gilliam's cult movie *Time Bandits*. There were plans for a sequel but Terry Gilliam later indefinitely shelved it after both Jack and David Rappaport, who played the other key role, suffered terrible tragedies. Jack was paralysed after his car rolled backwards and crushed him (he died six years later), while David, struggling with depression, killed himself in 1990.

Chapter Seven

Skating for Spielberg

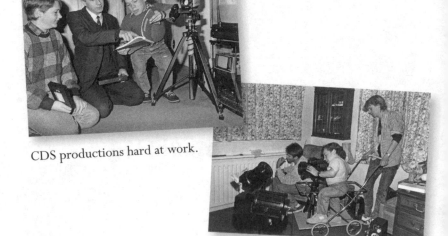

CDS productions hard at work.

We made a camera dolly out of a pram.
I don't know why we were filming a
radiator though.

Showing off our cinematic
awards (although I could only
manage third place in the BBC's
Screen Test Young Filmmaker of
the Year, the Oscars® for young
people – a travesty!).

The (very) odd couple: Daniel was into
Metallica while I was into Jean Michel
Jarre – but we were united by our love
for all things *Star Wars*.

My first major cinematic effort, *The Outing*, starring Mum's 2CV, my sister and friend Stuart, was inspired by BBC's *Rentaghost*. It involved lots of disappearing things, including Mum's car.

Me, over-acting while goose-stepping, from my short film *Russian Guard*.

'And all because the lady hated Milk Tray.'

Video Nasty, in which a man is eaten alive by his video cassette recorder (VCRs were about the size of mechanical diggers in those days).

Act I, Scene I from *Nightmare*: Just another average day, fourteen-year-olds drinking beer and playing poker – but it's about be disrupted by a possessed statue (which will later cause me to explode).

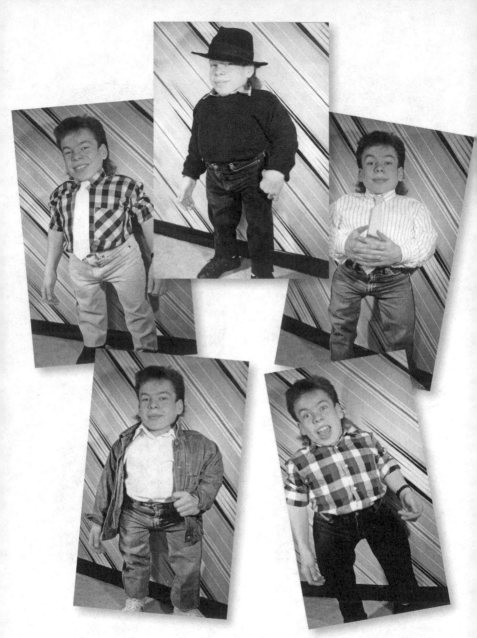

A selection of outfits from the Warwick Davis wardrobe. I don't know why I did this, I just thought it was a good idea at the time – can you guess which decade this was?

The careers officer came to give us advice. He took one look at me and raised his hands skywards in exasperation. 'Not the fire brigade?' I asked. 'I could get in all those hard to reach places.'[18]

While I still hadn't realised that acting could actually be my career, I thought that filmmaking made sense. Mum and Dad agreed; after all, I now had lots of connections in the biz and so I ended up doing my school work experience back at Elstree as a runner on *Who Framed Roger Rabbit?*

Yes, that's right, a runner. I thought runners were very cool. They used walkie-talkies and their main job seemed to be screaming at everyone to shut up before the filming of a scene started, something I knew I'd be very good at.

I was more than a little outraged when I discovered that 'running' was actually an important part of the job. I had to dash back and forth carrying scripts, papers, coffees, props and anything else they could think of between Robert Zemeckis, Bob Hoskins, Steven Spielberg and the entire production team. I was also given the most boring job in the world, photocopying and stamping every single page of every single script with a unique number, so if anyone sold a script to a journalist then the film company would know who to sack and sue.

---

[18] I did consider the police once they abandoned the height restriction, although I don't think I would have felt many collars.

On my second day I rolled into work on my roller skates, which helped considerably, but I was already certain that production wasn't for me.

A few days later I was rolling through the set when a man with a beard, glasses and baseball cap waved me over. 'Would you come here for a second?' he said.

I pointed at myself and said, 'Who, me?'

'Yes, you.'

I walked over to Steven Spielberg.

'I think,' he said, looking me up and down thoughtfully, 'that you'd be the perfect solution to a little problem we're having.'

By a stroke of luck, I was about the same height as Roger Rabbit and so I played the role of Roger for half a day during rehearsals, giving the actors something to focus on – that way their eyes were all looking at the right height when they came to shoot their scenes, making the animators' jobs a lot easier. Unfortunately, it was also at the end of my work experience and all too short-lived.

After *Jedi*, once I was back in the UK, I bought my own video camera and started making short films. My early twelve-year-old efforts centred on making animals, people and objects disappear à la *Rentaghost*. I loved the way it was possible to shoot, then pause and remove something – a rock for example – from a scene and then start recording again (without moving the camera) so it looked as if the rock had disappeared. My mother, my sister, my friends, everyone and everything vanished and then re-materialised all under my expert direction.

My first major production was *The Outing*, starring my sister and Stuart, one of my friends, who also supplied titles and music (he was good at calligraphy and liked to tinkle the ivories). They played an old couple having a picnic on Epsom Downs. They arrive in an orange and white Citroen 2CV (Mum's car), which then disappears. They're left sitting in their wigs and hats in the seats on the road. The seats of a 2CV were known as 'deckchairs' because they could be removed. Goodness knows why. Where on earth would you want to take a pair of car seats? They were extremely heavy and made for terribly uncomfortable deckchairs.[19]

There were very few young people making films then. It's completely different today, of course. It's so easy for kids if they want to get started now and they can get their work seen by thousands, if not millions of people on hosting sites such as YouTube. Back in the old days, all we had was *Screen Test* presented by the besuited and legendary Brian Trueman, the voice behind such children's TV classics as *Chorlton and the Wheelies, Jamie and the Magic Torch, Danger Mouse* and *Count Duckula*.

It was essentially an observational film quiz and was insanely popular. It also ran a 'Young Filmmaker of the Year' competition for budding Spielbergs. The prize was a plastic trophy. The most famous winner was Jan Pinkava who won in 1980. Nope, I'd never heard of him either, but he went on to win the Oscar[®] for best animated short in 1997 and then conceived the idea for and co-directed Pixar's Oscar[®]-winning 2007 film *Ratatouille*.

One tricky problem with stop start filming was trying to overcome the slight delay from pressing record and the actual moment when the camera started to record. Getting the cry of 'Action!' just right was key.

In one very early effort I played a disturbingly accurate Professor Filius Flitwick — which was pretty impressive, considering this

---

[19] When Mum said she was going into town to pick up a new car I was overjoyed and hung out the window looking for her on her way back. I was gutted when I saw a newer, black and yellow model of the 2CV straining its way up the hill towards us. She hadn't? She had.

was in 1982. There was no plot as such, I was simply a mad professor who made potions while wearing an extraordinarily ill-fitting Dennis the Menace black wig. I also hit my sister in the face with my geography textbook for no discernible reason and remember my performance involved a great deal of shouting about Cheddar cheese – one of my favourite foods.

My next production was a very sophisticated affair and involved a dramatic 1980s-style synth soundtrack. It was based on the famously patronising adverts for Milk Tray that featured the immortal endline: 'And All Because the Lady Loves Milk Tray'.

In those adverts a James Bond character would brave hell and high water to bring his lady (usually living in total luxury in a heavily guarded turret) her favourite chocolates. He'd sneak them in while she was in the bath or shower, only to mysteriously disappear, leaving only his calling card and the chocolates behind him.

I didn't have a real box of Milk Tray, so I made one. It was white with 'Milk Tray' scrawled across it in black marker in my terribly immature handwriting. The film also involved me waving a giant plastic fly over my sister (The Lady), not because it was necessary to the plot, you understand, but just because I had one. You could see my shadow, holding a long pole, in the shot. It turned out in this case that The Lady hated Milk Tray and killed The Man (me) after he'd made his delivery by throwing a rock at his head. This was my first stunt scene and I placed my wig on top of a cycle helmet so my sister could really throw the tiny stone at my head.[20]

The Russian Guard was another masterpiece, one that could have been influenced by Sergei M. Eisenstein. Again I played the lead in my Dennis the Menace wig, goose-stepping like a loon while

---

[20] I'd learned the importance of safety procedures from the stunt co-ordinators on *Jedi*.

carrying a spud gun and an old-fashioned gas lamp (even though it was broad daylight).

I still relied upon the old stop-and-shoot method, and I think that editing in-camera should be taught by film schools today because it really makes you think about how you're going to construct each scene, there's no room for error and it can't be fixed in post-production. As I was operating the camera, I'd often find myself trying to direct my sister while the film was rolling. Not wanting to be heard, I'd wave frantically, mouthing the word 'Go!' over and over again when I wanted her to walk, or 'Climb the tree!' You could tell when I was doing this because the camera would wobble.

My sister played the role of the thief who wanted to steal whatever it was I was guarding (a block of gold, cunningly disguised as a breeze block). To do this she shot at me with a spud gun; we used a stone to represent the bullet – it missed me, but only just.

Putting on my sternest Brezhnev face, I marched around in fury, outraged that someone has dared to shoot at me. Cut to sister half on and half off the shed roof, screaming 'I can't!' and me waving frantically, the camera wobbling. 'Yes, you can,' I mouth, 'Keep going!' She jumps down from the roof and we cut back to the Russian Guard who has now ratcheted the goose-stepping to Olympic levels. Finally, after falling for about thirty seconds, my sister lands on me, knocks me out and steals the breeze block, only to drop it on her foot during her getaway.

Cut to sister hopping her way Benny Hill-style across the field next to our house. I'd wanted to film her until she reached the other side but it was much further than we both realised and although she was getting tired as she hopped into the distance I waved at her frantically, mouthing, 'Keep hopping! Keep going!'

It was perhaps inevitable that when I left school I decided to study media at the nearby East Surrey College. The course consisted of film studies and video production. For our exam, we had to make a film based on the title 'New Year's Resolution', demonstrating all the techniques that we had learned during our year's study.

I employed my cousin Mark and my friend and fellow film student David Tulley, who gave two truly memorably dire performances in what became my first horror film. The soundtrack was made up of swirly Jean Michel Jarre synthesisers. The best thing we did was to manufacture an impressive dolly (essentially a camera on wheels which allows for smooth tracking shots) from the wheels of an old pram.

The story went like this. Mark is in the shower when David enters the house wearing a long black coat and hat, looking very suspicious. The synthesiser whirls itself up to feverish levels as David climbs the stairs towards the shower and . . . cue *Psycho* music . . . but no! David opens the bathroom door, shouts, 'Happy New Year!' and throws Mark his car keys.

I didn't realise it then but looking back on it now, this seems to me to have some slight homoerotic undertones. Two young men living together in a big house in the country – one of whom casually enters the shower without knocking and throws his friend the keys to his Ferrari. If anyone had walked in on me in the shower in real life I would have covered my privates and let the keys hit me in the face, before telling them to clear off.

Anyway, I'd had a kettle boiling in the bathroom for about half an hour to try and get some steam up, because the water just wasn't hot enough. It took us about twenty takes before the guys stopped fluffing their lines or falling about laughing – Mark kept dropping the keys because he had soap in his eyes. By the time they finally got their act together the hot water had run out; Mark left the shower shivering and as wrinkly as a Shar Pei dog. When we compiled the outtakes from this scene, they were longer than the actual film.

The next scene was downstairs where they shared a whisky from my father's drinks cabinet. After having a drink, David turns his wrist as if to look at his watch, but when filming actually forgot to look as all his powers of concentration were taken up with remembering his soliloquy: 'It's late. We should get to the party.'

One of our neighbours had a red Ferrari, which he was crazy enough to lend us for the film. We thought this was incredibly cool but we were also terrified of damaging it so David (who was a truly terrible driver) drove it off down a very long country lane in first gear at five miles an hour. It took forever to get out of the drive, which kind of reduced the Ferrari's impact.

Anyway, the party goes terribly wrong and Mark returns home alone, puts on the TV and falls asleep at midnight. We switch to the exterior of the house (where the sun has clearly just set – where were we? Lapland?) and my dad enters the house as the creepy murderer and kills Mark with an scythe while the TV plays 'Auld Lang Syne'.

The horror movies of the 1980s were a tremendous influence on me. I'd often use the music of horror maestro John Carpenter as the soundtrack to my home-made films. Like thousands of other teenage boys I went through the rite of passage of seeing 18-Certificate horror films when I was underage, *Nightmare on Elm Street* and *Halloween* being two particular favourites.

We saw *Nightmare on Elm Street* at a special midnight screening in Ewell, which seemed to have quite a relaxed attitude as to who could see an 18-Cert. In those days, cinemas were much larger (they've all been carved up into smaller screens today) and Ewell was about the same size as Cheddar Gorge with equivalent acoustics. If you were unlucky enough to end up at the back you'd end up hearing the movie about five seconds after the people at the front.

The cinema was pretty rough and had all the atmosphere of a bawdy East End pub. During the midnight screening we noticed that a haze had appeared in front of the screen. Some boisterous troublemakers had actually managed to set fire to one of the seats. The ushers threw a bucket of sand on it and we carried on watching, coughing through the smoke haze.

These days I hardly watch any horror movies at all, but one of my favourite films of all time remains Alfred Hitchcock's *Psycho*. Anthony Perkins' performance as Norman Bates made me really think about what it was possible to achieve as an actor for the first time – it wasn't just about delivering your lines in the right voice. His performance was so edgy, so different from the bloodthirsty movies Hollywood normally fed us.

Psycho also taught me about suspense, what was possible with sound and music. I bought the soundtrack and, as an avid sound-track collector, I still think it's one of the best scores ever recorded. I had a poster of Anthony Perkins holding a knife-shaped key to Room One of the Bates Motel on my wall throughout my teenage years, and I studied the movie in great depth at film school.

There were so many other wonderful films, aimed more specif-ically at my age group, at that time. *The Goonies, Gremlins, Inner Space* and so on. I don't mean to say there was some great golden age in the 1980s but I feel that films nowadays try to take them-selves too seriously; films then were much more rough and ready and audiences were happy to use their imagination during dodgy effects or forgive gaping plot holes as long as the movie was fun. They were so digestible and now I love nothing more than sharing

these films with my children, who love them just as much as I did
– especially *The Goonies*.

The mid-80s also saw the dawn of the pirate video. There
weren't many video recorders about then. We relied on our
wealthier neighbours in Kingswood who always seemed to get
these new gadgets first. They'd buy the very first video recorder,
the very first games console, the very first CD player, the very first
DVD player – which were all usually obsolete within a month, at
which point they'd then sell them on to the residents of Lower
Kingswood, my dad being a particularly good customer.

There was one friend who had a swimming pool, an Atari and
two video recorders (so he could record two things at once). The
recorders were about the same size as a small family car and they
sold one of these to Dad, who heaved it through our front door,
sweating, huffing and puffing. 'This is the future!' he exclaimed,
'And it's bloody heavy!' When he set the device down, the lounge
floor bowed slightly. It was a huge top-loader with giant dials and
knobs on the front: setting the timer was done using an analog
clock. The keys on the top were so big and heavy with such strong
springs that they were impossible for me to depress, even when
pushing down with both my feet. It was so complicated to operate
and relied on so many mechanisms that it never recorded anything
we wanted to watch. To me, it was just amazing to know that it
was technically possible to record TV.

A friend of mine got hold of a pirate copy of *ET: The Extra Terres-
trial* and we watched it at his house. We were all incredibly excited;
we were getting to see a great film for free! Of course, when we
played it, it was a dodgy copy of someone filming a cinema screen;
it was indecipherable. I'm very much against pirate videos these
days and if I see one I go crackers and try to take the tape/DVD
away from whoever has it. They are always of terrible quality and

are an insult to all the people who have done everything they can to make a film look and sound as amazing as possible.

My own teenage movie masterpiece was called *Nightmare*. There were three of us involved in this, all of us about fourteen. My co-producers were Alex Cotton and Courtland Stibbe (pronounced Stibbey), so we called ourselves CDS Productions.

Courtland was a dab hand at computing and he made some nifty titles on his Acorn computer. With the room darkened, I used my camera to zoom in on the monitor, to make it look as if the titles were coming towards the viewer.

And now for the plot. It centred on a cheap piece of tat that Alex had brought back from his family hols in Egypt, a clay model of Tutankhamun's head.

In the first scene we're all sitting around playing poker and drinking beer (as most fourteen-year-olds like to do) when Courtland, after suffering a heavy loss, marches off in a strop and has a sulk in the abandoned shed at the bottom of the garden, where he dislodges a floorboard, uncovering Tutankhamun's head.

I should point out that Alex had made it very clear to me, on pain of death, that the head should remain intact. So we used a rock as a stunt double whenever it was supposed to be thrown and we got pretty good at the old switcheroo.

Alex passes it to Courtland, who chucks it (the stunt double) onto the rubbish heap. Cue scary music. Alex then walks past the swimming pool in the garden and comes across the statue sitting on the wall. Strange. Surely it should be in the rubbish? He reaches out to touch it and – cue thunder and lightning effect – Alex is electrocuted and falls into the pool.

Cut to later on that day. I'm drinking beer (of course) and watching TV news (read by my mum). Cut to a shot of a pair of hands cutting the power line in the meter cupboard. I don't know where those hands came from, whose they were and where they went afterwards but don't worry, it's not important.

Cut back to me in the lounge. The power goes. I pull a face. Don't you just hate it when that happens? I pick up the phone, as obviously that's the first thing you do in that situation. The line is dead. I let the receiver fall to the floor. Things start being thrown about the room.

Odd? Yes. I go outside in my slippers (as Peter Kaye once pointed out, they're great for running in). There's a strange noise coming from – the statue. It increases in pitch and I run across the garden and still the noise increases. I run into the field and still the noise increases, it's shattering my eardrums. I can't take it any more!

Then I explode.

I should probably explain that last bit. We were all nerds and Courtland knew his way round a chemistry set. He knew that if we dismantled enough fireworks, we would be able to create a pretty nifty-sized explosion. We bought all the fireworks we could carry from a grateful newsagent, who'd overstocked the previous Guy Fawkes Night, and packed them loosely into a paper container with a kilo of flour. All we had to do then was film me running into shot, dropping to my knees, holding my ears.

'Cut!'

I sprinted to a safe distance (thank God for the slippers) as Courtland lit the blue touchpaper. The resulting flash and the mushroom cloud could be seen from Swindon.

If we had done that today we would have had the counter-terrorism squad round before you could say, 'The man in the newsagents sold them to us.'

Nonetheless, it was a great effect. But the film wasn't over yet. Oh no, you don't get off that lightly.

Once we were all dead, I switched the button on the camera marked 'negative'. The resulting tone and colour were supposed to represent us in the afterlife. Dressed in our best clothes (Alex was in a particularly fetching white shirt and white trousers), we worship the idol in front of a wall of flames (some petrol in one of Mum's baking trays placed just below camera) while *Carmina Burana*[21] plays. Then we place the artefact back under the floorboards in the shed. Goodness knows why it would kill to get back into that shed.

Finally, cut to me in bed. Aha, it was all a dream! But wait, the alarm clock starts ringing. I don't wake up – I'm dead!

And the credits roll. They were very specific; as owner of the clay statue, Alex was credited as 'Properties Manager'.

Unfortunately, I never got to find out what grade it would have got in college – by then I was starring in my own major motion picture.

---

[21] We all knew it from the TV adverts for Old Spice. The whole experience seemed to leave quite an impression on Courtland, who later became a monk.

Chapter Eight

Heroes Come in All Sizes

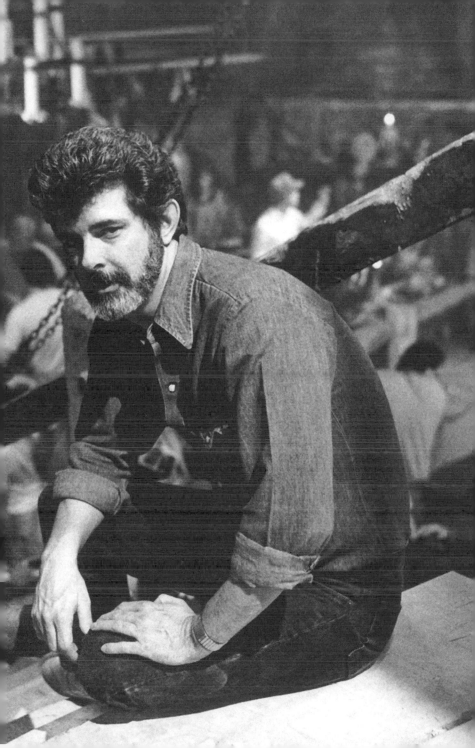

Val Kilmer and I didn't have to act our fear once we hit the mile-long glacier — I screamed until I ran out of air. 'Luckily', someone had the bright idea of piling up a mountain of loose powder snow right in our path to bring us to a halt.

Courtesy of Lucasfilm Ltd.

We repeated the sledging scene with a skier until Ron was certain he had enough footage of our terrified expressions.

Courtesy of Lucasfilm Ltd.

Discussing a scene with the wonderful Jean Marsh while director Ron Howard thoughtfully strokes his moustache. Jean played the evil sorceress Bavmorda with chilling conviction.

Courtesy of Lucasfilm Ltd.

Willow and Meegosh (aka David Steinberg), great friends both on-screen and off.

Courtesy of Lucasfilm Ltd.

'Stewpid Daikinis' George Lucas and Ron Howard.
Courtesy of Lucasfilm Ltd.

Val Kilmer, Ron Howard, me and Joanne Whalley. As can clearly be seen here, Joanne was madly in love with me but I broke her heart and she started dating Val on the rebound.
Courtesy of Lucasfilm Ltd.

'What are you trying to do? Drown me?' To add insult to injury, the storm scenes we filmed in Pinewood's reservoir were never used.

Courtesy of Lucasfilm Ltd.

Paddling towards trouble.

That smile wouldn't be on my face for much longer…
Courtesy of Lucasfilm Ltd.

MADMARTIGAN

ACTUAL
SIZE

Val and I did lots of public signings for *Willow*. Val, the joker, liked to write me amusing messages before he passed the photos over for me to sign.
Courtesy of Lucasfilm Ltd.

'Is *that* it?' I asked, and turned to look at Daniel. The 'that' was pronounced with a mixture of disgust and disappointment.

'Yup,' Daniel said with some uncertainty.

As far as I was concerned Cornwall was supposed to be an exciting land of smugglers' coves, warm cosy pubs, wild seas, rugged coasts and the pasty. What I was looking at here was a cottage that would be described in an estate agent's blurb as 'charming' and 'requiring extensive renovation and modernisation'.

In a *Withnail and I* moment, Daniel had convinced me to let him 'treat' me to a week's holiday with his family in remotest Cornwall. 'It's payback for you having taken me to the USA,' he said. Hmmm . . . Stepping over the threshold was like stepping back into Edwardian times. I could hear the damp cottage crumbling.

'Wow! Look at the TV!'

It actually had woodworm. I swear it was powered by a gas and valve system. I switched it on and it shook and hummed into life. I stared at the screen. And stared. The screen lightened fractionally.

'Maybe it'll have warmed up in half an hour or so,' Daniel said hopefully.

'I suppose you don't come on holiday to watch TV,' I said gloomily, not believing that to be true at all.

Outside it was raining cats and dogs but I had to admit, after a quick walk on a nearby wild beach, the scenery was really quite spectacular.

After two days of rain, as we still waited for the TV to warm up, I decided to call home. This was before the days of mobiles and meant I had to go in search of a public call box. 'I'll be back in a tick,' I said, and went on the hunt for a telephone. Luckily, I soon spotted the familiar red box in the local village.

Using a phone box was just one of many situations in which I had to employ a certain unusual ingenuity to compensate for my lack in height. After heaving open the heavy metal door, I then had to climb up the inside of the box, with one foot on either side, using the windowpanes as steps until I was halfway up. Then, pretty much doing the splits, I was able to make a precarious and short (it was quite tiring) phone call.[22] An old lady strolled past and did a double take.

'Mum?' I said, slightly breathlessly. 'It's me.'

'Oh, Warwick, thank goodness you've called!'

'What is it?' I asked, sensing the urgent tone in Mum's voice.

'It's George, he wants you to come and meet him and Ron Howard at Elstree Studios to talk about a new film.'

That was all I wanted to hear. 'I'll be right there!' I hung up, carefully made my way back down the interior of the phone box and ran back to Daniel. Once I'd explained, he insisted on accompanying me. Fortunately for us, his wonderful parents clearly understood that meeting George Lucas was about one million times more important to us than staying in Cornwall with them.

Ten minutes later we were packed and hopping up and down with excitement on the station platform. After a couple of slow starts, we got an express that whisked us back to London. Mum

---

[22] Thank goodness for mobile phones. I couldn't climb up the inside of the new call boxes they use these days as they're wider and have no footholds.

met us at the station and took both Daniel and I to meet George
and Ron at Elstree.

We were in a big office right at the far end of the building. As
usual, whenever he met anyone famous, Daniel turned into a
babbling wreck and just managed to introduce himself as my
'friend'.

'Warwick,' George said, 'this is a project I've had in mind for
some time. I told your mum back in '83 and we decided we
needed to wait until you were old enough.'

George said he and Ron were considering me for the title role
in *Willow*, a $40 million fantasy adventure.

'To be honest,' Ron said, 'I think you're too young. I mean, the
character we have in mind is a father – married with two kids – a
worldly kind of fellow.'

I resisted the temptation to insist that, at seventeen years old, I
was of course by now a worldly fellow. George was in my corner
and fought hard to persuade Ron. Eventually, he said to Ron:
'Well, you're the director so feel free to do more casting.' I was
going to have to fight for the part.

I was soon auditioning alongside hundreds upon hundreds of
little people as the casting director scoured the globe for actors to
play Willow and his wife and children. I went to several auditions
where I was paired up with various actors, to see who went with
who. Finally after about ten of these auditions, Ron asked me to
go to America and audition there.

Suddenly, there I was in Hollywood. Unbelievable. And I was
acting alongside rising star John Cusack, who was auditioning for
the role of Madmartigan, a wild mercenary. At the time, I didn't
really know who John was, but I was very excited about the next
actor – Max Headroom, a.k.a. Matt Frewer.

Ron had cast his net wide and was finally on the verge of casting. He was testing me and had me read with actor after actor, for eight hours straight. Taking on the role of Willow would push me mentally and physically and he needed to know I'd be able to cope.

By the time the last reading came round I was so shattered I didn't even notice the extraordinary actor I'd been paired with until he was stood right before me. He had wild, unkempt hair, his scruffy shirt was open to his belly button, he was wearing open-toed sandals, his jeans were worn and faded and his face was very, *very* red. 'I've driven for six hours across the desert with the top down,' he said in a deep, dry voice, scratching his stomach.

My God, he was *really* sunburned. I didn't realise that stood before me was one of the most famous men in the world at that time: Val Kilmer, a.k.a. 'Iceman' from *Top Gun*. It was no wonder – he looked like Iceman's exact opposite. He'd made a smart move by arriving in character.

Val had grabbed my attention and had woken me up. I launched into the read-through with renewed energy. As we spoke I was blown away by his energy; there had been an immediate spark between us.

I loved Val's quirkiness. The last of my fatigue vanished as we started to play the scene, yelling at one another, much to the amusement of Ron.

Val: Well, that was really stupid, peck!
Me: Don't call me a peck.
Val: Oh. I'm sorry . . . peck. Peck, peck, peck, peck.
Me: You be careful! I'm a powerful sorcerer. See this acorn?
I'll throw it, and turn you to stone.

Val: Whoo, I'm really scared. No, don't! Don't! There's a peck
here with an acorn pointed at me!

Me: Oh, I wouldn't want to waste it.

Val: Ha! Peck, peck, peck, peck, peck, peck, peck. peck,
peck!

'That was great, guys,' Ron said. 'Can we try the next scene?'
Val and I were already there.

Val: Mornin'. Rough night last night. wasn't it? I don't think I
introduced myself yesterday. My name is Madmartigan. And
you are, uh . . .

Me: You're dangerous.

Val: I am not.

Me: I suppose you're a warrior.

Val: I am the greatest swordsman that ever lived,

Me: Humph

Val: Say, uh, could I have some of that water? I guess I am
gonna die here. Who cares?

Me: Here.

Val: Thanks, friend.

Val winked. He knew and I knew we'd nailed it in just a couple of
short scenes. We looked at Ron, who smiled. 'Well, Warwick, if
you still want the part after all I've put you through, it's yours.'

We'd passed the test; we'd both won our parts, fair and square.
I still prefer to be cast against fellow actors today, so that I have to
win the role as opposed to being given the job straight out.

This meant I had to forget about college; I was now going to
play the title role in a major movie and would be away for eight
months. This was going to be an extremely demanding production

and I still didn't realise quite how massive a challenge it would be. And I had no idea this film would make me famous. When I told Daniel the good news, his response was 'Wicked! I'll be best mates with a proper star!'

This would be my first role with my face on camera. In the Ewok costume I had over-exaggerated the emotional expressions to bring them out in the physical behaviour of my character and Ron warned me about overacting. 'I want you to watch a few James Stewart movies,' he said, handing me VHS copies of *It's a Wonderful Life* and *Rear Window*. 'I want Willow to have a matter-of-fact style, like Stewart.' Ron would prove to be instrumental in turning me into a 'proper' actor. I think the fact that Ron had also started young – he had become a TV star at the tender age of five – meant that he was more than qualified to take me under his wing. He supported me every step of the way and always wore a smile, no matter how difficult and trying the days became.

Work began before we'd even signed the contract; there were numerous costume and wig fittings and I needed to be measured for props, such as weapons. I also went through a barrage of mental and physical health checks. It was kind of like being an astronaut. It seemed as though there were hundreds of people who were preparing me for this great adventure – which, of course, there were.

Then there were the dozens of sword-fighting and fencing lessons, not to mention the baby-handling classes. Various mothers brought their babies to Elstree thinking their child was going to be the star (the whole film centres around a lost baby, which I take care of). These infants were in fact the rejects from the castings and were handed over to me to practise holding, calming down, changing and how to carry them while running down a mountain being chased by a sorceress's evil minions.

While the fencing lessons were terrific,[23] I was horrified to learn that I also had to learn to ride a horse. My sister had once tried to teach me. She sat me on the thing, gave it a whack and it trotted off down the street with me perched unsteadily atop, unable to do anything to stop it.

'Couldn't a motorcycle be magically transported into the film?' I implored. Alas no. To make matters worse, when I was introduced to the trainer, she mistook my name for 'Merrick'. It rapidly developed into one of those awkward situations where I didn't correct her straight away and so it soon became impossible. For evermore I was 'Merrick' to her.

It was a nightmare – my short legs stuck out at right angles. 'You just don't have the equitation, Merrick,' the trainer told me. I didn't know about that, but one thing I knew for sure was that I couldn't control the damn creature and it would canter wherever it wanted, despite my yells. After two weeks of lessons I looked like one of those plastic toy cowboy figures that you sit on horses with their legs fixed in a permanent u-shape.

Val came over to London about two months before we were due to start shooting so we could rehearse. This would hopefully mean that when we were on location we would be able to knock out solid performances of each scene in one or two takes, saving time and money.

Val and I were together the whole time he was in the UK. He was loads of fun and completely crazy, a real maverick and totally unpredictable. He constantly improvised his lines, which really kept me on my toes. He was always thinking about his character, how far he could take him, how he would respond in almost any situation.

---

[23] I can still perform a nifty *derobement*.

Val wasn't afraid to speak his mind and was only too happy to pass on some acting tips, starting early on in rehearsals when he said, 'Hang on a minute, Warwick. Why aren't you breathing?'

I hadn't realised that whenever I spoke my lines I held my breath as I delivered them. Val, thank goodness, taught me to act and breathe at the same time.

Willow was the biggest casting call for little people in movie history, bigger than *Jedi* and *The Wizard of Oz*. In the end they found 240 little people from all over the world.

I felt there was some resentment among them towards me. I wasn't the most popular person on the set and I could understand it – some people would have given their right arm for my part (in the movie, I mean).

I tried not to hide in my own large 'superstar' trailer but sometimes, as the 'star', you can't help but be treated a certain way. For example, I was always called out to the set at the last minute, once everyone else had rehearsed and was in position and knew what they were doing. Some of my fellow little actors thought of me as a bit too big for my boots, but I'd been rehearsing most of the scenes for several months in England, and I usually had the longest day of all of the actors, so the production team were simply trying to conserve my energy. Still, it was a bit difficult and I sensed there was quite a bit of envy, although no one was especially nasty.

We started with the Newlyn village scenes, which were shot in Brocket Hall in Hertfordshire. I've heard rumours that the set was never dismantled and that the village is still there to this day, hidden by foliage and just next to a golf course. I can imagine errant golfers stumbling across it when hunting for lost balls and being thoroughly amazed and puzzled at this miniature-sized Stone Age-style encampment.

During filming those village huts were, er, ahem . . . 'well used' by the little people; after all, it's not that often we get to see so many of each other in one place – so things can get a little 'heated', shall we say. Sam, who I'd met on the set of *Labyrinth*, was in the film as an extra, but we didn't meet again until after the film.

There must have been something in the air as all the village pigs were at it too. Scenes were constantly being interrupted by their sudden and extremely noisy lovemaking. Buckets of water were eventually used to dampen the poor creatures' ardour. The pigs, that is, not the little people.

As George Lucas and Ron Howard were involved there was a huge media interest in the film from the UK press. Most of the journalists were kept away but I remember one young lady who managed to dip below the radar. She surprised me near my trailer.

'I'm doing a piece for *Look-In* magazine, for the back page where we put an interview with a famous actor and list their likes and dislikes,' she said, and started firing off a few questions. In my innocence I answered them freely. She asked me all sorts of silly little questions like 'What's your favourite colour?' and 'What's your favourite food?' and so on.

Little did I know that she was actually freelancing for the *News of the World*. From the answers I gave they conjured up the headline: 'I Want a Tall, Dark, Six-Foot Lover!' (confirming Sam's suspicions that I was a brat) and stuck it on the front page of the Sunday supplement magazine with a picture of me at the Cannes Film Festival wearing sunglasses and a sharp suit with a leggy woman (my sister) beside me.

At the time it was awful; my mum was horrified but that was nothing compared to Lucasfilm, who sent in their heaviest lawyers and got an apology from the *News of the World* printed in the next issue. Mind you, it wasn't much of an apology, and you had to look very hard to find it in between all the breasts.

With a roar another wave came crashing down, my boat span in the raging Force 10 wind, foam and air roaring like a jet engine. This had been a really bad idea. I could barely swim. I'm going to drown! I thought, fighting the panic as wave after wave crashed over me.

Water poured down on me from above. Finally, I felt the edge of the tank and grabbed hold. 'CUT!' Ron yelled.

I clambered over the side of Pinewood's million-litre reservoir as the storm, created by six airplane engines, countless pumps and wave machines, subsided.

'OK, people!' Ron yelled, 'let's go again!'

'What!?'

I'd spent the last two weeks in that reservoir being tossed and turned by wave machines. The tank is really a *huge* man-made lake. Any UK-made film that featured a lake, sea or river would be shot in it, including just about every Bond movie.

We were filming a long and complex storm sequence. In the film, Willow had to journey to an island to pick up the good sorceress Fin Raziel, who was disguised as a possum, but on our way back to the mainland, the evil sorceress cast a spell that whipped up a great storm in an attempt to drown us.

Part of the scene involved me swimming underwater for extended periods, using a respirator between takes. We shot this scene in a special underwater tank back at Elstree. As a proud seventeen-year-old, I was embarrassed to admit that I couldn't swim. I'm not as naturally buoyant as most and although this was normally a disadvantage, it also meant I could remain underwater with no difficulty at all, so as long as the respirator and safety divers were nearby I guessed I'd be OK.

After two weeks in the tank I was at the end of my tether but I remained determined to prove my staying power to Ron and the crew. It's amazing how far you will push yourself for a director like Ron. You can get to what you think is your limit but then somehow you manage to push through it.

I was never forced to do anything and Ron was always very careful not to work me too hard, but when you've got hundreds of people toiling round the clock to set up a scene which then all depends on your performance it's very, very hard to disappoint them and to admit that maybe you haven't the strength to continue. Or even just say you would very much like a break.

So I went again.

The enormous waves were created by giant water chutes at the top of which were suspended giant tip-tanks. These held thousands of gallons of water that, at the right moment, would be released down the fifty foot chutes into the tank, creating man-made tsunamis. I was supposed to try and ride these in my tiny boat for as long as possible before falling overboard.

I was just below two of these slides, standing on the boat, easing myself further into the centre of the tank, readying myself for the cry of 'Action!' when I heard a whooshing sound, which quickly turned into a roar. I looked up to see a wall of white water crashing down at me from above. Someone had released the door of one of the containers too early.

'Oh F—' was about as far as I got before I disappeared under tonnes of water. I popped up like a cork at the other end of the tank, found the little boat beside me and clambered aboard. I turned, looking for Ron, and saw him staring at me in shock.

I took a deep breath and yelled at the top of my voice: 'WHAT THE HELL ARE YOU TRYING TO DO, DROWN ME?'

As defiantly as I could, I stomped out of the wobbling boat and off the set in a huff. Although this was nothing compared to the huff that followed when Ron told me that the footage from these two sodden weeks wouldn't make it into the final cut! They had too much material and it was felt that this sequence did not add anything to the story – so it remains unseen to this day. The empty underwater tank is now hidden below the stage for *Who Wants to be a Millionaire*.

A few weeks later the entire cast and crew were flown to New Zealand on our own jumbo jet. I had arrived at the airport dressed in white and wearing fake Ray-Bans. I really thought I looked the business.

As I was about to step on the plane, Val came over to say 'Hi', or so I thought. Instead, he snatched the glasses off my face, snapped them in two and threw them in a nearby bin. Then he just stood there, smiling at me.

I was speechless. 'I . . . What? . . . Why? . . . My image, ruined!' was all I managed. What the hell was Val playing at? He was just standing there. In my path. Grinning.

'Here you go, Warwick,' he said, and presented me with two new pairs of genuine Ray-Bans. He'd just bought them in the airport. He turned, his shoulders shaking with laughter, and boarded the plane before my brain had time to readjust and thank him. That was typical of Val, completely unpredictable and generous to a fault.

Flying to New Zealand was an incredible experience. I was in first class and the seat, to me, was about the size of a four-poster bed. At one point in the flight I peeked between the gap in the seats and saw that Joanne Whalley – who played Sorsha, Madmartigan's love interest – and Val were getting very cosy indeed, and got more and more so the longer the flight went on.[24] Some scenes were reshot once they became a couple, because their sexual chemistry was then so much better.

I, on the other hand, brought out Joanne's motherly instincts. I seemed to have this effect quite often when I was younger and, like Carrie Fisher, Joanne always wanted to make sure I was well cared for.

I was being made up when a production assistant popped her head round the door.

'Is Warwick ready yet?' she asked.

'Just five more minutes,' the make-up artist replied.

'OK. I just wanted to let you know that the helicopter is ready and standing by, so just come straight over when you're done.'

As the door closed I suddenly sat up. 'Helicopter? Nobody mentioned a helicopter!'

And nobody had. We had to fly by helicopter to a remote location for one of the more action-packed sequences of the film. Most of the crew weren't so lucky and had to view the spectacular scenery from a bus, which wound its way along narrow mountain roads with 200-foot drops and hairpin bends galore.

Mum elected to take the bus because she was afraid of flying. I suspect she came to regret this decision when the bus turned one mountainside hairpin corner, skidded and came to a halt with its rear end hanging, à la *The Italian Job*, over a sheer drop.

'Nobody move!' the bus driver said. 'If we all keep still the bus won't slide any more. I'll call for help.'

The 'help' turned out to be a tractor, which, in its haste to reach

---

[24] They might not have become members but by the end of the flight they'd definitely filled out the application for 'The Mile-High Club'.

the stricken bus, lost control on the very same bend. It started skidding down the road towards the bus.

'Everybody out!' the driver yelled, triggering a mad scramble for the doors.

Fortunately, the tractor managed to stop just in time and towed the bus back onto the road.

Although I was a bit nervous about flying I thought it would be fantastic to fly over what had to be some of the most spectacular mountain scenery in the world. My excitement was quickly replaced by anxiety, however, when I saw what we would be travelling in.

'That's it?' The chopper had four seats. To me it looked like a flying lawnmower. Ron and Val were already on board. When I climbed into the capsule I looked up at the rotors that had started to turn above me and tried to stop thinking about the bolts that were holding them to the chopper's body.

I glanced at the pilot, a large moustachioed macho-looking American. 'Don't worry,' the production assistant said as he helped me into the chopper, 'Bud here flew hundreds of missions in 'Nam, he knows what he's doing.'

Before I had time to digest this fascinating new piece of information, Bud, who was chewing furiously on some gum, pulled back on the stick and took us straight up at a hundred miles an hour.[25] I felt my spine compressing and my shoulders sinking. 'Great,' I thought, 'by the time we get there I'm going to be even shorter.'

It was incredible flying in New Zealand. I never realised it had so many mountains, something I came to be very aware of as every time we flew over one we were hit by a tremendous updraught shooting us up a couple of hundred feet higher in a stomach-squeezing vertical climb.

---

[25] Well, that's what it felt like.

One time, when it was just Bud and me, we were forced to land due to bad weather. Bud, bless him, put us down in the middle of a swamp – luckily it was one of the firmer bits. It was truly amazing to be standing somewhere so incredibly remote, somewhere no human had ever been before.

Even though I was probably the only person in the entire world who didn't have to, I instinctively ducked my head whenever I climbed out of the helicopter. Val crouched down beside me and said, 'You really don't need to do that, you know.'

A short while later Val and I were sat on a tiny, frictionless and brakeless steel sledge on top of a New Zealand mountain. I stared down at the glacier that seemed to stretch off into infinity below us. Quoting Han Solo, Princess Leia and C-3PO, I said, 'I've got a bad feeling about this.'

In the film, the bad guys were chasing us and we were supposed to escape them by sliding down the mountain on a shield. I had thought this scene sounded like fun – until I saw the glacier as we swept up the mountain in the helicopter. All thoughts of the rotors falling off and of us plummeting to our doom were suddenly forgotten. What was the location scout on? Did he have any idea how long and steep this was?

I did have a stunt double who sometimes covered for me in distance shots. I say doubled, but Robert actually looked nothing like me, although he was roughly the same height. He was also the most accident prone and physically fragile man I've ever met. He disappeared down a hole in a field when we shot a sunset scene at Skywalker Ranch. He also nearly scalped himself when he caught his wig in a tree, no little achievement for someone less than four feet tall. Robert would trip over anything and everything, once falling over his own spear during a campfire scene – he almost turned himself into a shish kebab.

Goodness knows what would have happened to him on that mountain but, fortunately for Robert, Ron wanted the camera to be *on* the sledge, to show that this was actually us going down the mountain.

'It'll be fine,' Val said, but his customary confidence was a little lacking this time.

I got as far as 'Maybe we shouldn't –' before Ron yelled 'ACTION!' and someone gave us a good running shove in the manner of the bobsleigh, except they weren't silly enough to hop on for the ride.

Some of the crew had spent a few days helpfully polishing the ice for us, so we'd have a smooth and fast journey. They really shouldn't have bothered.

Cameras positioned all the way down the glacier captured our wide-eyed, non-acted terror as we zipped by at Mach 2, screaming at the top of our voices. Sparks flew behind us as we sheared through the ice in a blur. It was like the scene from *Star Wars* when the *Millennium Falcon* jumps into hyperspace and the stars become blurry streaks. Every so often I'd spot a cameraman desperately trying to keep us in shot as we flew past.

I screamed until I ran out of air and then kept on going silently, my mouth and eyes locked open. I could see where the ice ended and the rocky mountainside began. Luckily, someone had had the bright idea of piling up a mountain of loose powder snow right in our path and we hit it at the speed of sound, disappearing in a WHUMPF, shooting a little mushroom cloud of snowflakes into the sky.

After we'd been dug out, Val and I hugged. 'We're alive!' he shouted, and whooped with relief. I tried to unbend my fingers, with which I'd been clutching the sled. It wasn't easy.

Ron was in radio contact with the cameraman at the bottom and I heard him say excitedly, 'That was great, let's go again!'

Val and I looked at one another. Then we looked back up the mountain. 'You have to be kidding me. There's no way,' Val said. Nonetheless, still shaking, we climbed on a waiting snowmobile and were driven back up the slippery slope and did exactly the same thing all over again. The terror did not lessen in the slightest.

And then that, as it turned out, was Val's last ride on the sled. He refused point blank to get back on the thing. 'I've already fallen off two horses and nearly broken my damn foot on this movie, I'm not going to break my neck for you as well!'

It was true. On one of the first days of filming in New Zealand a steel cage fell on Val's foot. He had hopped off set in fury and refused to come out of his trailer. I watched from my own trailer window as first Ron and then George tried to persuade him to come out, only to be sent packing with a string of expletives. It took them half a day, but they got there in the end. If you look closely, you can see Val walking with a slight limp in some scenes.

As is typical for movies of this scale, there were quite a few accidents of this sort – Joanne stuck her sword in a stuntman's foot during a tavern scene, for example. There were also a few 'incidents' outside of work. We weren't really supposed to engage in risky activities whilst under contract but when we were in New Zealand about a dozen of us liked to go ice-skating at an outdoor rink. One evening we formed a line and started skating in circles around the rink. We got really good at this and started to build up some momentum. Little David Steinberg[26], who played Willow's best friend Meegosh, was on the outside end of the line and was therefore travelling faster than anyone else. Soon, we were travelling so fast that he was no longer able to hold on and his glove came off in the hand of the person he was holding onto.

---

[26] I can say that because he was even shorter than me.

I caught a brief glimpse of David zipping by at the speed of sound across the ice, his face frozen in terror as he shot towards the barrier that surrounded the rink. I half expected to find a 'David-shaped' hole in the barrier, but instead it had done a very good job of being a barrier and David had bounced back off it and ended up lying face down on the ice. Fortunately, he only needed a few stitches to his head and his bushy eyebrows covered those up.

That proved to be the end of our ice-skating exploits.

Although Val had had enough I, on the other hand, remained a glutton for punishment and agreed to go down a third time with a camera fixed to the front of the sledge, looking back towards me to make sure they got some nice close-ups of my 'frozen-in-terror' look.

A stunt double was found to replace Val and, as a bonus treat, we were told that we would be towed down the glacier by a stunt skier. 'You'll be fine,' Ron said, 'he's a real pro, he can do it backwards no problem.'

'Did he just say backwards?' I asked.

Sure enough, the skier pointed himself the wrong way down the mountain and set off while filming us with a Panavision camera, whizzing from side-to-side, narrowly missing boulders to make it 'more exciting' and adding some all new 'I'm going to die!' expressions to my repertoire.

As an actor and person, Val was amazing, he had a depth to him that's hard to describe. He really relished any chance to take his job to the limit; sometimes the production team would try and take advantage of this, not maliciously, but just because he was so good.

Years later I asked him about all the bad press coverage he got; he genuinely didn't know why it was they seemed to pick on him so often. He told me they hardly ever quoted him correctly.

Although he could sometimes come across as quite moody he was extremely mischievous and he never let me take things too seriously. His most-used word was 'fun'. 'Let's have a little fun, Warwick – oh sorry, no offence!'

Val loved his movie horse (a proper racing stallion) to be pumped up so it looked exciting on camera and he said I should do the same with mine.

'Heh, good luck with that,' I told him.

My own trusty steed was a former racehorse that had literally been rescued from the dog-food factory; it had been chosen for me especially because it was ancient, on its last legs and, no matter what you did, it simply wouldn't budge.

Nevertheless, Val knew every trick in the book when it came to horse riding and he often managed to wind my poor old nag up so much that it bounded off towards the horizon, with me bouncing in the saddle, screaming, 'You-ou-ou ba-a-as-ta-a-ard!'

When we were filming on other horses back in the UK, they were trained to go on the word 'Action!' so mine would take off down the road at the start of every scene until I asked if we could start using another phrase such as 'Begin acting!' The Shetland ponies were the worst. They were far feistier than normal-sized horses – like a terrier – and once they got going they really liked to try and throw me off. I suppose at least there wasn't so far to fall. There must be something about people and animals that come in small packages; what we lack in height we make up for in pluck.

I was sorry to leave New Zealand. I'm a big fan of extreme and snowy weather and it had plenty of both. It was also a truly beautiful and unspoiled country. If it wasn't for the fact that I need to be in the UK for work, then I'd be seriously tempted to move there.

It was back to Britain with a bump as filming continued in a Welsh quarry in Snowdonia – which also happened to be the coldest place on earth. We filmed the exteriors of the Nockmaar Castle and the transformation scenes in which the evil sorceress Queen Bavmorda, played by Jean Marsh, turned us into pigs.

The location was stunning but very dark, thanks to an abundance of slate and the fact it was situated between a lake and Elidir Fawr mountain. There was also an eerie rock formation known as the Lady of Snowdon because it had more than a passing resemblance to a human face.

We spent most of our time freezing to death in a caravan with no electricity. Poor Peter, another one of my stunt doubles, was so cold he wrapped himself in bin bags. We were so bored that we spent our days throwing playing cards at melons – if you threw them just right then you could get them to stick into the melon. Eventually we got so good at this we were able to flick them into cracks between cupboards and the joins in shelves.

One day, after filming had moved back to London, Val tapped me on the shoulder.

'What're you doing tonight?' he said with a grin.

I shrugged. 'Nothing.'

'Good. Tonight you're coming with me and having dinner with Tom Cruise and Mimi Rogers.'

Holy crap!

Tom was without doubt the number one star in Hollywood at the time (and the world's most successful little person). We ate in a restaurant in Covent Garden and while I'm sure the food and venue were both fantastic, I have no recollection of either. I was a complete unknown at this stage, and just seventeen years old. Tom and Mimi said 'Hello' and I mumbled something like 'Hmfglsltmu, heh, heh'. The waiters were just as starstruck and they spent the evening walking into pillars, dropping plates and colliding with each other as they passed.

All I could do was watch in fascination and with an open mouth as Tom and my mate Val reminisced about the *Top Gun* days, and all the jokes they used to play on one another, while other diners did a bad job of trying not to stare. Sadly, I can't remember the details. It all went over my head. There was a slight quibble as to who would pay the bill – although there was no way they were going to let me pay so I politely dropped out and let them fight over it.

I checked my watch and glanced out of the window anxiously. Mum was supposed to pick me up; she was under strict instructions not to embarrass me by parking her black and yellow Citroen 2CV in front of the restaurant's glass windows and to wait in a nearby street.

'Something wrong, Warwick?' Val asked.

'Not at all,' I replied in my finest 'Mr Cool' voice. 'It's been amazing but I've got an early start tomorrow. I'll just head off now and, you know, grab a cab from Covent Garden.'

We said our goodbyes and I headed towards the main door. It was then, with rising horror, that I saw it. My mum's 2CV slowed to a halt and pulled up right outside. I looked behind me. Tom, Val and Mimi still seemed deep in conversation about the bill. A waiter held the door open for me.

'Good evening, sir,' he said.

I looked back at him, checked the table one more time and sprinted out through the door at top speed, yanked the car door open and performed a commando-style dive into the back, yelling, 'Go, go, go!'

Mum floored the accelerator and we roared off at five miles an hour through Covent Garden.

'Now what was all that about?' Mum asked.

I glared at her. Mothers!

I just hoped that Tom, Mimi and Val hadn't turned in time to witness my extraordinary exit.

Willow was granted the honour of a Royal Premiere at Leicester Square in December 1988, attended by the Prince and Princess of Wales. I was driven there in a Bentley and felt every inch the superstar as it rolled up to the red carpet and I emerged to a hundred-flashgun salute.

Ever the conservative (by now) eighteen-year-old, I'd opted for the white dinner suit. Being the star of the film, I was sat next to Princess Diana, the most famous woman in the world; she could hardly see me behind my giant tower of popcorn.

She was absolutely charming and looked every inch the princess in her white evening gown, which sparkled in the glow of the screen. I watched her out of the corner of my eye and she laughed in all the right places. She came across as fun-loving and carefree; there were no obvious signs that her seven-year marriage to Prince Charles was in turmoil.

Afterwards, Princess Di and I had a little chat. Shyly, she said, 'You give us princesses a rough ride!' (The baby I was carrying throughout the film was a princess.) I did her the honour of turning bright red and mumbling incoherently.

After that, cast and crew went off for dinner at the Waldorf – Mum, Dad and sister Kim came too. Oddly enough, just by coincidence, I was sat next to Sam. We'd still barely met. She looked absolutely stunning in a gorgeous red dress. We even looked like a couple; me with my white dinner jacket and red handkerchief. But Sam was there on a date with Pete, the stunt double who was adept at throwing playing cards into melons. As we chatted I managed to undo some of the damage the *News of the World* had done to my character and did my best to erase my 'brat' image.

To promote *Willow* I flew from city to city all across Europe – Paris, Berlin, Copenhagen, Oslo, you name it, I was there doing press junket for *Willow*. It was a freezing cold December and I was somewhere different every day. Soon, I'd forgotten who I'd spoken to and what I'd said to them and constantly contradicted myself. I didn't mind, I loved everything – except for the food. Everybody always wanted me to try the local speciality but I simply can't stand foreign food. I made the mistake of saying, 'All I want is a nice piece of Cheddar,' while in Paris, the land of the stinky cheese, which didn't go down too well. This became my mantra as we travelled from city to city and various gofers were despatched to hunt down a piece of Cheddar or near substitute for Mr Bigshot.

While in one European capital, my ice-skating friend David Steinberg stopped by my hotel room to say 'hello'.

We chatted and caught up for a few minutes before he asked to use the bathroom.

'Sure,' I replied.

He returned a few mintues later. 'Gosh Warwick, that's impressive.'

'What is?'

'They've installed a sink for you so you can wash your hands.'

He'd only gone and washed his hands in the bidet.

'Oh yes, they do that for me now I'm a star,' I replied, trying to conceal a wicked grin.

'Wow, that's amazing.'

It was. Did David think a crack team of plumbers and tilers raced into each hotel before my arrival to install a new 'sink'? I like to imagine that for years after, whenever he arrived in a hotel room with a bidet, David thought, 'Wow, Warwick's been here!'[27]

Val and I did a few meet-the-fans signings. The routine was that we'd both sign the same photo; Val usually signed them first before passing them onto me. What he'd actually done was written a message to me on the photo such as 'When's lunch?' or 'She's hot!'

The initial reviews for *Willow* were somewhat mixed. *Time* magazine said that Lucasfilm had 'hit its dark age' and that *Willow* was simply 'a reprise of his *Star Wars* plot' while the *New York Times* praised my 'earnest performance' and *Variety* said, 'kids will love it'.

It was a hit at the box office, grossing $57.27 million from a $35million budget in the United States and, while this wasn't as profitable as George had hoped, it was a slow grower. Its popularity has increased over time and it is arguably regarded as a bit of a cult movie today. I've lost count of the number of times people have told me that they wore out their VHS copy of the film from playing it so much. Thank goodness for DVD.[28] I think its success is down to its timelessness. It isn't particularly dated and certainly follows no particular fashion.

Audiences seem to enjoy underdogs and they don't come much more underdog than Willow. It's filled with interesting characters and, as George always said, the focus is on the characters, not the special effects: 'The special effects are there to help tell the story, that's all.'

There's romance and comedy, especially with the tiny sidekicks, the Brownies. Willow and Madmartigan have a really interesting relationship and are a real odd couple. It's one of those films where everybody can get something out of it, from an eight-year-old to

---

[27] Sadly, David is no longer with us – a great talent much missed.
[28] As a bonus feature, there's a DVD commentary by yours truly.

an eighty-year-old. Trying to find a film at the local video store that the whole family can watch and enjoy can be quite tricky, they're either too boring for adults or too violent for children. I rented *Kindergarten Cop* the other day to watch with my kids and I'd forgotten just how surprisingly violent it was.

I'm asked almost every day if there's going to be a sequel to *Willow*. Well, I asked George Lucas and Ron Howard that very question at a party a couple of years ago. 'I'd love to,' Ron said, 'but you'd better check with George.'

I found George and asked him. 'Ron and I talked about it for a while,' he replied, 'and I thought about doing a TV series,' adding in his deadpan voice (but with a glint in his eye), 'Of course when we do it we'll have to recast, you'd be too old to play Willow now.'

So the jury is still out. Lots of talented screenwriters have sent in scripts for *Willow II* but George just isn't interested, he only develops projects that he's written or come up with himself.

Back then, however, I had plenty of my own projects to worry about.

'I WANT A TALL, DARK 6FT LOVER!' EXCLUSIVE

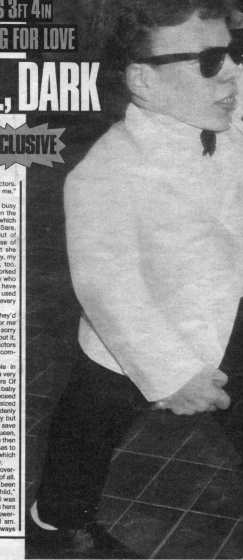

● Warwick Davis, star of the new blockbuster movie, Willow, is desperate to destroy the myth that men like their women a couple of inches shorter than themselves. Being only 3ft 4in tall himself, he says: "Girls of 3ft 2in just do not turn me on..." He goes on, "I want a tall girl. She must also be dark-haired and have a great sense of humour to match mine. I just can't bear the idea that people think because I'm a short person, I'm looking for a short girl – in fact, 6ft is nearer the mark!

"For a start, the chances of finding a short girl are pretty slim. For the film, Willow, the producer George Lucas had to scour half of Europe to find 200 extras and I certainly didn't fancy any of them." In the movie Warwick actually plays opposite a mini wife. But watching the romantic scenes, you can tell when he's hugging and touching her that, really, he's not physically attracted to her.

"Obviously I am sad there is no romance in my life at the moment," Warwick adds. "But I am only 18. I haven't given up. I don't simply sit around and think of all the difficulties I've had to cope with – I just get on with it. A full-sized girlfriend isn't too much to ask for, is it? After all everything else about me, except my height, is perfectly normal.

"I'd also like to dispel the myth that all small men want to dominate their partners because they think they have to prove they are macho just because of their lack of inches. I think a bit of domination would be quite nice to keep me in order."

Warwick was discovered by top producer George Lucas 7 years ago when he was cast as one of the Ewoks in the movie, Return Of The Jedi. "But actually my grandmother answered a request she heard on Capital Radio calling for 3ft actors. She's always had great faith in me," he explains.

Since then he's been kept busy with plenty of TV and a part in the feature film Legend, during which he fell in love with actress Mia Sara, who played the princess. "But of course with Mia, it was a case of adoration from afar. I thought she was really beautiful – physically, my ideal woman and very sweet, too.

"In fact, all the girls I've worked with, including Joanne Whalley who plays the princess in Willow, have been very nice. Carrie Fisher used to bring me milk and cookies every day which was kind.

"I'd hate to think, though, they'd been nice purely out of pity for me because I certainly don't feel sorry for myself. When you think about it, there aren't that many 3ft 4in actors – so I am lucky. I've got less competition at auditions."

Warwick plays the title role in Willow, a fantasy extravaganza very much in the Star Wars, Raiders Of The Lost Ark style. Willow finds a baby in a stream one day. He's supposed to take it back to the normal-sized people's land. But then he suddenly discovers it's no ordinary baby but a princess, who's destined to save the world from the wicked queen, played by Jean Marsh. The film then follows his adventures as he has to fend off the evil queen's army which is ordered to capture the baby.

For the role, Warwick had to overcome one of his biggest fears of all. He had to ride a horse. "I've been afraid of horses since I was a child," he explains. "Ever since when I was very young my sister put me on hers and it bolted. They are so powerful and so much bigger than I am. Also, it is quite humiliating always

10

Warwick as Willow with his family of little people in the soon-to-be released blockbuster. And posing with his big friends before setting off for a glitzy night out on the town – in search of 6ft romance?

'A bit of domination would be quite nice to keep me in order'

having to be lifted up and plonked on the horse's back.

"They started off teaching me on Shetland ponies, but I was still petrified. It was really important to the story, though. I had to go through with it. In the movie I have to travel half way across New Zealand with the baby.

"There were actually 75 babies in all, including a mechanical one for dangerous shots – which we called motor baby. All the real ones were really quite revolting. They had to have orange curly wigs which were stuck on with syrup because normal spirit gum affected their skin. Every time I held one I just got covered in yukky goo, not to mention the constant wailing. It put me right off."

Warwick has a very matter-of-fact attitude about his lack of height. "There's nothing about myself that I'd change," he says quite firmly. "I certainly don't crave my lost inches. I think my attitude is due to the way I have been brought up. I went to a normal school, all my friends are tall. And I never get embarrassed about my height – although sometimes other people do.

"I'm very grateful that I didn't go to a special school," he continues. "My school days were very happy. But I'm sure things would have been a lot different if I'd gone to a school where you are made to feel that there is something wrong with you. I was never bullied. I have quite a strong character and if anyone tried to tease me I was perfectly capable of standing up for myself

"Most of the people who are the ... I've met ▷

NEWS OF THE WORLD

Sunday

73 STONE
INSIDE FAT HOTEL
EVERYONE'S A WHOPPER!

3FT 4IN

DWARF FILM STAR SEEKS SEXY 6FT LOVER!

11

'Weren't you in *Time Bandits*?'

It may look like it but Sam and I weren't going out together here. This was the night of the *Willow* party, when we first started to hit it off.

Chapter Nine

Oh, Rats!

I spent a truly incredible day with George Lucas, Steven Spielberg and Harrison Ford on the set of *Indiana Jones and the Last Crusade*. I even got to see Sean Connery 'shot' by a Walter PPK.

Courtesy of Lucasfilm Ltd.

J ust before I was due to attend the UK premiere of *Willow*, David Tomblin, the man behind *Return of the Ewok* and George's assistant director, called me at home.

'Why don't you come up to Elstree this weekend?'

'Sure, mind if I bring a friend?'

David had invited me to Elstree a couple of times since *Jedi* and I was getting quite used to it. For Daniel, my best mate and obsessive Princess Leia fan, this would prove to be an entirely novel and overwhelming experience.

We arrived on Saturday morning and sought out David. When we finally found the right studio we couldn't believe our eyes.

Hundreds of crew members were frantically going about their business on an enormous set. They were sawing, hammering, yelling and piling up mountains of sand. In one corner, some men were stacking huge mesh cages containing thousands of enormous live rats.

A woman was rearranging dozens of silver, gold and bejewelled goblets on an old wooden table. Hydraulic systems hissed and clanked below her. Gantry cameras whirred past. A dozen men in Nazi uniforms were smoking cigarettes, checking their guns and brushing their trousers. The atmosphere was electric. It was clear that something very big was about to happen.

'There's something strangely familiar about all this,' I said to Daniel.

Daniel was looking over my shoulder, mouth agape. Something

tapped me on the head.

'Hi, shortstuff.'

I turned and looked up.

It was Indiana Jones.

'Harrison!'

Harrison Ford was in full costume, hat on head, whip in hand (he'd just used it to tap me on the head). I felt my hair reverentially. I'd just been tapped on the head by Indiana Jones's whip. Unbelievable. But it was him all right, down to the last detail, right down to the scar on his chin.

'Come to join us for the last day, have you?' he asked. 'I'm pretty certain there's no Ewoks in this. Who's your friend?'

'Who him?' I said, amazed that Harrison would be interested. 'He's only Daniel.'

Daniel was doing a very good impression of a zombie at this point. He was staring fixedly ahead, his mouth wide open and he looked even more pale than usual.

'What's up with you?' I asked.

'Uhm . . . uhm . . .' Daniel replied as Sean Connery ambled up, also in full costume.

'Hi,' Sean said, 'who's this then?'

Harrison did the introductions. It was very surreal to have Indiana Jones introduce my friend Daniel to Sean Connery. All Daniel could manage was 'Uhm'.

'I'm only twelve years older than him, you know,' Sean said, pointing at Harrison, 'but I'm supposed to play his father!'

'Yeah, well. He never tires of telling people that. C'mon, George is here, let's go find him.'

We left Daniel in a trance-like state, turning this way and that to see a constant stream of wonders pour into the set from every direction. I spotted a familiar face among all the noise and chaos.

George Lucas, who was executive producer, was with a very excitable man with glasses, beard and a V-neck golfing jumper: Steven Spielberg. He was buzzing, full of energy, something I'd seen before in George when he was setting the stage for a grand finale.

They were just finishing a conversation. 'That's it exactly!' Spielberg was saying, 'OK, I can see the whole thing unfolding now.'

Spielberg loves movies that rely on craft and collaboration, where every single department is as motivated as every other. 'No computers!' used to be his motto (although there would be a famous bit of digital manipulation, when Julian Glover's character drinks from the wrong grail cup at the end of the movie and starts to age very rapidly – this scene would help the film win the Oscar® for best effects).

'Hello, Warwick!' George said, 'Come and meet Steven.'

I sidled up alongside the great director.

'Willow!' Steven said. 'You were great in that. We must work together some day.'[29]

Steven explained this was the last day of shooting for the third and final Indiana Jones movie (as we all thought it was back then): *Indiana Jones and the Last Crusade*.

'This is old Hollywood-style filmmaking,' Steven said. 'Have you seen the rats yet? Alison said she could handle them but when you see two thousand of them all running around loose, well.'

He was referring to the stunning Alison Doody, who played the blonde Austrian Nazi turncoat, Dr Elsa Schneider. In the film, she tries to kill Indy by sealing him in a tomb – not before sleeping with both him and his father (not at the same time, I hasten to add).

---

[29] I'm still waiting for the call.

Rat breeders (sounds like more of an insult than a job title) had raised two thousand rats especially for this scene — which was set in a Venetian sewer. And these weren't your average sewer rats; they'd been especially isolated and fed on vitamin-rich supplements so they wouldn't be riddled with disease. Finally, once they were released on set, a rat orgy kicked off — they'd been isolated for so long that they were feeling extremely frisky.

'Poor Alison,' Spielberg said. 'Do we have any shame? No, we don't!'

Someone thrust a rat in my face. 'Aaarrgh!' I yelled in disgust, only to see it was made of rubber. 'Present for you, Warwick. One of our talented extras.'

Apart from the rubber ones there were hundreds of mechanical rats. Now *they* were scary. They wiggled and thrashed so they could swim through the sewers. Their jaws, filled with huge fangs, shut with a vicious snapping motion, like hundreds of those clockwork chattering teeth that were so strangely popular in the 1980s.

Harrison was constantly joking around and he'd managed to get his hands on a live rat that he cradled and cuddled. 'Used to be a nature guide when I was a kid and had a couple of rats as pets. They have personalities, you know, not like snakes. Rats are fine creatures.'

I swear the rat wagged its tail as Harrison petted and then kissed it. Harrison then jokingly ran through the script with the rat, making sure it knew what it was supposed to do and exactly when it was supposed to jump into Alison's hair.

The on-set activity increased to feverish levels as Steven walked over to the director's chair. He conducted the film from behind a monitor which was remotely linked to a camera perched on the end of an enormous thirty-foot-long crane. He controlled the camera while directing a crane operator; who moved it up and down, backwards and forwards. This way Steven was able to 'fly' all over the set.

The plan was to film the famous 'Oh, rats!' scene as well as the finale of the film, where Indiana finally gets his hands on the Grail, albeit fleetingly. The Grail scene was up next.

Harrison nudged me. 'Try and take it off,' he said, pointing at his hat, bending over so I could reach it.

Thrilled to have a chance to try it on, I yanked but it wouldn't budge. I gave it a really good tug, but nothing.

'See?' Harrison said, 'It's stuck on. Impossible to remove. If it falls off, we stop filming and have to go again. In Jordan we had to reshoot the damn tank chase scene about thirty times. This is what I have to do to make a living, stick a hat to my head with glue and tape.'

Terry Gilliam was there as well,[30] admiring the mechanical rats. Fresh from the critically acclaimed but commercial flop of *Brazil*, Terry had already embarked on his next madcap venture *The Adventures of Baron Munchausen*. Apparently it was being filmed in Spain, so I had no idea what had brought him to Elstree.

Daniel was pretty much where I'd left him, except now he was agog at Alison Doody, who still looked rather attractive, despite her Nazi costume.

Eventually, when Spielberg called action, the set fell completely silent. Indiana and his dad were being held at gunpoint by the Nazis in the temple that held the Grail. Indy was the only one able to get the Grail back but both he and his dad agreed they'd rather be shot than hand the Grail over to the Germans.

---

[30] No, I wasn't in *Time Bandits*.

When the clapperboard finally fell, I watched as Julian Glover (a.k.a. evil Nazi sympathiser Walter Donovan) spoke his lines. I was instantly mesmerised, completely caught up in the drama.

'Step back now, Dr Schneider. Give Dr Jones some room. He's going to recover the Grail for us. Impossible? What do you say? Ready to go down in history?'

Suddenly Donovan turned his Walter PPK (yes, I know, clever isn't it?) onto Sean Connery and shot him in the stomach. I actually jumped with shock and watched with horror as Sean fell to the floor.

He can't die! Can he?

'The healing power of the Grail is the only thing that can save your father now. It's time to ask yourself what to believe.'

'CUT!'

'Wow.' I was completely blown away. What on earth was coming next?

George told me that the film was all about leaps of faith, as well as the love between father and son, something that was close to Spielberg's own heart – like Indy's dad, his father hadn't been around when he was young.

By the end of the film, Indy and his dad would realise that being with each other was more important than everything else that was going on around them – they'd have a meeting of minds and hearts.

'So his dad doesn't die, then?' I asked hopefully. George grinned.

The rest of the day zipped by in a blur as one amazing sequence followed another. I saw the temple set break up and move on five, incredibly powerful hydraulic systems which simulated an earth-quake and the collapsing temple; I saw Alison fall from Harrison's hand to her 'death'; I watched as Harrison hung over a 'precipice', his fingertips brushing the grail as Sean held his other hand, and saw everything that was going on around them, the hundreds of people that made it all look so good. Harrison had one foot on a stepladder as Sean pulled him up from the precipice. About a dozen men were off camera, busy with smoke and wind machines.

I saw 5,000 rats – 2,000 real, 500 mechanical and 2,498[31] rubber ones – terrorise a beautiful blonde. After the scene was shot it took a dozen men about twenty-four hours to find and home all the real ones.

Finally, Daniel and I reluctantly admitted it was time to go home and so we collected our rubber rats and strolled off into the Elstree sunset, going over and over this most incredible of days, determined that we would never, ever forget it.

---

[31] Once he saw I had one, Daniel had to have one too.

Chapter Ten

Hiii-Hooooooooo!

As Reepicheep in the BBC productions of *Prince Caspian* and *The Voyage of the Dawn Treader*.
Courtesy of the BBC.

I sense another storm scene coming…

I really knew how to cultivate my image in those days.

D espite having starred in a major motion picture, I still hadn't realised that my career as an actor was well and truly under way. In fact, I never had a defining moment where I said 'I want to act' or 'I am now an actor'.

I still thought of myself as a budding film director and continued to make short films with my friends, entering several festivals. Horror works really well as a genre for the short film; you don't need much of a story and the idea — as far as I was concerned — was to try and shock the audience.

Up until this point I'd only recruited my friends to act in CDS Productions but I decided to find a professional for my new solo project, *Video Nasty*. Eventually, I persuaded my friend, voice coach and normal-sized *Willow* extra David Sibley to act for free. As ever, the set was the Davis family home.

Video Nasty was the story of a man who watches TV twenty-four hours a day (he takes pills to keep himself awake). One day he gets eaten by his video recorder and ends up trapped inside the TV but gets spat out during a commercial break. There were some pretty sophisticated special effects in there (I went through a fair bit of fishing wire to achieve most of them) for the time and I was so pleased with the end result that I sent it into the Holy Grail for young filmmakers: the *Screen Test* 'Young Filmmaker of the Year' competition.

I was delighted but not surprised when I heard I'd been selected for the final. I went off to appear on the programme and, so I thought, to collect my trophy. I was therefore left reeling when presenter Brian Trueman announced I was in third place and was now the proud owner of a certificate stating as much. I left the studio feeling a little short-changed.

In those days it was very hard for kids like me to make a film. While I was writing this book I taught my kids how to use Apple's editing software and how to do 'stop-motion' animation using digital cameras. It's amazing; you can even keep a ghost image of the previous frame on screen while you move your model to position it for the next frame. And if anything looks a bit untoward it can always be fixed in post-production.

While my filmmaking career hadn't exactly entered hyperspace, my acting career was moving along nicely. Mum was still my agent; she took the calls and did the paperwork. And not long after I'd finished filming *Willow*, the BBC called her to offer me the role of Reepicheep the talking mouse in their adaptations of *Prince Caspian* and *The Voyage of the Dawn Treader*, from C.S. Lewis's wonderful *Chronicles of Narnia*. These BBC children's dramas were a real institution and a major televisual event broadcast on Sunday evenings.

It was amazing to work on a BBC drama; most of the series was shot on location on beaches in Wales and Milford Haven (I would return to the exact same beach many years later for *Harry Potter and the Deathly Hallows*) and on board a full-scale replica of the *Dawn Treader*. The deck and everything above looked completely authentic, while a production studio was below decks.

The storm scenes were filmed at London's Ealing Studios where the special-effects team had built a mock-up of the *Dawn Treader*'s upper deck. This had been mounted on a hydraulic system, which would simulate the boat at sea in a violent storm.

I was in a fairly bulky foam mouse bodysuit, complete with screw-on tail. I was also wearing a glued-on foam-latex mouse nose, complete with whiskers made from stripped feathers.

When the 'storm' started, I wobbled and rolled my way back and forth across the boat. After what seemed to me to be an eternity the director finally yelled 'Cut!'

Relieved the ordeal was over, I tried to return to my starting position. I couldn't move. The problem was that my foam suit had now absorbed so much water that it had turned into an extremely heavy water suit. It sagged dramatically, giving me a rather unfortunate knee-level potbelly. My once perky foam nose drooped impotently.

After a quick discussion, it was decided that I needed to be 'wrung out' before the next take. To save time, the make-up girl placed her hands round the nose and twisted in opposite directions. This was followed by a sudden undignified nasal downpour. Fortunately, they let me out of my body suit before they wrung that dry.

I was delighted to follow *Dawn Treader* with a performance as Glimfeather the Owl in *The Silver Chair,* the next book in the series. For Glimfeather, I decided to do some preparation and went to an owl sanctuary to study their behaviour. However, apart from learning that the collective noun for owls is a parliament, it was of limited benefit. I couldn't, no matter how hard I tried, turn my head all the way round, tuck my head under my arm or produce a shower of tiny pellets every twenty minutes or so.

Luckily, my voice was a few octaves higher in those days, so I was able to do a pretty good 'twit-twoo' and spoke every sentence with an 'oo' on the end or in the middle, so lines became 'Pleased to meet yoooooooou,' and 'She's oooover there.' I'd sometimes carry it on after a loooong day, withooooout thinking.

A real highlight of this production was meeting and acting with Tom Baker during *The Silver Chair*; he was still hugely famous then for playing the best Doctor *Doctor Who* had ever seen.[32]

Tom's wonderful voice – later put to good use as the narrator for *Little Britain* – was a delight to hear and I tried to get him to talk as much as possible. I found him to be a wonderfully honest person with a very peculiar dark side. He had the kind of stare that snakes use to hypnotise small furry animals before they swallow them whole.

He loved talking about death, ghouls and spooky places. He once said, 'All my life I have felt myself to be on the edge of things. All my life I have suffered from bad dreams. All my life I have had difficulty in knowing whether I am awake or in a nightmare.'

In fact we've both shared the same nightmare, having filmed in the same freezing Welsh quarry, me in *The Hitchhiker's Guide to the Galaxy*, Tom in *Doctor Who*. The TARDIS materialises in the same quarry in almost every episode of *Doctor Who* – that quarry must be the centre of the universe.

Tom and I also shared almost precisely the same view about acting; he never took the job for granted and considered himself extremely fortunate to have had as much success as he did. He added that *Doctor Who* was the best job he'd ever had. 'All I had to do was speak complete gobbledygook with utter conviction.' Nobody's done it better.

I was delighted to bump into him at a sci-fi convention in 1990. 'Where's your scarf?' I joked, referring to the fact that he wasn't wearing his trademark nine-foot scarf. He smiled suddenly, and I felt like a small furry animal in the gaze of a king cobra – which, as a former Ewok, was only natural I suppose.

---

[32] Back off, Peter Davison fans.

After I'd finished filming *Dawn Treader* and while *Willow* was still in cinemas – Robert, my accident-prone Willow stuntman 'double' was appearing in *Snow White* at the Cambridge Arts Theatre with the late[33], great singer and comedienne Marti Caine as the Evil Queen, and I popped along to see the show. I hadn't seen a panto since I was a child and wasn't expecting much, so it was with some surprise that I discovered it had a deliciously infectious atmosphere and I found myself shouting, 'He's behind you!' along with everyone else. It looked chaotic but it seemed as though the actors were having enormous fun and the energy coming from the crowd was like nothing I'd ever experienced.

I admired the abilities of one performer in particular, the Queen's Cat – called Catsmeat – who at one stage leapt into the audience and nimbly ran along the backs of the chairs, over kids' screaming heads. Quite an amazing feat. He turned out to be an exceptional choreographer, Paul Harris, whom I'd work with very closely on another famous project, far in the future.

After the performance, I saw a man with a rather stressed and frazzled appearance marching towards me. He came straight to the point: 'I'm directing this travesty,' he opined. 'Our leading dwarf is a raging alcoholic, I've just fired him. Do you want the role?'

This was a bit sudden. I hesitated.

'I've got to let him go. He's been caught stinking of booze in front of the children once too often. Luckily, he's playing Sleepy so we've got away with it so far.'

'I don't know,' I began.

'We keep an eighth dwarf spare so he can take over but we'd

---

[33] She wasn't late then, of course – that would have been quite something. It is well known in panto-lore that all the Snow Whites eventually become Evil Queens. That must be a rough day, when you get the call, 'We'd love you for panto, except this year we want you to play . . . er . . . the Evil Queen.'

love to have you as Sleepy if possible, otherwise we don't have an eighth man.'

I then spotted Samantha on stage, who'd been a Newlyn villager in *Willow* and whom I'd admired from afar on the set of *Labyrinth*. I recalled the night we'd finally met properly during the *Willow* dinner at the Waldorf and how well we'd got on. I then thought, in true Leslie Phillips style, 'Well, *hellooo*'.

'OK, why not?' I said.

'Great, you can start tomorrow.'

'Hang on . . .'

Taking to the stage in a nightshirt was a very strange experience at first, but I loved every minute. It was odd because at the time my name was everywhere on cinema billboards, newspapers and magazines, as *Willow* was still showing. But as Sleepy in *Snow White* I wasn't given any billing whatsoever and I don't think anybody in the audience realised who I was.

Almost every actor will tell you that there's nothing quite like performing in front of a live audience. There's no second take so you have to get it right first time. If you don't, the audience lets you know straight away. Fortunately, panto is the home of the live cock-up, although the worst thing that happened during this version of *Snow White* was a blackout. In another, more recent production, Grumpy (played by my father-in-law) and Dopey got stuck in a lift on the way to the stage, which brought proceedings to a sudden halt for a few minutes before they were successfully extracted by a caretaker with a crowbar.

Although the happy squeals of delight from the kids in the audience gave me a pretty big ego-boost, I soon found out that panto took great discipline and stamina. We did three shows every Saturday and two every other day of the week, except for Mondays, with 10 a.m. matinees for the littlest children – who were also our toughest audience. For everyone, actors and audience alike, panto is great fun and all involved have a brilliant time.

Since then I've acted in *Snow White* dozens of times – as the tabloids say every year at Christmas, there's always a – wait for it – 'Dwarf Shortage', so demand is very high.

Once, a few years later in Dartford, there was a bomb scare just as we were reaching the grand finale and everyone had to evacuate the building. Once we were outside a policeman told us it could take a while, so the seven dwarves went down a local boozer with the wicked queen (who happened to be male and smoked a pipe) for seven halves and a pint of Guinness. We took great delight, sitting there in the smoky, quite grim pub, watching locals enter and not know where to look or what to say as we shouted: 'It's your round!'

'Oh no it isn't!'

'Oh yes it is!' and so on.

During that very first special *Snow White* in Cambridge, after exchanging a handful of waves and a smattering of nice words, Sam and I slowly started to get to know one another; there are always lots of Christmas parties for panto folk. I presented Sam with a Christmas card with a long message in it, telling her how much I enjoyed her company and so on. It was very reserved and polite, although I think it was clear that romance was on my mind.

I opened Sam's card to me. It read 'from Sam'.

I sighed. 'Patience, Warwick,' I thought, 'just hang in there.'

After the last show of the day on New Year's Eve, everyone was busy zooming out to join the festivities in town. New Year's Day was a rare day off so most people wanted to make the most of it. I wasn't in any mad hurry and the theatre was almost deserted by the time I was about to leave. The exit was on the far side of the stage and the dressing rooms were on the other side, so you had to cross the stage to leave the building. I was halfway across the stage when I saw Sam coming the other way. The stage was dimly lit, there was no one about and the curtain was down.

Something inside told me it was now or never. I was nervous, I was shorter than Sam and I wondered how this would go.

I needn't have worried. It went perfectly.

As we kissed, alone on that stage in what was a flawless moment, I half-expected the curtains to open and an audience to leap to a standing ovation. This was, after all, my finest performance.

It was around this time that I was finally able to drive my first car – a brand new Mini. I actually bought it a while before I'd passed my driving test[34] and had it customised. It was black and I had the interior redone in black leather, with wood strips along the doors and dashboard, a made-to-measure driver's seat and, of course, raised pedals. The only catch came when applying for insurance, as I had to mention the modifications. This meant that they needed to know my height and weight. I was at home when someone from the insurance company phoned to check my details.

'There seems to be a mistake with your form,' he said, 'your height is down as three-foot-six; we need to know your height, not your child's.'

'But I am three-foot-six,' I said.

This was followed by a short silence.

'Are you sure?'

'Quite sure. I'm very aware, more than most people, of my exact height.'

---

[34] Before I got my licence, Daniel and I used to sit in the mini in the garage, listening to music on the car stereo. We'd also put on our Ray-Bans, switch on the hazard lights and pretend we were the Blues Brothers.

I explained why I was smaller than average but this didn't seem to help matters.

'But there aren't any numbers low enough on our system for me to input your height.'

'Well, I'm sorry to hear that but it's not my problem, is it?'

'But I can't accept it, it doesn't fit on our system.'

'Can't you just put a note on the system?'

And on and on the conversation went. I was simply a blip in the system. However, once I got to speak to someone senior enough, I eventually got my insurance. It's the same with passports, life insurance, visas – anything that requires height and weight, including – believe it or not – the taxman (of whom, more later).

Being able to drive offered me a new-found freedom. I didn't much care for travelling by bus – my friends always wanted to sit upstairs, which inevitably involved death-defying ascents and descents of the insanely steep staircases they have on buses. They posed an extra-special challenge as I was too short to reach the support rail. I'd never complain; I just tried to get myself up those damn stairs. I find that most problems to do with being short can be overcome with a little determination. Then, it seemed to me at least, no one expected anything from the world – now it's as if people who are different automatically feel as if the world should be altered to suit them. But while I was (not) growing up, I had to make do with the world as it was and find the best way round the obstacles it put in my path.

Needless to say, as soon as I got my driving licence, I drove everywhere I could.[35] I drove Sam to and from college and gave her lifts to wherever else she wanted to go. We were soul mates. Being with Sam was the best and easiest thing in the world.

---

[35] The mini finally had enough after 100,000 miles, after which it fell apart faster than a clown car.

When she wasn't acting, Sam was studying hairdressing and beauty therapy. She told me that her college were having an end-of-year make-up competition in which students would create crazy designs to show off their skills.

Ever one to take a challenge to the limit, I hatched a dastardly prize-winning plan. I got my hands on some fake fur and two chamois leathers and Sam did the rest. When it was Sam's turn to show off her creation, I leapt onto the catwalk screaming and beating my chest with one hand, waving my banana in the other, doing my finest Cheetah impersonation. I circled the stunned judges, thumping my hands on the floor, before throwing my banana in the air and galloping out – with first prize. Tarzan would have been so proud.

By now, as any woman whose boyfriend has dressed up as a monkey for them will tell you, I was madly in love. I bent down on one knee and proposed (after removing the monkey get-up). Sam said 'Yes'.

Me in monkey make-up as designed and painted by Sam, who's holding the first prize certificate. I knew we'd win if I waved my banana at the judges.

In my adapted mini – yes it really is that simple. Bolt on a raised seat and a set of adapter pedals and you're away – although you should always make sure your nuts are tight.

I'm first on the left: Sam is second from right. That stage was the setting for a very romantic scene between us.

Mr Cool himself.

Chapter Eleven
Willow's Shotgun Wedding

The odd couple. Me and my beanpole best man and idiot, Daniel.

Our dress requirements were a tad unusual but the tailor came up trumps.

With our bridesmaids and page boy, Luke.

Us, mums, dads and grandparents.

In the year following our engagement, Sam and I decided to buy a house and found a semidetached in Peterborough where Sam was still at college. Surrey, where my parents lived, was still ridiculously expensive as far as I was concerned, while Peterborough was fairly central, and not too distant from various studios and popular filming locations.

Then Sam uttered the two little words that send the pulses of men racing into panic mode: 'I'm pregnant.'

It was a bit of a shock-horror moment. We were both so young, having just turned twenty, and although we planned to get married the following year we hadn't intended to start a family quite so soon. The knowledge that a child was on the way meant that everything was suddenly turned on its head – including our outlook on life. We decided to continue with our wedding plans regardless, as the baby was due after our chosen date.

Sam had a beautiful pregnancy; she stayed active and retained the title of Chief Wedding Organiser. She had five bridesmaids and one page boy. What we'd originally planned as a small affair soon spiralled into a huge event for 120 people. Obviously, the wedding dress was a bit of a challenge for the dressmaker and I had to arrange for some extreme re-tailoring of a morning suit. But although it was a busy time we were very happy and excited, life couldn't have been better.

And then, from nowhere, I suddenly fell into dire financial straits. Actors have very different accounts from normal self-employed people and I wasn't at all up on what I should have known about tax. I had thought that my accountant had taken care of everything but he had somehow failed to notice that I should have registered for VAT almost ten years earlier. It was only when I moved to a new accountant that they noticed this – along with about ten years' worth of other anomalies.

Suddenly, almost overnight, I was horrendously in debt.

At one point the bailiffs turned up at my parents' house just as I'd packed all of my stuff into a van, ready to move to Peterborough. They must have thought that very convenient and they spent a lot of time eyeing up my precious mini. Luckily, my new accountant managed to call them off.

Every penny I earned had to go towards paying back the tax. Luckily for me, Lucasfilm and the Jim Henson Organisation accepted that I should have been paid VAT on my earnings and so they paid that part off for me.

It was awful; I really hadn't done anything wrong, yet the taxman was breathing down my neck treating me like a criminal. I once answered the phone and a voice said, with no introduction: 'We've been watching you, we know you've got a car and we will have that.'

'Fine,' I replied, 'take it, it's on hire purchase so I don't own it anyway.'

During all this, and while we were rapidly approaching the wedding, a tax inspector turned up at my door. His mouth dropped open when he saw me. He looked like a college professor. I noticed he still had his bicycle clips around his trousers.

'Oh dear,' he said in the tone of a natural born bureaucrat, 'they didn't warn me.'

'What do you mean?' I asked.

'The office is supposed to tell me if people I'm going to visit are "different".'

I didn't much care for the tone in which he said 'different', almost with a sneer.

'Different? What do you mean, different?' I asked testily.

'Well, "black", for example.'

'Black?'

'I didn't know you were going to be short.'

'Why does it matter?'

He couldn't give me an answer and mumbled incoherently. Even though I decided that he was a very unpleasant man, I felt obliged to let him in and he got to work in my office – a.k.a. the spare room with a desk and a chair. Whenever he saw Sam or I he shook his head worriedly.

On the third day he asked: 'What are you?'

'Right! That's it!'

I wrote to Customs and Excise and complained in no uncertain terms about this man and, more importantly, about this bigoted behaviour. I received an official apology and, in what turned out to be a major victory, Customs and Excise changed their policy so that no personal information about colour, size or any other 'difference' about any person would be kept on their files.

They didn't let me off a penny of the tax I owed, though.

The one thing this horrible experience taught me was that I should always be proactive in my career. When you've got work, it's very easy to sit back and forget to hunt out new jobs until the present one dries up. Ever since then I'm always thinking of the future, what I'm going to do next and how to go about it and make it happen. No actor can afford to just sit back and wait for the phone to ring. Even major stars, particularly British ones, are not as wealthy as most people think. You have to knock on a lot of doors and keep on at people.[36] It also made me appreciate what we have now, as back then we had to watch absolutely every penny.

I was desperately skint. I had paid for the wedding and honeymoon before the tax debacle had begun and couldn't get the money back. We sat in our newly bought house (which I was fighting to keep hold of) and watched a tiny portable black-and-white telly, which we had perched on top of a cardboard box while sitting on an old hand-me-down sofa, surviving off beans on toast.

It was odd being in such a desperate financial position at the same time as having such an extravagant celebration to prepare for. And to make things worse, I had significant worries about Daniel's Best Man capabilities. Although he was my best friend, he was also an idiot. Daniel still didn't have any idea what he wanted to do in life. I worried he might end up working at McDonald's – I don't mean to put McDonald's down – and I'm still surprised Daniel passed his driving test.

He also still looked completely mental, like an anorexic member of Metallica. He was unkempt, skeletal, had long strawberry-blond hair and was still totally obsessed with heavy metal, movies, and women. His parents were lovely, so I had no idea where it all came from. But I'll say one thing for him; he showed me how to make the most of being the centre of attention. By making people laugh, Daniel was able to get on the right side of both pupils and teachers and I was quick to pick up on this. Although looking different attracts attention, it's your personality that really counts in the long run.

Incidentally, Daniel wasn't the only one with long hair. I had

---

[36] Just ask George Lucas.

also grown a fashionably long mullet of which I was extremely proud. In fact, it grew to be as long as Willow's (that was a wig in the film). Then, just before the tax disaster, I had a curious urge, which gradually grew into an all-consuming desire, to have a wave put in. But for some reason, the local hairdresser interpreted the word 'wave' as 'tight perm' – perhaps because they seemed to be all the rage at this time. So I emerged from the hairdresser with a head full of ringlets and went straight to Debenhams where I bought a flat cap to cover them up. I spent a couple of days looking like a very short footballer before I found another hairdresser to iron the perm out.

Anyway, I digress. Daniel came over to our house the night before the wedding. Our house then was tiny – not me-tiny, just smaller than average – and Daniel came bounding in through the back door, full of excitement ahead of the big day. It had started to rain and Sam said we needed to get the washing in. Daniel, wanting to be helpful, yelled, 'I'll do it!'

He zipped around the garden, plucking the washing off the line before giving it to Sam in the kitchen. He then zipped around the dining room, kitchen and lounge like Tigger the Tiger before pawing his way up the stairs looking for me, babbling on like a fool the whole time.

It was then that Sam noticed a peculiar aroma. During his little run round our back garden, Daniel had managed to tread in a dog poo the size of a cowpat. This mess was now spread throughout our entire house – on our brown carpet, which disguised the poo very effectively. This meant we couldn't see where the poo was but, boy, could we smell it. So Sam and I spent the night before our wedding carpet cleaning. Our two dogs, Pepi and Wicket watched from a distance, both of them looking as guilty as hell.

Yes, I was quite worried about Daniel's Best Man capabilities.

The big day, 29 June, dawned fine and dry. As was the tradition, I'd spent the night before the wedding – after cleaning up all the dog poo, of course – in a fancy hotel. I went for a swim in the hotel pool in the morning. Sam had a much more stressful start to the day – hair-do, make up, bridesmaid dressing. I was ready in five minutes, just popped on my morning suit and *voila*.

As a treat to herself, Sam's Nan had stayed at the hotel too. As I made my way to breakfast, she emerged from her room ahead of me. She looked quite frazzled.

'Everything all right, Nan?'

'Oh no,' she said with a croak, 'I've been up all night sucking on a Fisherman's Friend.'

I had a friend video the entire wedding and, although he was involved in TV, I belatedly realised that he had nothing to do with actual camerawork. When we played it back I thought we'd mistakenly just got the cuts from the edit. All he did was point it in our general direction while he nattered away to somebody else. I tried to edit it but it was impossible; the best bits were when he filmed the table decorations during the speeches, and an extended shot of a polished hubcap (while we were getting out of the car outside the church). You could just see me in the reflection.

Daniel was grinning like a Cheshire cat when I joined him at the front of the church. 'You should have seen the choir's faces when I arrived,' he said. He did look quite extraordinary in his morning suit; with the top hat he was about seven feet tall. 'But that was nothing compared to when they saw you.'

It was true, the poor things were all over the shop; I could tell Sam was on her way down the aisle from all the notes they were missing, even the organist was playing about as well as a blind monkey.

I turned to see my fiancée coming towards me. She looked

absolute stunning. It was quite something. I take most things in my stride but getting married was about as emotional as it gets. I'm sure other grooms will know what I'm talking about when I say there's nothing quite like the moment when you hear the triumphant opening bars of the *Wedding March* and your bride enters the church. As I stood there and watched Sam walk down the aisle in front of our closest friends and family, I understood why marriage is the ultimate declaration of love.

The ceremony, I'm relieved to say, ran very smoothly – Daniel hadn't lost the rings and nobody fluffed their lines.

However, things got a lot more 'interesting' after the ceremony. As we left the church someone with a gravelly voice yelled, 'Over 'ere, Mr and Mrs Davis!' We turned and were caught in the gaze of one lone paparazzo who'd gate-crashed the wedding. No celebs were invited but this guy still thought it would be worth it – he spotted that Sam was five months pregnant and in the next day's *News of the World* we saw ourselves pictured under the headline: 'Willow's Shotgun Wedding'.

We made it to the reception and, after we'd eaten a magnificent meal, Daniel tapped his glass. Everybody turned to listen. I was more than a little nervous as to what he was about to say.

'I've known Warwick for just about my whole life,' Daniel began, 'and I can safely say we've been through a great deal together and nothing ever caused our friendship to founder . . . Although there was one occasion when we nearly lost it and it was over a woman.' He grinned.

I looked at Sam and smiled nervously. What the hell was he talking about?

Daniel pulled out a very old, very crumpled bit of paper. I could see it had been ripped into dozens of tiny pieces but someone had stuck all the little bits back together with sticky tape.

Oh dear.

The penny had dropped. It was the letter I had written all those years ago detailing why Daniel didn't like a girl that I was interested in. 'Goodness, is it me or is it hot in here?' I said, reaching for a glass of champagne and trying not to turn bright red as Daniel started to read the letter in the voice of a teenager.

'Hello, *mon cheri,* that's French for "my dear". I'm sitting bored in my French lesson thinking of you . . .'

My toes curled until I looked like I was wearing a pair of Persian slippers.

'How about *Le Kiss?*'

It was so, so painful to hear but I knew that worse was yet to come.

'P.S. You know Daniel said he couldn't go to the party with you, well that's because he doesn't want to go with you. But I'll go with you. How about it?'

Daniel had read it brilliantly, in a mock love-struck style, and the entire room erupted into laughter as he got to my accidental *double-entendre*: 'How about it?'

I had to admit it was a brilliant speech.

'I've been waiting to do that for ten years,' Daniel said, 'and it was even better than I imagined.'

'You just wait until your wedding,' I joked, 'you'll be lucky if your bride, if you ever find one, stays with you long enough to go on the honeymoon.'

We honeymooned in San Francisco. George had invited us to his annual Lucasfilm family picnic at the Skywalker Ranch on 4 July. The ranch is on Lucas Valley Road and this, so I'm led to believe, is a coincidence; it was already called that before George moved in. The invite said: 'Bring a dish for pot luck.' Guests all bring a dish that goes on a huge table and everyone just digs in. It was a really incredibly idyllic family event, you could swim the beautiful man-made Lake Ewok or visit the on-site fire station for a ride in a fire truck. Then there was the animal barn, the fruit gardens and the vineyards – and if none of the food on display took your fancy, you could visit the on-site restaurant for a fresh steak before taking in a movie in 'The Stag' – the 300-seater Art-Deco-style cinema.

So when George said, 'Warwick, why don't you and Sam stay on the ranch for a few days?' I only had to think it over for a nanosecond. 'I'll cancel our hotel reservations,' I replied.

The house we stayed in was amazing; every single room had a TV and video player. The windows were made from specially commissioned stained-glass designs. There was a huge station clock in the hallway, the biggest I'd ever seen. The main bedroom was so spectacular that we decided we wouldn't spoil its perfection and slept in the children's room.

We didn't want to outstay our welcome, so after a couple of days we continued our honeymoon as planned. After having lunch with George we bade him farewell and headed to San Francisco to get some wheels.

We rented a red Ford Thunderbird. It came with a basic set of hand controls. You simply pulled back a lever on the steering wheel with your right hand and the car accelerated; and to brake, you just pushed back down. After a short practice run around the car park, I felt able to take on the streets of San Francisco.

We drove up Lombard Street, home to James Stewart's character in *Vertigo*. It was indeed a street designed to cause light-headedness. It was on a thirty-degree hill and snaked its way up in a series of hairpin bends. It's understandably known as the 'crookedest street in the world'.

'Bring it on,' I thought. I was keen to get to the top and have a look at San Francisco from the surrounding hills. Almost as soon as we started to climb we were caught in a traffic jam. As we slowed to a halt, I looked for the handbrake.

'Where's the handbrake?' I asked Sam, trying to balance the car, frantically pushing and pulling the lever back and forth.

We couldn't see it anywhere. Eventually, Sam looked on the floor. 'It's down here!'

'Why, in a car adapted for disabled people, would they put the handbrake near their feet?' I wondered.

We were trapped. The street was one-way, there were no U-turns and no parking, so there was no choice. The only way was up. We were now stuck in this traffic jam, unable to reach the handbrake, so I sat there yanking at the 'stop' and 'go' control, alternately trying to stop us crashing into the cars in front and behind. They must have thought I was insane. I could see the driver in front nervously checking his rear-view mirror, looking at two petrified little people sweating profusely and growing larger as we rocketed towards him before skidding to an abrupt halt, in a car doing a pretty good impression of a pimpmobile with hydraulic suspension. I'd then release the brake and we'd roll back down towards the driver behind us with looks of dread on our faces before I thrust the lever back to compensate for the incline, spun the wheels and shot forwards again.

Finally, seventeen hair-raising hairpin turns later, we made it to the top. I was exhausted.

'Right,' I said, turning to Sam, dripping with sweat, 'Seen enough of San Francisco?'

Sam nodded. We hit the Pacific Coast Highway, one of the world's greatest drives, and cruised south, past the picturesque Half Moon Bay and Big Sur with the Santa Lucia Mountains poking above the distant haze. We didn't have a particular plan, we'd just stop once it got dark and stay in the first motel we could find – nearly all of them reminded me of the Bates Motel from *Psycho*.

It was incredible but all too soon we were on our way back to the much humbler-sounding Peterborough – just in time for the Stilton Cheese Rolling Championships.

When we returned from our honeymoon, everything was great – except for one thing.

We were flat broke.

Everything we owned was second-hand or had been donated to us by friends and family. The only new things we had were presents for our unborn baby (we'd opted to wait and see whether Sam was carrying a boy or a girl), who was now due in a few weeks. A brand new cot was loaded with toys, clothes and other baby essentials.

Although Sam's pregnancy had been incredibly smooth, the doctors told us that the baby's potentially large size meant she would need a Caesarean – so we already knew the birthday.

However, just as I'd finally decided to become an actor, the work had suddenly dried up. I had found an excellent agent, Paul Lyon-Maris, and constantly pestered him but at the time there was nothing for a short actor. Had this been a wise decision? Was I going to have to get a job selling insurance?

On the day we were due to go to the hospital for the birth, I heard something very heavy thud through the letterbox.

Could that be . . . a script?

It was.

The return address was Hollywood, California. I excitedly tore the bulky packet open, pulled out a wad of paper and looked at the front page. It had one word on it:

Leprechaun.

'Aha!' I thought, 'this is more like it.' Just then it was time to head for the hospital. The plan was for Sam to give birth by Caesarean. We travelled down with Denise, Sam's mum, and it was soon time to say goodbye. All I could do was tell Sam I loved her before the porter wheeled her away.

The next time I'd see Sam she'd be with our son or daughter and life would never be the same again. I was incredibly excited; I knew this was going to be the greatest moment in my whole life but I was still terribly nervous for Sam. My stomach was turning butterflies – goodness knows what Sam was feeling at that point. Now I knew how my father had felt when I was born. I just hoped and prayed there wouldn't be any problems.

The appropriately named Mr Hackman was going to perform the Caesarean and he had assembled a crack team of nurses, paediatricians and specialist doctors to deal with every eventuality.

I took a seat in the waiting room with Denise, who began fretting at me. After a few minutes I decided to go and get a cup of tea. On my way back I remembered the script which I'd thrown in the back of the car, so I went and grabbed it and started reading to take my mind off the worry and to try and stop Denise from making me even more nervous than I already was.

The birth, on Wednesday 11 September 1991, couldn't have gone more smoothly. Dr Tuck, one of the specialist paediatricians, gave our baby an examination and told Sam: 'He's perfect,' adding with a grin, 'I'm delighted to say you don't need me,' before rushing off to tell me.

He! It was a boy!

We'd already picked a name. It had no particular significance for us apart from the fact that Sam and I both really liked it: Lloyd. I thought that Lloyd Davis sounded like a good actor name.

Lloyd weighed six pounds and three ounces, which was more or less average-sized, and he looked to be in great health. Everybody was ecstatic. Both Sam's parents were there by now and they were walking on air, as was I. Life didn't get any more perfect than this.

Two hours later as we stared in wide-eyed wonder at our beautiful son, Sam said, 'He feels a bit cold.' The nurse fetched a heated blanket but it didn't help. Lloyd was struggling to breathe. A doctor came in and took Lloyd away to the special care baby unit. Mr Hackman appeared and he reassured me that Lloyd was fine.

At 10 p.m. Dr Tuck said that Lloyd needed to be put on a ventilator. 'There are only four of these at the unit in Peterborough,' he said, 'and they're all in use so we're going to have to move Lloyd to another specialist neonatal unit in Nottingham.'

'But that's almost fifty miles away!'

I couldn't believe that our son had to be taken to another hospital; surely this was putting his already fragile life in even more danger? Unfortunately there was nothing nearer, so Nottingham it had to be.

Sam still couldn't move at this time. A nurse sat with her and told her when the ambulance had arrived. 'Can you bring Lloyd to me before he goes?' she asked. They wheeled him in at 1.30 a.m. in a big portable ventilator.

The same nurse stayed with Sam all night and helped her get ready to follow in an ambulance to Nottingham. When we got there Lloyd looked fine. He was the biggest and healthiest-looking baby out of all the kids on ventilators.

On Friday the 13th at 5.45 p.m. a doctor came in, sat down with us and said, 'Lloyd is very poorly. We don't know if he's going to make it. There's a genetic factor we don't know about which means his lungs are underdeveloped.'

It was as if all the air had been sucked out of me. I was nauseous, dizzy; a tremendous suffocating weight seemed to be pressing down from above. Our son might die? It made no sense to us. He looked so healthy and active. We stayed with Lloyd the whole time. Although we were able to interact with him for a bit it was very difficult with all the tubes, wires and the ventilator mask. We couldn't pick him up at all. Despite this, in a very short span of time we began to feel a bit like parents.

Sam was still exhausted, however, and had to go back to bed to rest. Just after she did so Lloyd took a drastic turn for the worse and poor Sam was dragged back just in time to see him being resuscitated.

'His body can't take it,' the doctors told us. 'His lungs are too small.'

The following Friday, Dr Nigel Ruggins, a paediatrician from the special care baby unit, came to see us. 'I have the best job in the world but sometimes it's also the worst. This is the day when it's the worst. I had thought I might arrive here this morning to find that Lloyd had died in his sleep, so I didn't have to have this conversation with you.'

Sam and I held hands.

'I know he looks pink and healthy at the moment but Lloyd can't take many more attempts at resuscitation. The longer we keep him on the ventilator the worse his condition will become. His kidneys will fail, then his liver. You wouldn't want Lloyd to go through all that, would you?'

We didn't.

After we'd given consent at about three o'clock that afternoon, we watched as Nurse Melanie, who'd become good friends with us in a very short space of time, took Lloyd off the machine and gently handed him over to us.

We were given a special quiet room, so we could have some privacy with our son. We cuddled and told Lloyd we loved him so much. For a little while, we were a family together, and we got to know our son. He moved a little, he looked so alive, so healthy. It seemed like a strange thing to do at the time but I'm very glad we took a photograph. You need these things, the mementos.

About thirty minutes later, Lloyd passed away.

He had given us nine unforgettable days and we treasured every single one.

Leaving him at that point and saying goodbye was the hardest thing Sam and I have ever had to do. There is nothing in life that can prepare you to face something like that, nothing.

The drive back to Peterborough was awful. We just didn't want to go home, not to our unfurnished house, filled only with brightly coloured baby toys, cards from well-wishers and a freshly painted nursery. It hurt so much. It's as if your arms ache with emptiness, with the impossible desire to hold your child.

But we didn't know where else we could go.

Later that night as we cuddled up in bed, Sam said, 'I want the pain to go away, Warwick. I want to fast-forward a few years so I don't have to feel like this.'

It was very hard for us to accept Lloyd's death. We'd gone from the happiest moment in our lives to the saddest within a few days. It was very difficult to accept that medical science had been unable to save our son. But in Lloyd's case, there really was nothing they could have done differently. We had to come to terms with the fact that there's no magic in medicine.

Lloyd was buried at our local church. On the day of the funeral we were door-stepped by a journalist, angling for an interview. Although we like to help journalists whenever possible and we do now happily speak about Lloyd, back then it was too awful. It seemed like something we couldn't possibly ever face. It didn't help when an American magazine, not stopping to consider the time difference, phoned us at 4 a.m. – again to ask for an interview.

Any routine became a major ordeal. Our world had collapsed. To then just go back to the mundane stuff, like going to the shops, answering letters and paying bills, it all felt so pointless. What difference did it make if we paid the bills? This was such an awful low point, an incredibly difficult time for both Sam and me.

Sam was also physically exhausted. She had gone through a Caesarean and her body had been prepared for a baby. She had to readjust to not being pregnant and also not being a mother. She was physically shattered and needed time to recover.

It was hard for friends and relatives as well. They were there for us, but there's not much to talk about, they didn't know Lloyd, they'd never seen him and so this only served to isolate us further. It made grieving very difficult.

Sam and I are very happy people and our house was always full of laughter, noise and activity. But after Lloyd's death, it was hard to start laughing again.

It didn't help that we were still broke. I had no prospect of work, and spent my days worrying about our future and how we were going to keep repaying the taxman. I wondered how we were ever going to come back from this.

Then I remembered the script.

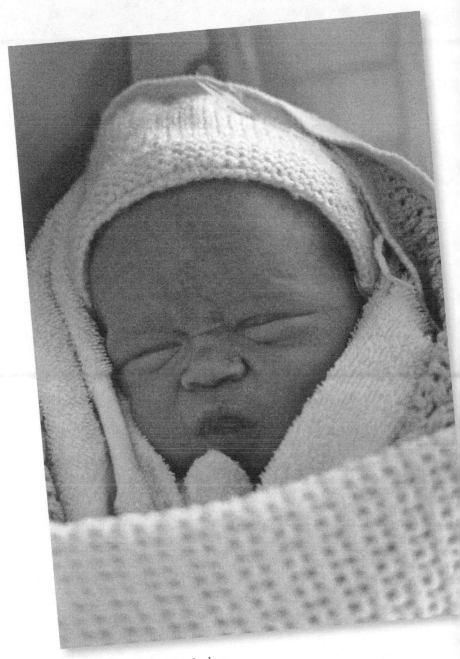

Lloyd, our wonderful baby boy.

Chapter Twelve

Lep in the Hood

Me, as the Leprechaun with Sam and Daniel.

With Mark Jones, writer, creator and director of the first *Leprechaun*.
He almost burned down his home in an effort to impress me.

Insane genius make-up artist Gabe Bartalos (he's on the left).
Gabe is responsible for more upset stomachs than the Delhi Belly.

About to grab a very famous pair of legs – they belonged to Jennifer Aniston. *Leprechaun* was her first big screen role.

'Seriously, *you're* Warwick Davis?' the amazed voice on the other end of the line said.

Mark Jones, the writer and director of *Leprechaun*, couldn't believe 'Willow' had called him back. After all, this was the craziest idea for a movie he'd ever had. He wanted me to star as an evil leprechaun in a tongue-in-cheek children's horror flick.

What could I say? It was . . . interesting. I'd never played a bad guy, and this was a chance to go against type, an idea I loved. The further you step away from your own character the more challenging and fun it becomes and the Leprechaun went about as far as it was possible to go. I also knew a change of scene would make all the difference both personally and professionally right then – and it would pay just enough to keep the Inland Revenue at bay.

As Mark and I chatted, we really gelled. I could tell this was going to work.

Sam was all for it and one week later we were on our way to Heathrow, ready to catch our flight to Los Angeles. This was just what we needed. It was as if we had been magically airlifted out of our gloom. Of course, we would never forget Lloyd. You always feel some sadness and wish things could have turned out better. But with time the sadness becomes manageable, you learn to accept it and the experience becomes part of who you are. We were still grieving for Lloyd then, of course, but we were so grateful for the chance to be somewhere new. We knew that life still had many things to offer us and this opportunity gave our spirits a much-needed boost.

Airports are interesting places. These days, if I'm flying on business I'll fly first class, but when I'm paying, I'll fly economy. You'd have to be crazy to spend thousands on first class. Nonetheless, because I'm an actor, lots of people assume that I belong in first class and this sometimes includes the people at the check-in desk.

When we rolled up to check in at the British Airways section in Heathrow, we were greeted by a very smart uniformed gentleman who clicked his heels in salute. He then swept up our bags, loaded them onto a trolley and ushered us past the queues to the first-class section.

He delivered our bags with a flourish and beamed. 'There you are, sir.'

'Ah, right,' I said.

'Something the matter, sir?'

'Oh no, no, but er . . . We're not flying first class. We're economy. Any chance of an upgrade?'

It never works but I always ask or try some silly scheme. I sometimes strategically put a few photos of me in my various film roles inside my passport and let them accidentally spill out onto the counter as I check in. 'Oops, sorry about that, I always have to keep a few handy for fans, you know?'

They always notice in the USA but then invariably apologise and say, 'First class is full, sir,' in a treacly voice – peppered with strychnine. In the UK they simply pretend not to see them.

I nearly missed a flight once. 'Sorry I'm late,' I said. 'Autograph hunters.'

The desk clerk looked over my head and said, completely

deadpan: 'Why, is there somebody famous in the airport?'

It sounds extremely odd but I really do need the legroom. My legs stick straight out over the edge of the seat – I can't bend them as my knees are too far back. So when someone in front puts their seat back I'm suddenly concertinaed into my chair. It's also very hard for me to get in and out if I'm not in the aisle seat. If the person next to me is asleep, I'll usually just balance on the armrests and walk across. I've never woken a fellow passenger yet, although I dread the day when someone opens their eyes to find me nose-to-nose with them just as I'm straddling their chair.

Despite these hurdles, I still fly an awful lot. On another flight with Sam, I'd really tried my damnedest to get us an upgrade. At check-in they'd told me it was full but now I was on the plane I could see there were loads of empty seats in business class. Sam didn't mind and went to sleep.

Imagine my delight, then, when the film started and I couldn't see it (this was still in the days before TV screens were in the backs of every seat, when they used to show in-flight movies on a screen in the middle of the plane).

'Aha,' I thought, 'this could be my ticket to an upgrade.' I called over a stewardess.

'I can't see the screen.'

'Oh my goodness, I'm so sorry about that. Hang on, let me see what I can do.'

This was more like it. Business class here I come. I started to gather my things in preparation.

The stewardess returned five minutes later and handed me a metallic flight case.

'What's this?'

'Sit on that and you'll be able to see.'

With the hard, ice-cold metallic suitcase below me, I could see about half of the screen. Then I realised I was sitting in the exit row. The rule is that if you feel you can't open the emergency hatch then you shouldn't be sitting next to it. I called the stewardess.

'So sorry to disturb you, only I've just noticed where we're sitting and I don't feel confident I can open the door in an emergency.'

'Oh my goodness,' she said, 'you've got a good point there. Hang on.'

I rubbed my hands in anticipation as she headed off again. She returned two minutes later.

'I've just asked someone in another row and they've very kindly agreed to swap with you.'

As my smile faded, she gestured to the row just in front of us.

Now I was still in economy, with less legroom, sitting on an uncomfortable metal box and watching a film I didn't want to see.

'Hmmm,' I said, thinking out loud, as Sam settled down beside me and tried to get back to sleep. 'Perhaps I could –'

Sam's eyes snapped open. 'Just leave it, Warwick.'

Once we were in California, Sam and I met Mark Jones at his house in the Hollywood hills. He was a successful TV writer who'd produced scripts for many popular 80s TV shows, including *The A-Team*, and now wanted to make movies. It was a hot September day and he put on a very pleasant lunch.

Mark showed us round his house, he was especially proud of the fact that he had a real fireplace.

'Let me show you how good it looks when it's lit,' he said enthusiastically.

'No, really, you don't have to.'

'But I insist. I've never had an English person stay with me before so I've never had an excuse to light it.'

I'm still not sure what he meant by that exactly but I let him start the fire and the house quickly turned into a baker's oven.

'Is it me,' I said a few minutes later, 'or is there a slight smoke haze in here?'

The smoke alarm went off.

'Aw jeez, that's embarrassing,' Mark said.

'Why?' I asked.

'The alarm's connected straight to the fire department.'

Minutes later the house was full of macho firemen stomping around demanding to know what was going on and where the fire was, and then why anyone would want to light an open fire on a balmy September evening in California.

It turned out Mark hadn't realised that he was supposed to open something called 'the chimney vent'. He was deeply embarrassed that our first meeting had turned out the way it had. So was I. But despite being a little char-grilled and a bit worried about Mark's sanity, I signed up for the movie.

The 'plot' involved a bloodthirsty leprechaun (who spoke almost exclusively in rhyming couplets), a pot of gold, lost teenagers, a deserted house and a magical four-leaf clover. My nemesis was a very attractive young woman, who, at the end of the film, would have the dubious honour of sending me to my doom at the bottom of a well. Her name meant nothing to me then: Jennifer Aniston

Ask Jennifer about *Leprechaun* today and she will deny everything. I don't blame her. Once during filming, when Ron Howard called me and asked what I was up to in LA, I admit that even I was a bit reluctant to confess. When I finally told him, his advice was, 'Whatever you do, don't make another one.'

After I'd agreed to do it, I had to audition for the all-important 'moneymen', the producers who were financing the film. But while they may have been financially astute, they weren't terribly creative. They all sat in line behind a table in true *X-Factor* style while Mark and I came out and did our thing, talked through the plot and played out a few scenes. I'd developed a special 'Leprechaun voice', more of a creature voice with a hint of Irish than a full accent.

The suits seemed to be happy that the film would make money and we started shooting at Valencia Studios, just as they were clearing out all the gear from *Terminator 2: Judgment Day.*

We also shot scenes at the Big Sky Ranch where *Little House on the Prairie* and *The Waltons* were both filmed. These were insanely popular TV dramas and it felt a little blasphemous to be turning these sets, known for their incredibly saccharine family-friendly dramas, into a comedy horror location – especially the scene in the local store where I cruelly crush the store owner's chest and stomach by hopping on him with a pogo stick. *Prairie* was also famous for its opening credits where three children run down a hill. I broke a cop's neck at the bottom of that hill. Oh yes, this was quality horror.

The suits were quite hands-on. They were always on set, watching where every penny was going. There was one who came to visit while I was in the make-up trailer being transformed into the Leprechaun. Gabe Bartalos, the make-up artist, was a boomingly loud, dark-haired giant of Hungarian descent who was completely crazy and a real delight to work with. He held complete mastery over horror make-up and had worked on several cult horror classics, such as *Brain Dead* and the *Cremaster Cycle*, an extraordinary film/art project that earned a special exhibition at the Guggenheim Museum in New York.

On that particular day, Gabe had been showing me various things he'd created for the film. 'Take a look at this,' he said, proudly passing me a little cardboard box. I opened it and inside, lying on a bed of cotton wool, was a finger that had been severed, or rather yanked out of a hand; it had all the tendons trailing from it. It was even wearing a ring and looked absolutely 100 per cent realistic, and I said so.

It was then that one of the producers knocked at the door. 'Hang on a minute,' I said, as Gabe went to answer, 'watch this!' I took the finger and pretended that when the door opened it had somehow ripped off my hand. 'Aaaaaaargh!' I screamed, waving the severed appendage in the producer's face. I looked insane, I was half-naked and half-made-up as the Leprechaun.

The producer's reaction was not what I had been expecting.

He stayed completely deadpan and said, 'When I was in college, I was fooling around in the shower and when I jumped up to throw something over the top of the shower curtain, I caught my ring finger on the rail, slipped and fell and ripped it clean off. It looked exactly like that.'

I looked down and saw that his ring finger was indeed missing.

A few days later Gabe showed me a severed hand. 'Yes, very nice,' I said, and left it well alone.

Work on *Leprechaun* had started so quickly that Sam and I hadn't been able to hire a car and now, thanks to my hectic work schedule, we didn't have time to. Los Angeles is known as the City of the Car; it wasn't the sort of place you can get about easily on foot. This left us feeling a bit trapped in our hotel. When I mentioned this to crazy make-up artist Gabe at the hotel, he threw me his car keys. 'I'm flying to New York for the weekend, why don't you use my Caddy while I'm away?'

'Well . . . um.'

I had thought it was obvious why not, but after a while cabin fever had really taken hold, so I decided to have a go; after all, temptation breeds innovation. I piled the seat with pillows from the hotel so I could see out of the window. I then took off my right shoe and tied a sturdy shoebox lengthwise to my foot. I reckoned that this would be enough for me to press down on the accelerator and the brake.

Sam decided to join me.

'So,' she said, 'where are we going to go?'

'Erm . . . to the shop.'

I set off down Wilshire Boulevard in the Cadillac, looking for a seven-eleven. I had no idea what I was going to get when I got there – I was doing this for the experience not because I needed a gallon of milk and a box of Oreos.

What made it tricky, however, was the fact that it was very hard to judge how hard to push down to brake and accelerate, so my progress was very jerky. I just hoped the cardboard box would survive the journey.

Wilshire Boulevard is twelve miles long and one of the main East-West roads in LA. It's named after Gaylord Wilshire (shame they didn't choose the first name – Gaylord Boulevard has a much nicer ring to it) who cleared a path in his barley field there in the 1890s. If he had seen his road one hundred years on, I'm sure it would have blown Gaylord's mind. Lined with skyscrapers, one part of it is known as Miracle Mile – it'll be a miracle if you survive the journey because it's so congested and it contains one infamous ten-lane intersection. This, combined with all the neon lights, must make Wilshire Boulevard look like a Christmas tree from outer space.

Unfortunately, I missed all this and somehow sailed through the ten-lane intersection without knowing it. I was far too busy trying to find the brake and accelerator with my cardboard box.

I drove past the spectacular Ambassador Hotel, where Robert

Kennedy had been assassinated, and past the Academy of Motion Picture Arts and Sciences (the place where they hand out those little Oscar® statuettes) and daydreamed about receiving the Oscar® for *Leprechaun*. 'I don't know what to say, it was so unexpected. This just goes to show what a little guy with big dreams can achieve.'

We eventually spotted a grocery store, found a parking space and I was about to climb out when I realised the shoebox was still fastened to my foot. I removed it and then searched for my shoe.

'Oh, bugger.'

I'd forgotten it.

But that wasn't going to stop me. I'd come this far. After all, I'd just driven a Cadillac through central LA using a shoebox and I'd be damned if I'd turn back now.

So, I emerged from the huge car, one shoe on and one shoe off, and tried to ignore the stares from the people in the grocery store. Being in LA, I presumed they saw a lot of strange sights, but obviously never a one-shoed little person.

Sam, who was giggling at my predicament, bought some juice and snacks. I limped my way out to the Cadillac, clambered back in, re-tied my shoebox and drove us, very carefully, back to the hotel. By the time we got back I was exhausted.

'Well,' Sam said, 'that was interesting.'

I don't know about that but it certainly cured my cabin fever.

During the filming of *Leprechaun* I had a number of scenes with Jennifer Aniston. You could tell even then she was going places. She was extremely professional, knew her way round a film set and nailed everything on the first take, an essential ability in a movie like *Leprechaun*, which had a tiny budget and a limited shooting time of just three weeks.

One scene involved me chasing Jennifer through an old people's home using a wheelchair. When Mark had written the script, he hadn't realised just how impractical this would be – I could barely reach the wheels of the wheelchair, let alone pump them around with my arms at the necessary speed.

The answer was to shoot at twelve frames per second. When the film was played back it looked like a leprechaun version of Benny Hill was chasing a terrified Jennifer Aniston up and down the nursing home corridors while she screamed over a standard horror soundtrack. In reality, Jennifer ran in slow motion so I could keep up.

Although stuntmen were available, I did most of my own stunts. At one point I crashed through a fence on my roller skates, leaving a leprechaun-shaped hole behind. I also got to drive a super-powered go-kart in a car chase with the cops. We had to go back and reshoot more violent versions of several scenes after the suits declared that a scary children's movie would not be as profitable as an adult horror film. Mark obliged and turned the gore up to eleven.

Everyone on set got on well, we had a good time making it, there were no egos and we were all just grateful to be working. I never really got to know Jennifer personally, only professionally. When I was in costume it was quite tricky – attempts at idle chit-chat really don't work when you're dressed as an evil leprechaun. Once she won her part in *Friends,* for a while I entertained the futile hope that I'd get the call from the show's producers to make a special guest-star appearance as the Leprechaun.

A lot of the plot of *Leprechaun* was suspiciously similar to my childhood favourite *Scooby-Doo* (Mark had written for Hanna-Barbera, the makers of said programme). It involved four kids hunting for a four-leaf clover, the only thing that would kill me. They finally succeed when one of them wraps up a clover in some chewing gum and catapults it into my open mouth. I swallow, choke, stagger to the edge of a well (where the wall is partially broken) and start to decompose and then tumble back down into the bottomless hole. All that was missing was for me to shout, 'And I would have gotten away with it if it wasn't for those meddling kids!'

For the decomposing scene, I had to wear an acrylic jawbone which Gabe inserted into my prosthetics before supergluing several tubes to my body. All sorts of goo, gunk and smoke was blown out through these tubes to make it look as if I was melting. It was actually somebody's job to smoke a cigar and puff smoke into one of the tubes, so it looked as if my chest was burning as I dissolved.

We filmed from 4 p.m. until 6 a.m. every day on location in the high desert outside LA, where the wind chill brought the temperature down to below freezing. Contrary to what you might expect, the layers of foam prosthetics didn't protect me at all. The cold crept up through my little shoes, up my legs, through my Leprechaun hands and straight up my arms like a rapidly rising icy tide.

The schedule was relentless. I'd get back to the hotel at 7 a.m. where I'd have breakfast and then, after a day's sleep, upon arriving back on set I'd have breakfast again. It was exhausting; I had to be in bed by 8 a.m. or I wouldn't make it through the next day's shoot.

I was delighted when filming finally wrapped and we could go home. I'd loved making *Leprechaun* but it had been a gruelling few weeks.

Another reason to get back to the UK was to see a genetic counsellor who would explain some of the complications Sam and I would face when trying to start a family. We'd never even heard of such a thing until Lloyd had fallen ill and a doctor suggested that we should consider it.

We each had our own reasons for being small; mine was an extremely rare genetic condition that occurs in about one in a million people called spondyloepexpalidcious.

No, hang on, that's not it. Even the most experienced doctors have to take a few runs at the pronunciation: spondyloepiphyseal dysplasia congenita, SED for short (thank goodness). SED is an inherited disorder of bone growth where the ends of the bones don't fully develop and this results in short stature and some skeletal abnormalities. There are a host of other connected problems that people with SED may or may not have, such as a cleft palate, club foot (which I'd had), high risk of retinal detachment and potential neck problems.

Sam has achondroplasia, the more common type of dwarfism, also a genetic condition. We had no idea what the effect of combining our genes would be; medical knowledge of my condition and the effect of having children with Sam was literally nonexistent. In fact, as numerous doctors told us, we were the first such couple they'd ever come across. The doctors in Nottingham tried to console us with the fact that they had learned a great deal from Lloyd; his was the first case of its kind in the world, they said.

Researchers later discovered that when both of our genes are combined, there's a one in four chance that our children could be tall, or could be like Sam, or like me, or share both of our genetic material. The fourth option was the most dangerous and that was what had happened to Lloyd.

So when Sam fell pregnant again, we were cautiously excited. Sam went through another textbook pregnancy but this time our baby was born 'asleep' at University College Hospital in central London. We named him George. The loss was almost too painful to bear, we were devastated and I left the hospital after the birth, without even seeing George, just to walk the streets and to try and clear my head. It seemed crazy that in the world outside, everything was just carrying on as normal.

When I came back to the hospital, Sam, who was still really weak, said, 'You should see him, Warwick, it will help.'

Reluctantly, I agreed. I thought that seeing our son would make the pain all the worse.

But it didn't. I was able to say hello and goodbye. It was exactly what I needed to do. Although my heart ached, he looked so perfect, as if he really were sleeping.

On what was another agonising drive home, I stopped when we were just outside Peterborough. 'Thank you,' I said, hugging Sam, 'thank you for making me see my son.'

These experiences drew Sam and I even closer. We ended up learning things about ourselves we would never have learned had we not lost Lloyd and George. Of course, these are the sorts of lessons no one should ever have to learn and I wish this was something we hadn't had to go through, but in the process we discovered just how much we were able to cope with. It also convinced us that we truly were soul mates; that we were meant to be together because together we could face anything.

Our experience with Lloyd also left Sam and I passionate about helping Peterborough's Special Care Baby Unit buy more ventilators so that sick babies and their parents wouldn't have to be transferred for treatment elsewhere as we were. Whenever I donate my time to a good cause (opening a school fete, a local fair, a charity auction, etc.), the organisers usually ask if there's anything they can do in return, so I ask them to make a donation or organise a collection for the baby unit.

Our decision to try again was by no means taken lightly. I worried that the risk of becoming attached to another baby might have been too much to bear. I hadn't expected the bond I felt towards Lloyd and George to be as intense as it was so soon after they were born and I wasn't sure I could cope with the pain of loss again.

Sam, meanwhile, was adamant: we *would* have a child.

In the meantime, *Leprechaun* was released in 620 cinemas across North America to overwhelmingly terrible reviews. One reviewer described it as 'Mildly diverting horror silliness' full of 'ill-advised slapstick twists', while another said it was 'incredibly bad and boring' and that 'Jennifer Aniston shows that, in different circumstances, she might be competent'. The *New York Times*, however, did point out that 'it does feature what is possibly a movie first: a murder committed by a leprechaun riding a pogo stick'. Excellent!

Fortunately, cinema-goers disagreed with the majority of the critics and *Leprechaun* soon achieved a notorious degree of popularity among teenagers. It cost about $900,000 to make and took ten times that at the US box office on its first release.

Mark and I remain proud of it to this day, and I'm always delighted when people mention the Leprechaun in lists of other classic horror characters. Alongside Freddy, Chucky and Jason, I'm in good company.

It was one of those films CDS Productions would have loved to have made if only we'd had the idea – and if *Leprechaun* had come out when I was fourteen or fifteen I would have been first in the queue to see it at Ewell cinema.

As it was a commercial success, the producers decided to finance a sequel (*Leprechaun 2: One Wedding and Lots of Funerals*) and although Mark was attached to the project he wasn't going to direct this time; that would fall to a chap called Rodman Flender, who'd directed a lot of television and would go on to helm the teen-horror movie *Idle Hands* starring the then almost unknown eighteen-year-old actress, Jessica Alba. (The plot of *Idle Hands* concerned a young man whose right hand becomes possessed by Satan – yeah, yeah, we've all used that excuse!)

I was amazed that I was now starring in my own quirky horror franchise and was delighted to sign on the dotted line for *Leprechaun 2*.

Once again, we had an extremely low budget and just three weeks in which to shoot the film. We had to shoot relentlessly through the night in an operation that was run like a production line and we whizzed through several pages of script every night. Looking back, comparing *Leprechaun 2* to *Harry Potter* (not something many people do, I realise), the process couldn't be more different. On *Harry Potter* a whole day can be spent on just one shot.

I enjoyed the fast pace, as it gave my character energy and kept us all on our toes, but some of the crew found it hard to keep up. We seemed to burn through cameramen at an extraordinary rate. Every time I looked up another new face was staring at me through the eyepiece.

Rodman also came up with his own bizarre set of Leprechaun rules. He decided the Leprechaun couldn't touch anything made of wrought iron and so the entire movie revolved around me touching or being imprisoned by iron (the Leprechaun has to trick his way out of an iron safe at one point).

According to mystic legend (a.k.a. Rodman), the Leprechaun can have the hand of any damsel who sneezes three times, explained in the immortal line: 'She sneezes once, she sneezes twice, she'll be me bride when she sneezes thrice!'

One can only presume there weren't many allergies hundreds of years ago. After the heroine, in this case Bridget (played by a beautiful blonde Shevonne Durkin) has sneezed the requisite three times, I tie her up in preparation for marriage.

In one very gross scene, I had to lick poor Shevonne's face. Gabe, the crazy make-up guy, told me he had something very special in mind for this scene. He revealed he'd made a three-inch tongue extension that he wanted me to try. What's more, the tongue had a fork, much like a snake's.

'I can't wear that!'

'I just have to dry your tongue and glue this on, it'll be fine, trust me.'

Once it was fastened, he emptied half a tube of slime into my mouth so I could drool all over the unfortunate Shevonne before I gagged on the fake tongue. I've had to play some fairly outrageous scenes in my career but this was the most grotesque by far. Shevonne didn't have to act when she winced in disgust.

Leprechaun 2 was made for even less money than the first and despite the snooty, if accurate reviews (*Variety* described it as 'a nasty piece of business that revels in chicanery and gore', although I appreciated the comment **'Davis brings zest to his role despite having to manoeuvre through a ton of makeup'**; damn right!), it was a roaring financial success.

This was bolstered somewhat by *Wayne's World 2*, when Wayne (Mike Myers) induces a panic attack in Garth (Dana Carvey) by doing his impression of me as the Leprechaun. *Wayne's World* and its sequel were two of the most popular movies of the early 90s and that reference undoubtedly gave *Leprechaun 2* a great lift and kept the franchise going.

Even though the Leprechaun exploded at the end of *Leprechaun 2*,[37] the producers had no trouble resurrecting him in *Leprechaun 3* (*Welcome to Vegas – the Odds Are You Won't Leave Alive!*). It was directed

---

[37] He blew up after being impaled on an iron bar.

by Brian Trenchard-Smith, who was known for his magical ability to make movies look expensive even though they'd been shot on a shoestring. He'd directed a number of cult Australian Exploitation films (a.k.a. Ozploitation), including *Turkey Shoot* (1982), which reached number one in the UK box office charts on its release. Quentin Tarantino recently cited Brian as one of his favourite filmmakers.

Much of the shooting took place in the basement kitchens of the infamous Ambassador Hotel, where the first Academy Awards took place and where Sirhan Sirhan assassinated Robert F. Kennedy in 1968. There's an 'X' scored into a tile in the kitchen which marks the spot where he fell. The place had a really eerie feel at night and several of the crew said they saw strange things (probably just me in costume dashing to and from the loo).

The set designers turned the main ballroom (where Kennedy had given his last speech) into a casino with gaming machines that had been especially licensed so they could be used in California.

Even though the film was set in Vegas, our budget was such that we could film in Las Vegas for one night only. We stayed in the Mirage Hotel, an enormous 3,044-room monster that opened in 1989 – it had cost an incredible $630million to build. It's famous for its volcano fountain that erupts every night at 9 p.m. and for Siegfried and Roy's magic show featuring a man-eating white tiger.[38]

Gabe turned my room into the make-up trailer, which was fine except for the fact that I had to then walk across the casino floor made up as the evil Leprechaun. Trying to look inconspicuous when you look like a cross between a Gremlin, the Grinch and Yoda isn't easy – you'll only ever have a limited degree of success.

---

[38] It lived up to its name a few years later when the tiger ate Siegfried. Or was it Roy? I can never remember.

A large pancake-faced man wearing a Hawaiian shirt stopped me. He bent down and asked, 'Hey, and who are you supposed to be, sonny?'

'What do you mean?' I asked. 'I'm just here for a good time.'

He did a double take. Gabe had done such a good job with the make-up that a horrified look of awareness that I might be real slowly crept across the man's broad sweaty features.

I carried on through the casino where some people were daft enough to think I was a lucky leprechaun and tried to touch me for good fortune. I guess that out of all the cities in the world, Las Vegas was the one place we could get away with this. An evil leprechaun was no big deal in a hotel full of white man-eating tigers, ventriloquists, seven-foot go-go dancers and an entire circus in its parking lot.

If I'd done this in London I think the reaction would have been somewhat different: no one would dare say anything and would pretend they'd seen nothing, apart from the children of course, who would be quickly whisked away by their embarrassed parents. And in Los Angeles I think I would probably have become a target for sharpshooters.

Brian kept us on such a shoestring that we didn't even have all our filming permits, so this was a 'guerrilla shoot'. I had to leap out of our van, run out into the streets followed by the camera and sound teams, start filming, hopefully get the shot we needed in one take, and then run off before the cops appeared and demanded to see our permission slips.

'Run around and behave like the Leprechaun!' was Brian's only direction for most of these scenes. Filming was immediately interrupted on Sunset Strip when some teenagers recognised me from the first film.

'Get rid of them! Walk down the Strip!' Brian yelled, looking around anxiously for cops. 'Just act; do stuff!'

It was the weirdest feeling. I gradually got further away from the crew until I was on my own, walking through downtown Vegas. Behave like the Leprechaun, he says? Right, I'll show him!

The costume gave me freedom to misbehave; I was no longer Warwick, I was an evil little leprechaun! I tried to hitch rides and gave the finger when the cars wouldn't pick me up. I hopped up and down and shook my fist at them. This was great! I could get away with anything!

Eventually, the van pulled up alongside me with a screech of tyres, the door slid open and I jumped inside. 'That was great, Warwick,' Brian said, and with that our guerrilla shoot was concluded.

I was keen to appear on screen in a Leprechaun movie without my make-up and suggested to Brian that I make a cameo appearance as myself sitting in the background in one of the casino scenes. He thought it was a great idea, so the next day we visited a casino where I sat in front of a one-armed bandit with Samantha.

'I don't know,' Brian said, 'people might still recognise you too easily. You look like the Leprechaun.'

'Oh, cheers for that,' I said.

Despite the fact I looked nothing like that monster, Brian still insisted I wear a hat and plonked his fedora on my head. But at least the scene made the final cut, and if you're watching very carefully you'll spot Sam and me (it also made it into the trailer) working the slot machines, looking a bit like underage gamblers.

Leprechaun 3 was another underground hit and plans were soon under way for number four, but before the script was ready I had to fly back over to the UK for some urgent stilt-walking lessons.

My three-hour transformation into the Leprechaun.

Chapter Thirteen
Love and Biscuits

On the set of *Leprechaun in Space*. Why's he in space? Surely we don't need to explain that do we? The extraordinary creature in just his pants is Guy 'My Little Tank' Siner of '*Allo 'Allo* fame.

I had been whisked off to deepest Norfolk to meet an old clown who lived, much like Yoda, in a little bungalow in the swampy fens. As I climbed onto the stilts under the clown's watchful gaze, I mumbled, 'This really is something I thought I'd never have to do.'

'All right up there?' the old clown croaked. Wobbling like a man trying to stand to attention on a giant blancmange, I nodded gingerly.

'Good,' he replied, and promptly pushed me over.

'What the hell?!' I yelled, my voice slightly muffled by the soft turf. He grinned.

'First rule of stilt-walking; overcome the fear of falling.'

His technique did not quite work as he had hoped. I developed a healthy fear of being pushed over by the nutty clown and became quite adept at walking away from him at great speed. This did help me to learn more quickly but not quite in the manner he'd hoped.

I needed to stilt-walk so that I could tower over Ted Danson in a scene for the American TV production of *Gulliver's Travels*. I was supposed to be jealous that someone even shorter than me had shown up in Brobdingnag (the land of the giants) and had taken my place to become the Queen's favourite jester.

It was great seeing the world from a 'normal height' for once.

One day, while practising in the clown's garden, getting more and more used to the stilts, I wandered into his kitchen. 'Wow, this is great,' I thought. I could reach his kettle and cupboards so I made us a cup of tea, and wondered whether stilts might have a practical application for Sam and me. In particular, I hadn't been able to afford to have our kitchen customised and we'd never even opened the top cupboards.

Cooking, especially using frying pans on the hob, was a nightmare that involved several stools, nerves of steel and a steady hand. Perhaps stilts would be a cheap solution. When I showed up with a pair under my arm, Sam was quick to respond.

'No way! I'm not having you stagger about on those with pans of boiling water.'

'Awww.'

So I travelled with my stilts to Portugal, where the filming was due to take place. I was horrified to learn that the location for my scene was a magnificent palace, complete with polished marble floors, hardly the same thing as the soft, peaty soil of Norfolk. Typical. Risking life and limb in the name of art once more.

I was, however, delighted to be playing opposite Ted Danson. Over eighty million people had recently watched his swansong on the hugely popular TV sitcom *Cheers* and this was his first major role since. It was an extraordinary production, one of those rare TV jewels where the special effects and costumes constantly dazzle alongside some terrific performances by an all-star cast.

Apart from stilt-walking on slippery floors,[39] the most amazing thing about filming *Gulliver's Travels* was working with Peter O'Toole, Robert Hardy and Edward Fox, mainly because they were all as mad as the proverbial box of frogs.

For example, during a break I went outside to stretch my legs and saw Peter and Edward silently playing catch with a piece of rubble. They were completely deadpan, they even looked a little bored, but

---

[39] I didn't fall over.

there was simply nothing else to do. Actors find the oddest things to pass the long time between scenes. These days we can count our blessings because we have our iPhones to keep us amused.

On *Gulliver's Travels*, one of the producers had a new-fangled invention called a mobile telephone. It was the same size and weight as a brick. We gazed in wonder as he called another producer who was on his car phone on Hollywood Boulevard.

'Show off,' Robert said.

'Damn him and his phone,' said O'Toole.

The very next day the same producer was struck by lightning while on the phone.[40]

The production was a huge success; it was the first to adapt all four parts of Jonathan Swift's 1726 novel and it collected Emmys, BAFTAs and Royal Television Society Awards – almost as quickly as Ricky Gervais.

Eventually it was time to hang up my stilts and return to Peter borough. Looking at the local paper I saw that hypnotist Paul McKenna's show had arrived at the Corn Exchange in Cambridge. I was really interested in hypnosis and neurolinguistics and so Sam and I went along.

I leapt up when he asked for volunteers and marched on stage with dozens of other people to the sound of Jean Michel Jarre. When Paul saw me he gave me a friendly wink before choosing me as one of the final ten volunteers who would take part in his show.

When Paul hypnotised me it felt *wonderful*. It was so relaxing, every time he said 'Sleep', I gratefully retreated into this beautiful, warm and comforting place.

---

[40] He was fine, although he smelt of burned hair and ozone for a few days.

Paul made me think I was about to get into the ring to fight Mike Tyson and he had me jumping in the air and throwing punches in no time. It was so strange, I knew it wasn't real, but at the same time I could see Tyson right there in front of me, I could hear the roar of the crowd and felt my punches hit home.

'OK, Warwick, that's enough, sleep, sleep, sleep, sleep.'

I relaxed into my tranquil trance.

'OK, Warwick, I now want you to give me your definition of true love. Think about this carefully, take your time, just say whatever is in your heart.'

I stood for a moment, calmly evaluating all the options. Hmmmm. What could it be? Aha! Suddenly I had it!

'So, Warwick, what is your definition of true love?'

Speaking in a loud clear voice I said: 'Chocolate biscuits.'

Sam was not amused. Perhaps my saying chocolate biscuits was the expression of a subconscious desire for the thing I found most comforting, because there was nothing I loved more than sharing a pot of tea and a packet of McVitie's choccy digestives with Sam of an evening.[41]

Well, that's my theory anyway and I'm sticking to it.

After the show was over, I left feeling terrific, really energised, and this stayed with me for several days.

Not long after, I met Paul at the premiere of *Apollo 13* in Planet Hollywood in London. I asked him if it might be possible to hypnotise a director to give me a part.

'Oh, most certainly,' he said and winked.

I wasn't sure if he was serious or not but he did tell me that we all have a safety mechanism built in which won't let us do anything that doesn't fit in with our own personal system of beliefs.

---

[41] Note to McVitie's: I prefer plain chocolate.

I was so fascinated by the concept that we can essentially make adjustments to our brains' software using hypnosis and neuro-linguistics that I took lessons in hypnosis at the same school as Paul had. I've only ever used it on myself to reinforce positive thoughts and ambitions – to make sure life's biscuit tin was always full.

Also squeezed in between the *Leprechaun* films was a project I'd really rather not mention. In fact, until I came to write this book, I'd almost managed to forget all about it. It was called *Prince Valiant*, and was based on the famous comic strip of the same name, and it was an absolute disaster from start to finish. As Pechet, Prince Valiant's squire, I had quite a big part. Although the idea was great, it was poorly executed and very little about the production made any sense. The director seemed intent on partying all night long and giving roles to his friends – and the one and only Chesney Hawkes (not that there's anything wrong with Chesney, of course, he's a delightful man, it's just that he wasn't suited for the role of stable hand). Even the wonderful Joanna Lumley – who still managed to put in an amazing performance as Morgan le Fay – couldn't save it.

Most of the actors were just happy to emerge with their careers still intact and hurriedly found other work before the film was premiered, panned and bombed. It was with no little relief that I grabbed the script for the next *Leprechaun* movie and ran for the Hollywood Hills. But then I opened the script and . . . what was this? Leprechaun in *space*?

I have no idea what actually happened but I can imagine the production meeting went something like this.

Suit One: What to do with the Leprechaun next?
Suit Two: Put him in space!
Suit Three: How did he get there?

Suit Two: Doesn't matter.

Suit Three: But he died in the last film.

Suit Two: Doesn't matter.

Suit Three: Get Brian Trenchard-Smith back, he can polish a turd, just look at *Leprechaun 3*.

Well, Brian polished for all he was worth on the truly unforgettable *Leprechaun 4: In Space: One Small Step For Man . . . One Giant Leap of Terror*, and actually did a pretty amazing job. He created extraordinary comic horrors out of nothing. Yes, I know it shows but that was the whole point – the trashier the *Leprechaun* films looked, the more the horror fans seemed to like them.

In fact, one of my favourite moments of my acting career came in that movie. It's the scene in which the Leprechaun is zapped by some kind of laser, which causes him to expand to gigantic proportions – he then does a lot of slow-motion stomping around a space station.

To pull it off the special-effects guys built a scaled-down replica set with lots of crates made of tiny plastic boxes. I think I was enjoying myself a little too much – even bashing my head on the ceiling was a new treat. 'Warwick, that was great,' Brian said, 'but we're going to have to do that again, this time try not to make the sound effects.'

I realised then that I'd been producing the sound effects myself. I thought they were in my head but every time I'd stomped my foot on the ground I'd growled, 'Boom!' and every time I'd smashed a crate I'd yelled, 'Smash!'

The one thing I couldn't understand about this film was that after the Leprechaun becomes big, he looks down the front of his trousers and admires his enlarged manhood. This never made sense to me, as proportionately speaking, it would still look the same size to him. Still, it was never mine to reason why, this was a *Leprechaun* film; nothing was supposed to make sense.

I was delighted to be acting alongside Debbe Dunning, the Tool Time Girl from Tim Allen's hugely popular TV show *Home Improvement*. Her character, Delores Costello, was named after a silent-movie star – the grandmother of Drew Barrymore.

But I was most honoured to be working alongside a true legend, Guy Siner, a.k.a. Lieutenant Hubert Gruber from classic British Sitcom *'Allo, 'Allo!* He played Dr Mittenhand, who was half-man and half-machine, a bit like Davros from *DoctorWho*. Poor Guy was forced to suffer so much indignity during that film. He staggered around night and day with no clothes on from the waist up and seemed to be glued to more prosthetics than any other character in acting history. Most of the film's budget went on Guy's make-up and costume; I imagine the local glue factory had to hire more staff and work through the night.

In the film the Leprechaun injects Dr Mittenhand in the head with a mixture of crushed up spider and scorpion juice he's made in a blender. This turns poor old Mittenhand into a . . . a . . . Well, I suppose you'd call it a scorpion-spiderman.

I saw Guy at a convention several years later (he's since been in both *DoctorWho* and *Star Trek*) and we had a fun chat about the good old days, in particular the agony he went through being an arachnid. The spider costume was so massive and heavy that he couldn't do anything once he was glued in – he couldn't even go to the toilet so wouldn't drink anything and would end the day dizzy with dehydration. Despite this (or perhaps because of it) he gave a truly crazy, brilliant performance screaming his desire for flies once he was transformed. He sounded like a cross between Gruber's older, evil twin brother and Dr Strangelove. I remember Guy saying, 'I am like the Wizard of Oz, am I not? Running things from behind a curtain. Only this wizard IS NOT A FAKE!'

Unfortunately it didn't end well for Dr Mittenhand and me. At the end of the film I drift off into space and explode while Mittenhand is frozen by a blast of liquid hydrogen and shatters.

Why? How? Doesn't matter. There were a lot of shots of a former Miss Teen USA runner-up carrying a gun and running around in her underwear to take viewers' minds off any plot holes. Besides that there were some gratuitous breast shots, six corpses, a light-sabre duel, a dash of cross-dressing, public urination, space discos, kung fu fighting, flame throwing, face flattening, bug blending, electrocution and a shrink ray (and reverse shrink ray). All good, clean, family fun.

Ron Howard called me again during the making of *Leprechaun 4* and asked me what I'd been up to. Recalling that he'd told me not to make any more after the first one, I reluctantly confessed: 'Well, I've made another three *Leprechaun* films since.'

'Well,' he said, 'my daughter and her boyfriend loved that first *Leprechaun* film, so I guess anything they like is fine by me too. Besides, my brother's in one of them.'

Sure enough, Ron's infamously ugly brother, Clint Howard, was there in *Leprechaun 2* as 'The Tourist'. Clint had appeared in hundreds of films, including nearly all of Ron's; some say that Clint's face served as the model for the dragon in *Willow*.

As production finally wound up, Sam and I flew home. We had plenty to think about on the flight back.

Sam was pregnant again.

Chapter Fourteen

Annabelle

Sam and I with baby Annabelle.

Nice shades!

Annabelle has inherited my obsession for McVitie's biscuits.

rofessor Charles Rodeck was calm, confident and reassuring. 'Foetal medicine has come a long way over the past couple of years,' he said with a smile, 'and this little unit is the best in the world.'

He was right. The three noticeboards full of pictures of happy parents and babies on his office walls were testament to that.

Professor Rodeck was a pioneer in foetal medicine based at University College Hospital in Central London. He had devised a test, which was not without an element of risk, but which we decided in our case was clearly worth doing. It would tell us if the baby was likely to survive by pinpointing some of the genes it had inherited. Although any test that involves sticking a large hypodermic syringe into a womb is risky, the odds of losing our baby to this procedure were slim – less than two hundred to one. Nevertheless, I held my breath as I watched the Prof carefully pass the needle into Sam's womb. It's a very delicate procedure. Both Sam *and* the baby had to keep very still.

We then had to spend a nerve-wracking two weeks waiting for the result. We still didn't know which gene produced my condition, but when the results came through Professor Rodeck was able to tell us that Sam's gene, the gene that caused achondroplasia, wasn't present.

That meant our baby was either going to be a tall child or an SED child (like me). The most important factor was the brilliant news that she didn't have the lethal double-dominant combination of both of our genes. She would survive the birth. Yes! Full of optimism, I got on with redecorating the nursery and Sam and I shopped for all things baby-related.

Sam went into Peterborough Hospital on 28 March 1997. We knew most of the doctors and nurses pretty well by now and it was great to see so many friendly faces; they really took care of us from day one.

Emotions were running pretty high. Everyone was determined that this time we would leave the hospital with our child – the doctors, Mr Hackman included, put themselves under tremendous pressure. 'We're going to win this time,' he told us with a confident smile.

Sam was knocked out for the Caesarean birth. Mr Hackman wouldn't let me in his theatre, which was fine by me; I doubt I would have stayed conscious had I been present. Despite having starred in half-a-dozen gore fests, I have a low tolerance for live surgery.

When Mr Hackman yelled, 'It's a girl!' my first reaction was 'What?' I couldn't believe it. For some reason I'd convinced myself and everyone else that we were having a boy. I'd even chosen a name: Rodney.

Sam and I were both big *Only Fools and Horses* fans. I also thought it was very distinctive (nobody's called Rodney these days) and that Rodney Davis would make another excellent actor's name. I hadn't even thought about choosing a girl's name, but inspiration hit on almost the first page of a baby names book, which told us that Annabelle meant 'fortunate and beautiful'.

Annabelle – who was little – was born fighting for her life and was put on a ventilator. Despite just having had major surgery, Sam joined me downstairs so we could see our daughter together. We hardly dared to say anything. Neither of us could face having to grieve again.

While Annabelle battled away, Sam and I played detective with the paediatrician, Dr Yong, and various other doctors who were trying to figure out what was wrong. This was something entirely new to them; so many decisions had to be made in response to sudden changes in Annabelle's condition.

To other parents in the same situation I'd recommend being proactive. Question the doctors. Trust them by all means, but just make sure you know what they're doing, why they're doing it and what the consequences might be. We'd learned so much already from our previous experiences and so understood a bit of the lingo by now.

The hours grew into days and still Annabelle hung in there. Neither of us dared to voice our hopes.

One morning a nurse came in to fetch Sam. 'You need to pop down and see Annabelle and Warwick,' she said. 'Nothing's wrong, but I think you should go down.'

I turned as Sam arrived at the intensive care unit. She could tell from my smile. It was the largest I'd ever pulled in my life. I showed more teeth than the smile I pulled when I knew I was going to be in a *Star Wars* movie, and broader than the grin I wore when I won the part for *Willow*. It was a smile of pure, utterly uncontained joy.

Sam walked towards me. 'Look,' I said, 'look at Annabelle.'

She was off the ventilator.

Sam gasped with joy and started to wobble; I caught her as she fell.

'Annabelle is here to stay!' I said.

It was the greatest day of our lives.

It took another seven weeks before Annabelle was healthy enough to leave hospital. It was such a joy to finally bring one of our children home. To us Annabelle was even more precious because of what we'd been through with Lloyd and George. Every day we had to remind ourselves that this was real – that Annabelle was here to stay.

As ever, I didn't have much time to reflect. We'd literally just settled in when I received another life-changing phone call.

It was George Lucas. 'Warwick, you finally talked me into it; it's time . . .'

Chapter Fifteen
The Little Menace

With Jake Lloyd (aka Anakin Skywalker) on the ferry back from Tunisia after filming the Tatooine scenes for *The Phantom Menace*.

Me as Wald, Anakin's best pal.
Courtesy of Lucasfilm Ltd.

Holding a fuel pipe while badgering George for a part in yet another scene.
Courtesy of Lucasfilm Ltd.

The now infamous 'Willow scene'.
Courtesy of Lucasfilm Ltd.

Rumours had been circulating for years about a new *Star Wars* film. I'd used every available chance to drop every kind of hint I could think of to George Lucas, old buddy, old pal, dear friend – usually by fax – to let him know that I would make myself available if and when filming commenced.

Whenever I spoke to George I'd always say something like: 'For goodness' sake, when are you going to make another *Star Wars* movie?'

And all he would say was: 'Soon, Warwick. Soon.'

So yes, some people have since said that *The Phantom Menace* was my fault.

Not long after the phone call, a letter arrived postmarked Skywalker Ranch. George had given me the part of Wald, Anakin Skywalker's best friend.

'Excellent!'

Anakin is the central character in *Phantom Menace*, the kid who goes on to become Darth Vader, so I reckoned that as his best friend I'd have a lot of screen time. It would also mean that we'd be very, very close at long, long last to paying back the taxman.

One of the downsides, of course, was that as my character was a youngster I wouldn't get to play with a light sabre or laser guns and the chances of killing any Stormtroopers would be remote. I didn't mind, I was just delighted to be in the new *Star Wars* movie.

Wald was a little green alien with saucer eyes, antennae and a froglike skin. As I shared none of those physical characteristics, this meant I would have to wear a rubber head. I sighed. I'd come a long way since *Jedi* but now here I was, about to go back into yet another rubber head. Oh well, I'd asked for it, I suppose.

But George was way ahead of me, of course. He called me and said he felt bad about giving me the role of a masked character and he'd found something else for me to do as a humanoid background character. So I showed up at Leavesden Studios extremely excited. George was there and told me I'd be filming a scene from the pod race with the second unit.

I headed over to make-up where the hair designer, who shall remain nameless, looked me up and down and said, 'You need hair extensions.'

'Fair enough,' I thought, and took a seat where for several hours many hair extensions were glued onto my hair with a waxy, rubbery substance. When she'd finished I stared at the mirror. I looked like a tramp who'd spent a night sleeping in a hedge full of angry badgers.

'Oh yes,' I said, in the tone of a man who had made the mistake of telling a young high street hairdresser to do whatever they wanted, 'I can see what you've done here, yes, it's good. Excellent. Yes. Um.'

Once in costume, suitably attired for a day at the space races, I dashed off and found the stage, just in time to start shooting scenes from Anakin's pod race.[42]

'What's Willow doing here?' a production assistant asked.

'What do you mean?'

'You're dressed as Willow, are they making a sequel? This is the stage for *Star Wars Episode I*,[43] you know.'

---

[42] Five years later I would be standing on exactly the same stage, except on that occasion I'd be watching a Quidditch match.

[43] For a long time Ep. 1 didn't have a 'name' and *The Phantom Menace* was chosen at the last minute.

It was true. I hadn't realised until then but I looked like an older, scruffier version of Willow — albeit a version who hadn't washed his hair for a few years. Sure enough, by the time the film came to be edited the scene became known as the 'Willow shot'.

Interestingly (for the gee–, sorry, fans), this link was expanded upon and, as an April Fool joke, StarWars.com ran a story saying that *Willow* had been absorbed into the *StarWars* universe. It worked well because there are various similarities between the two films. They both have a lead character with great imagination and hidden potential (Luke and Willow) and a loveable rogue-turned-hero (Han Solo and Madmartigan). Also Skywalker is the English translation of the Sanskrit word 'Daikini', which is the name of the 'human' species in Willow. But as far as I know there are no plans to merge the two . . . yet.

In the 'Willow shot' we were supposed to be watching a pod race and making bets on the outcomes. A mass of enormous studio lights were used to replicate the blinding suns of Tatooine and aircraft propellers to simulate the backdraught of the pods as they raced by. The actors had to picture the pod race happening right in front of them and I also had to imagine I was sat next to Watto, a CGI character (he's the greedy Toydarian second-hand goods seller who 'owns' Anakin, his mother and C-3PO).

Now, as we were in a sports stadium watching a pod race, it made sense that there were various alien beings selling snacks and drinks. As the cameras began to roll, a girl came into view with space-age-looking crisps (I think they were Walkers with a blob of food colouring on them) and a weird gloopy fruit juice. It was served in intergalactic Tupperware, the same sort of beakers and plates used by Luke when he's having dinner with his family on Tatooine in *Episode IV*.

We were supposed to look full of anticipation, excited at the prospect of a great race, and then we had to leap up as the race began. As the crisps came past, I thought 'Why not?' and grabbed a handful and then took some juice to wash them down.

'Cut! That was great, let's go again, everyone!'

Because it was a special-effects shot, numerous takes of us performing exactly the same actions were required. So six large handfuls of crisps and a couple of pints of space juice later, I started feeling rather ill. I'd also managed to develop a very painful migraine, thanks to the extremely bright and hot studio lights. After the seventh take, I shut my eyes and leaned backwards in my chair in an effort to ease my aching head and a growing feeling of nausea.

Someone was tapping on my foot. Where was I? Who on earth would be tapping my foot? I opened one eye. Oh, cock! It was George. This was my first day on the movie and I'd fallen asleep. Twenty years of pestering and this was how I showed my gratitude.

I decided to play it cool and stayed just as I was, leaning back in my chair.

'Hiya, George, just resting my eyes from the bright lights.'

George's eyes twinkled. I could tell he knew.

'I was snoring, wasn't I?'

I wondered how I always managed to do this. I always tried to be on my best behaviour around George but I always managed to embarrass myself. It had happened on the set of *Willow*. Daniel and I had been regaling the crew with a story about how a few days earlier I'd been stranded in one of the Portaloos in total darkness without any toilet paper and I'd had to yell out of the window for help. Daniel got very graphic and quite rude and despite my best efforts to get him to shut up he had continued, blissfully unaware that George was standing right behind him. Luckily (on both occasions) George didn't seem to be offended.

After we'd wrapped, I went back to the changing room and spent an hour wrestling with the hair extensions.

I found a passing make-up artist. 'Excuse me, could you help?' I pleaded.

After another few minutes of wrangling she gave up. 'I don't think they're meant to come out,' she said suddenly, and then quickly left the room.

I turned and looked in the mirror. 'Good God!' I exclaimed. She'd managed to make them look even worse. I looked like TV scarecrow Worzel Gummidge after he'd been zapped by an electric chair. My hair, real and fake, was perpendicular to my skull. I yanked and yanked at the extensions and eventually I had most of them out but the glue stayed put and knotted my hair. The damn stuff simply wouldn't wash out.

I ran from the studio straight to the nearest hairdressers. As I came in they all pulled expressions that said, 'I'm not touching that, you do it,' and I saw that any chance of rescue was hopeless. I sighed despondently.

'All right, just shave it off then.'

Location filming was done in the deserts of Tunisia. I wanted Anna-belle and Sam to come but it was just too hot and a tad risky, espe-cially by my standards. My general rule of travel is not to fly anywhere where injections are required. Generally speaking, these areas tend to contain animals, large and small, that like to eat or poison humans. Tunisia required lots of injections. I didn't really want to go but the producers weren't going to move the location just for me; besides, everybody else was already there. I was the last to arrive.

I flew overnight to Tunis. 'A driver will meet you tomorrow to take you to the location,' the production assistant said. 'Bring lots of water.'

The following morning, carrying two enormous bottles of water and a suitcase, I was met by a short man (well, shorter than average) in the tiniest car I had ever seen. It was of an uncertain model (I think it may have been Libyan) and vintage.

'They take you there,' the man said over and over, 'they take you there, nice car. They take you there, nice car.'

'Nice car, yes,' I said loudly, exaggerating my mouth movements as one does when trying to speak to someone whose English isn't that great. I threw my suitcase in the back seat and climbed on top of it so I could see out the window. We bounced madly on a very rough street and I banged my head on the car roof, a first.

'How long?' I asked, hoping this would be a short journey.

'Eight day,' he replied with a cheery smile.

It was about then that I experienced one of those alarming moments when you seriously question yourself: What am I doing here? What have I done? Why haven't they sent a helicopter?

These questions only grew louder in my mind when the driver suddenly took a turn off the dusty main road and into a little town. It looked like something out of Indiana Jones. We navigated our way through smaller and smaller roads until we were driving through little more than alleyways.

'Where are we going?' I asked.

'Carpet,' he replied, as he pulled up outside a little building.

He climbed out and beckoned me onwards, 'Come, come, come, come.'

'Oh God,' I said to myself, 'I've been kidnapped.' I half-expected to walk in and see half the cast tied up and being photographed holding the latest copy of the *Tunis Times*. The house was full, all right, but it was full of people all smiling at me and pointing at the walls.

After a few minutes I realised they were trying to sell me a rug. Ah! I thought. Now I know where I am. But if there's one thing I am good at, it is saying 'no' and I take especial delight in doing this to salesmen – from any country and for anything.

These guys were persistent, I had to admit, but so was I.

'You buy carpet.'

'No.'

'This one?'

'No.'

'This one?'

'No.' And on it went. Hours passed. Eventually they gave up and the driver, with a gloomy expression, waved me back to the car. I got in, a smug smile upon my face. 'Well, that was fun,' I said.

We carried on through the desert and arrived at a small oasis just as the sun was setting. We carried on through a tiny town, which looked like it had been hit by a bomb and only partially rebuilt. It turned out that unfinished buildings were exempt from building tax so nobody ever completed their homes.

I was relieved to see that the hotel had been properly finished and it looked fabulously exotic. As I checked in I noted that the luggage room was full of rolled-up rugs. I guessed that not everybody had been able to say no to the persistent rug-selling driver.

My room was perfect and, much relieved, I threw my suitcase on the bed and popped it open. It looked as if I was an international biscuit smuggler. It was filled with two dozen packets of McVitie's dark-chocolate digestives.

I'm dreadfully paranoid about foreign food, so I had reasoned that as long as I had my biscuits and a ready supply of drinking water, I would survive. I steered clear of the local cuisine and rotated between two staple foods, pasta with tomato sauce and pizza margarita; no salad and no fruit. It worked, in that while lots of other people got sick, I didn't.

The crew call was 4 a.m. every day. On my first morning, I

walked into the corridor and joined the cast and crew as we all quietly shuffled our way through the hotel to the lobby. Although at that time of the morning we looked like a troop of miserable zombies who hadn't so much as sniffed a fresh brain for weeks, we were all terrifically excited to be working on the new *Star Wars* movie.

Outside, a huge convoy of jeeps were waiting. George was at the front in 'Yoda 1'. We climbed aboard and off we went, heading into the desert as a distant pink glow signalled the coming dawn.

We arrived at an enormous city of tents. These would be our trailers. They were arranged on decking, so they were off the ground and an old lady was busily sweeping the last traces of sand from them as we arrived. I wondered at what ungodly hour she had been forced to rise.

Everyone climbed out, still not speaking much, and we searched for our tents. Once I found mine, I entered with some trepidation. It was pitch black inside and I worried what creatures might be hiding there. Sure enough, I saw something small lurking in the corner.

'Awight, Warwick!'

It was the one and only Kenny Baker, a.k.a. R2-D2.

I sighed with relief. I was delighted to see Kenny again and we chatted as I got myself settled in. It was surprisingly cool inside the tent. An advantage of being so small was that we were the only people able to stand up straight once inside. But I was about to find out that my lack of height brought with it a much greater disadvantage.

I noticed that a trench had been dug all around the camp.

'I wonder why that is?' I asked Kenny, who shrugged.

I watched as two men made their way round the trench, which was about four feet deep. They were staring at their feet and every now and again they stopped and grabbed something with a stick and shoved whatever it was into a canvas bag. They grinned at me as they went past and it was then that I saw they were collecting snakes and scorpions that had fallen in overnight. The trench was supposed to keep them out of our tent city.

'I wouldn't want to fall in there,' Kenny said.

Damn right, we'd never get out.

'I hope it works,' I muttered, 'it's bad enough having to put up with your snoring without having to worry about snakes slithering into our tent.'

Shooting started before sunrise and we would keep going until about two or three in the afternoon, when the sun would be too strong – especially for those in rubber heads. It was amazing how quickly the shadows disappeared as the sun rose. People were quickly caught out if they hadn't drunk enough water. Actors were passing out all over the place. I was so used to wearing rubber heads, and knew my limits pretty well, so as long as I kept well hydrated I knew I'd be OK. There was one crowd scene, in which everyone was supposed to leap to their feet. When George cried 'Action!' dozens of aliens leapt up and half of them promptly fainted.

I wanted to make the most of the experience and so on my days off I'd go and watch the filming. I wanted to witness a little piece of movie history being made. One day George spotted me hanging about. 'What are you doing here today, Warwick?' he said, checking the schedule on a clipboard. 'We're not filming you, are we?'

'I just wanted to watch.'

'Well, seeing as you're here, you can make yourself useful then. I'm going to put you in this scene. Run off to the make-up room and go and make yourself look different.'

'Like what?'

'I'm sure you'll work it out with them.'

I quickly dashed off and found a free make-up person, explained I was going to be in a shot and they should make me look 'different'.

The make-up and costume tents were amazing, all the costumes were hung up together on one side like a galactic Oxfam. The creature suits were all hung up on the other side of the tent, which resembled an alien slaughterhouse.

The make-up artist plastered my face with black greasepaint, which gave the appearance of a healthy growth of stubble. The costume department then did a mix-and-match of Wald's and the 'Willow shot' character's costumes. The effect was to make me look like a local Bedouin that had somehow lost his camel and wandered onto the set.

I ran back to George, who did a double take. 'Err . . . great![44] Well, not bad . . . I suppose. What I want you to do is to walk alongside that incredibly tall guy over there with the black-and-white face, just behind where Liam is going to walk across the road with Jake.' (Jake Lloyd played Anakin Skywalker.)

I'd noticed that a tall blonde lady was dashing about the set and was busy photographing the stars. It turned out that this was the world-famous photographer Annie Leibovitz, who was shooting a massive feature for *Vanity Fair* on *Episode I*, featuring all the *Star Wars* characters.

Everyone who was anyone seemed to be on set that day, so Annie decided that today was the day for a massive group shoot that would appear as a double-page spread in the world's most famous magazine. One advantage of being small was that I was naturally thrust towards

---

[44] 'Great' is George's favourite and most-used word.

the front of the group shot, and in the end Annie positioned me right between R2-D2 and C-3PO, front and centre.

This character was barely visible in the film, I was just in the background for a few seconds and so my appearance front and centre in this shoot created enormous debate about his importance among *Star Wars* fans. They speculated whether he would come to have later significance in the next two films in the series (he didn't). They eventually christened this mysterious character 'Grimey'.

Another scene that caused much debate is when Qui-Gon Jinn (Liam Neeson) tells Anakin that he's a 'special child'. Anakin has been having a fight with another Rodian, the same species as my rubber-headed character, and I had been in the background, egging Anakin on. Qui-Gon stops the fight.

Always looking for an opportunity, I asked George if I could have a line.

'Yes,' George said, 'why not?' I spotted that glint in his eye. 'Let's give the fans something to talk about.'

Now, *Star Wars* aficionados will remember Greedo from the 'original' 1977 film, he was the green alien shot dead by Han Solo in the cantina on Tatooine.

George decided to make the character that Anakin was fighting into the young Greedo. George said to me, 'After the fight's done, say to Greedo, "Keep that sort of thing up and you'll come to a bad end."'

'Cool!'

'We won't use it,' George said, taking the wind out of my sails somewhat, 'but we'll put it on the DVD extras and it'll be debated at conventions.' Which it was.

To deliver my lines, I had to learn Huttese, the official language of the Rodians, created by Oscar®-winning sound designer (and the voice of Wall-e), Ben Burt. I even got my own training tape, just as you would use to learn any other language, and I can still recall some to this day.

I'm sure you can imagine my joy when I was told we were moving from our palatial residence to film in a more 'remote' area. I fretted. My supply of chocolate digestives was running dangerously low. However, I was relieved to see that George was staying at the same hotel as the rest of us; this was generally a sign that the hotel would be pretty good.

And it was true – the hotel was the best in town.

It was also the only hotel in town.

There were no windows in the thick stone walls, just a collection of holes. The bed was lumpier than the Leprechaun's skin and dozens of insects bustled their way across the floor and chattered through the night. I slept with one eye open, watching the digestives.

I couldn't understand why we'd moved from one patch of sand to another but then I realised that George wanted to use the amazing houses the locals lived in as a location. They looked a bit like white, smooth honeycombs and the people that lived there were very welcoming and put up with an awful lot as we turned their village into a film set for a few days.

The only tricky part came was when the call to prayer came at midday. Men spent the rest of the day taking it in turns to climb to the top of little towers that were dotted around the town and shriek at the top of their voices for an hour or so. In the end we had no choice but to carry on filming through the cacophony – a bit of a challenge for the sound engineers.

I remember waking up on the morning we were due to leave with pure joy in my heart. I was down to my last couple of melted and crumbled digestives, so the end came just in the nick of time.

I travelled with Jake Lloyd and his dad by ferry to the island of Djerba, the Blackpool of Tunisia and the location for some of the scenes from the original *Star Wars* movie (including the Mos Eisley spaceport exteriors).

Jake was as overjoyed as I was to be returning to civilisation. He'd already done a fair bit of acting prior to *The Phantom Menace* so it wasn't as if the movie biz was new to him. We didn't really talk too much about the film during the journey. I really liked Jake, he spoke to me as if we were on the same level, as if I were just another ten-year-old. He even tried to sell me a lizard; goodness knows where he found the poor creature. We've since kept in touch and these days he's much more interested in making films than appearing in them.

We had to spend one night in Djerba before flying back to the UK and while the cast and crew went wild with the food, drink and ice after weeks of being careful, I decided to keep up my precautions until we were off the continent, and tucked into the very last of my crushed and melted McVitie's. Everyone else came down with food poisoning. My beloved chocolate digestives had saved me.

Once all the location filming had been done, George went off to edit. After this was completed it was time to film the pick-ups in a second wave of filming where any missing bits were added. These scenes were filmed at Ealing Studios in the UK.

I was very surprised to be called by Robin Gurland, the casting director. I really wasn't expecting to have to film any more of my parts. 'George wants you as Yoda in a scene,' she said.

'You must be mistaken,' I said. 'Yoda's a puppet and I'm not having Frank Oz putting his hand —'

'Well, yes he is, but now George needs him to walk across the ground with the other characters near the end of the film and Frank can't do that.'

Wow, I was going to be Yoda! Because I'm a bit larger than the actual puppet, the costume department made me my own Yoda outfit, complete with walking stick. They also gave me Frank Oz's Yoda gloves, which had Frank's name on the inside of the cuff.

Sam was called in at the last minute to act in the same scene, as the original little actress playing Even Piell was away on holiday. It took place at the end of the film when Anakin and Obi-Wan (Ewan McGregor) and members of the Jedi Council exit a space cruiser and are met by Senator Palpatine (Ian McDiarmid) and Queen Padme (Natalie Portman).

On the day, producer Rick McCallum was directing. As I was so excited to be playing Yoda I couldn't help myself and slipped into my occasional bad habit of adding my own sound effects. I grumbled and hurrumphed in Yoda's voice as I made my way down the gangway. Sam, unrecognisable in her prosthetics, was right beside me.

A few seconds later, I heard 'Cut, cut!' Rick then said, 'Warwick, I need you to hurry up a bit and keep up with everyone else.'

'But I'm Yoda,' I said. 'He can't walk fast and neither can I in this costume.'

At this point I had no idea that Yoda was going to bounce around like a nutter in all of the prequels. Added to this was the complication that I would be naturally slower as my legs were half the length of everyone else's. I couldn't exactly jog down a gangway in my Yoda costume.

'I'm not a sprinter!' I said as we lined up to try yet another take. I had to focus on the character's integrity – I didn't want to turn him into Charlie Chaplin, but at the same time I still had to keep up with everybody else. Thankfully we got it in the end. But I made the entire cast walk up and down that gangplank about half a dozen times before I did – and after all that you have to look very carefully to spot me as Yoda. I considered it a great honour to have played the Jedi Master, albeit for a tiny amount of screen time.

As I've mentioned earlier, I'm a big fan of film soundtracks and have been collecting them since I was a kid. So after the filming and editing was completed I asked George if I could come to the recording of the score to *The Phantom Menace*. To my surprise and delight he said yes. It was recorded at the famed Abbey Road Studios in London; George was there on the day and I watched spellbound as John Williams and the London Philharmonic ran straight into the main theme, one of the most recognisable pieces of film music ever written. It was incredible; I could hardly believe I was sat there with George, watching the film play out on a screen while a world-class orchestra played the music live.

I'd brought David Sibley, my dialogue coach, with whom I'd filmed in my student days, along as well. We were both in the studio when the orchestra suddenly launched into the opening *Star Wars* fanfare. If you've ever stood next to a full orchestra then you'll know just how incredibly loud they can be – it's like standing next to the *QE2*'s foghorn. Poor David was so surprised by the volume, he jumped back as if he'd been shot by a blaster, knocking into a huge speaker which toppled from its stand and crashed to the floor, BANG! The orchestra crashed to a cacophonic halt and poor David turned bright purple as John Williams and the entire London Philharmonic turned round to glare at him.

I looked at John Williams and said in a matter-of-fact voice: 'So, are those speakers expensive then?'

A couple of hours later, I was sitting with George in the recording booth when my mysterious scruffy character from the 'Willow shot' appeared on screen.

'George,' I said.

'Yes, Warwick.'

'What are we going to call this guy?'

'I don't know, what do you think he should be called?'

'Well,' I said, 'in all of your films my characters' names start with the letter "W". There's Willow, Wicket W. Warrick[45] and Wald, so I suppose it has to start with a "W".'

'OK, let's call this guy Weazel.' He paused, adding, 'With a "zee".'

This led me nicely to a subject that I'd been meaning to ask George about for some time.

'George, can I ask you a question?'

'Sure, Warwick.'

'Why do my characters' names always start with "W"?'

I knew George's middle name was Walton and I wondered whether it had something to do with that. Or was it just W for Warwick?

'I'm not telling,' he said, 'my little secret.'

And that was that.

The Phantom Menace was probably the most eagerly awaited sequel of the twentieth century and it was perhaps inevitable that it would come in for a lot of criticism. Kids loved it, and I think that's the point, it's a *Star Wars* film for a new generation. For those of us who grew up with the original trilogy it's difficult to accept a new version; and if there's one thing I've learned, it's that people get extremely militant and passionate about every aspect of *Star Wars* (just ask Carrie Fisher). Some fans can't stand Ewoks, never mind Jar Jar Binks, but, as George has said, these characters are there

---

[45] The US spelling. The 'W Warrick' was added to the character name on merchandise for *Return of the Jedi*.

for children. The films are supposed to appeal to everyone – but they're primarily for younger people.

At *Star Wars* conventions I always have a brilliant time talking to people who are passionate about the films and who are very clear about their likes and dislikes. For me, one of the best things about these conferences comes from seeing grandparents arrive with their very young grandchildren. *Star Wars* was something they could all share; I consider myself very lucky to have had a foot in both the prequels and the classic trilogy.

By now, life had stabilised somewhat, thanks in part to the fact that I was busy with work and Sam and I were enjoying life with Annabelle. Even so, I was keen to look to our future security and so never stopped seeking new opportunities.

Inspiration struck one day while reading an article about the smash hit film, *The Full Monty*.

Chapter Sixteen

The Half Monty

Inch High Productions
presents

THE HALF MONTY

You've seen **"The Full Monty"**, you've heard of **"The Chippendales"**, but prepare yourself 'cos you've seen no[...]

Directed & Choreograph[...]

FOR "THE HALF MONTY" BOOKING or INFO[...]

© 1998 INCH HIGH PRO[...]

During my early career as an actor I never had an agent as such (my mum did a fantastic job of representing me professionally until I was eighteen); I generally waited for the phone to ring or a script to drop through the letterbox. In my experience, some agents that represented a lot of little people treated them more like a commodity rather than talent.

They'd ask something like: 'How many do you want?' and would reduce their rates according to the size of the order. The little actors' particular talents didn't come into the equation; they just sold them short.

This unsatisfactory situation inspired my father-in-law Peter Burroughs and me to set up Willow Personal Management in 1995. Out of courtesy, I called George Lucas and checked with him that he was OK with me using the name – of course, this also let him know that if he needed short actors then he knew where to find them.

I'm very grateful to Kevin Wood, a panto producer who offered us space in his office and the use of his staff to get us started. Now all we had to do was wait for the phone to ring. It didn't, and we spent the first few weeks staring at it. When the first job came in (looking for a girl four feet tall to appear on a book cover), I suddenly realised I hadn't a clue how to negotiate.

And it wasn't easy persuading short actors to join; after all, I was also the competition. Whenever I rolled up at auditions, because I was quite well known and had a high profile (especially among little people), I'd hear things like 'Oh God, Willow's here, we can forget it.' It made the audition very uncomfortable but I took their point – their fear was that if they joined my agency, then I would take all the best work for myself, leaving them all the bit parts – it would be like playing the lottery except I got to choose the numbers.

In reality it's not like that at all – every single person brings different skills and abilities to a role. Besides, casting directors sent us very specific briefs, e.g., someone precisely four feet tall who can do an Irish accent. Obviously, someone who is three-foot-six from Surrey who can't do an accent to save their life is not going to get the role.

We constantly argued that we were trying to make things better for short actors, that by matching people to the right part we'd improve the standing of little people in the acting community and therefore bigger and better parts would be written for them. We got off to a slow start but in the end Willow Management was saved by Christmas.

Every year lazy tabloid hacks take great delight in digging out and dusting off the headline 'Dwarf Shortage' as panto season gets under way – just Google it and see. Soon business was booming and we were dishing out seven dwarves left, right and centre, resolving disagreements between potential Dopeys and Docs about who should play who. Kevin's decision to let us share some of his office space proved to be a canny one as he was always able to have first choice of little actors for the pantos he was producing.

One of the most rewarding things about Willow Management is when someone I've sent to an audition gets the part. Sometimes this proves to be a life-changing moment for the person involved, increasing their self-esteem as well as the width of their wallet.

Day to day, my father-in law Peter answers the phone, does the deals and smokes the big cigar. Running the agency is a full-time job for him and requires a lot of hard work. He'll often still be in the office negotiating deals long after my own agent has stubbed out his cigar.

Lots of agents shut the door on people without experience, which is crazy; many potentially great actors never even get a shot. If someone comes to me who's genuinely enthusiastic and has the drive, I'll give them a chance.

I also take great delight in talent spotting. There was a boy who appeared in a play at Annabelle's school who I thought was fantastic. He really wanted to act, so I put him in touch with a well-known casting director and he's since appeared in several commercials and TV programmes.

Willow Management now represents over 120 short actors below five feet tall (we're probably the world's largest agency for short actors) and we've found work for all of them (and I happily admit this is thanks to good old pantomime[46]).

Our success meant I started to receive a few enquiries from tall actors, asking if there was a similar agency for big people. There wasn't, and so we added that string to our bow as well and created a new division called Willow Tall. We now represent actors over seven feet tall, including the UK's tallest man, Neil Fingleton (seven-foot-seven) and second tallest Chris Greener (three-quarters of an inch below Neil), who had been the record holder until Neil showed up.

As it happened it fell to me to break the news to Chris that he was no longer the UK's tallest man; it was only afterwards that I realised how humiliating that must have seemed, coming from someone who was three-foot-six.

I think I'm actually better off being 'too small' as opposed to 'too tall' because I can fit in all sorts of places, whereas Chris and

---

[46] Oh yes it is!

Neil struggle to fit into cars, plane seats, toilets, restaurants, cinemas, etc. Of course, being small does mean I face a few unusual hazards, for example, the more expensive the hotel, the higher the bed. So if I'm in a five-star hotel and a bit sleepy, I sometimes forget I'm not at home and end up wishing I'd worn a parachute with my pyjamas.

For some reason, the agency began receiving more and more requests for little people to appear at nightclubs and this led Peter and I to come up with the idea for a twenty-minute show based on *The Full Monty* – the now infamous *Half Monty*.

I soon had a bunch of little guys who were prepared to bare all in the name of entertainment. They were Gee Williams, Phil Holden, Ray Griffiths, Chris Chapman and Big Dave.[47]

I hired a very camp, very strict and very brilliant choreographer, Paul Harris, who had played the very agile Catsmeat in the first panto I'd appeared in. I explained my idea and he got it straight away. 'Fantastic!' he exclaimed, throwing his arms out wide before skipping across the room with excitement. 'I can see it all now! Leave it with me!'

Paul's mantra was 'Fame hurts!' He envisaged the Village People and put together routines for our troop of little guys dressed as an American Indian, builder, strongman, cowboy and soldier. When they were all dressed I couldn't help but think of them as the 'Model' Village People. The show started with 'You Sexy Thing' and closed with 'You Can Leave Your Hat On'.

Sam made the costumes at lightning speed while we rehearsed in a dance studio in Dartford. The costumes were extraordinarily difficult to make; everything had to be fixed with Velcro so it could

---

[47] What Dave Vear lacked in height he did his best to make up for in girth.

be put on and – more importantly – removed in a flash. Sam needed to get it just right because we couldn't afford any 'wardrobe malfunctions'.

I don't think the lads knew what had hit them when Paul got started. He actually began with the line: 'You're gonna be the best but you're gonna have to sweat blood!' He even straddled the chair backwards and rehearsals turned out to be a cross between *Boot Camp* and *Fame Academy*. None of the guys had ever danced professionally before but, thanks to Paul's fanatical approach, they all got it in the end. It was dance or die trying.

One of the first routines Paul came up with was 'Jailhouse Rock', where all the guys danced with fold-up chairs while wearing prisoners' uniforms complete with arrows.

I wasn't going to dance. This was the limit of my extroversion, but what I did do was sell the concept. This turned out to be the easiest job in the world. I'd call a nightclub and would say something like: 'Five guys, all under four feet tall, do the Full Monty.'

'I get it. It's fantastic. When can they come?'

The first night was in Batley in Yorkshire, in one of those enormous super-clubs. I was more nervous than the guys but it went down an absolute storm. Afterwards the guys were buzzing. 'The girls went mad!' Ray said, grinning from ear to ear after his 'I just wanna make love to you' finale, 'they even stole my G-string!'

Sam sighed. 'I'll get my needle and thread then, shall I?' This turned out to be a real problem – female fans sometimes stormed the stage and fought tooth and manicured nail for trophies. Poor Sam often had to work through the night making repairs or producing yet another pair of security guard's trousers.

Peter and I were also kept pretty busy. We were inundated with booking requests once the word of mouth spread, and soon we were fully booked for *two years* in advance – all round Europe.

The lads toured everywhere with Peter accompanying them as their 'roadie'. One of the strangest gigs they did was at a private party in Stevenage where they were asked to perform the show in someone's lounge. This was a tight squeeze – even for them – and so Paul and I went along to make sure none of the audience had their knees broken during the chair-swinging sequence in 'Jailhouse Rock'.

The *Half Monty* created a lot of press controversy but it was not at all exploitative, it was professionally performed, and I can categorically say that the girls loved it as much as the performers. We had two versions of the act: The 'Full Monty', which left nothing to the imagination, and the 'Not-Quite-Full-Monty' version where the G-strings stayed on.

However, one booking that did raise all of our eyebrows was for an all-girls' Catholic school graduation party.

'Yes, we let the girls choose whom they'd like to perform,' the mother superior said, speaking in exactly the prim sort of voice you'd expect from a Catholic headmistress. 'But I am instructing you that under no circumstances are you to go the – uhm – "Full Monty".'

I assured her that the G-strings would most definitely stay on and wondered how on earth the girls had managed to talk her into letting us perform in the first place.

Paul, who could sometimes be quite terrifyingly hysterical, would often turn up at shows as a 'secret shopper' to make sure the lads were putting everything into their performance. He made a surprise appearance at the school and – for reasons that still remain unclear to all of us – demanded that the lads do the Full Monty.

'But we can't,' protested Big Dave in his strongman outfit, 'Warwick's had to promise the mother superior.'

'Nonsense! I've spoken to the head girl and she wants you to do the Full Monty! Do you think for a moment that she would demand such a thing without the permission of the mother superior?'

Five little guys looked at each other and shuffled their feet uncomfortably. 'Well . . .' Ray began.

'Exactly!' Paul boomed. 'If you don't get out there and get all your kit off right now then I'm going to sack the lot of you. There's plenty of other men out there ready to climb into your thongs!'

The first thing I knew about all this was 9 a.m. on Monday morning when a hysterical mother superior called me. 'We have let the girls decide their end-of-year entertainment for over fifty years!' she shrieked, forcing me to hold the phone away from my ear. 'After this ungodly act we can never let them choose again! You've ruined it for everybody!'

I was tempted to say, 'At least you'll have the memories,' followed by 'To whom should we send the invoice?' Instead, I apologised and quickly hung up, my ears ringing.

Paul was a genius but a real force to be reckoned with. During rehearsals at one nightclub, Paul yelled at Gee the fire-eater[48] so much he became flustered and knocked over his fuel, which burst into flames, causing his lighter to explode and shoot a column of fire up to the ceiling. There we were, half a dozen little people and one very camp hysterical man running around a column of fire, everyone shouting at once. It looked like some bizarre pagan ritual where a witch doctor had shrunk the Village People.

I sprinted out to the lobby where a receptionist sat behind a high counter was filing her nails.

'We need a fire extinguisher!' I yelled.

---

[48] He danced to 'Hot! Hot! Hot!'

She peered over the top of her desk and watched as I flapped around in a panic below her.

'Oh,' she said in a thick Essex accent, 'I'm not sure we've got one.' She placed a finger to her lips and pondered. The shouts from the rehearsal room were getting louder.

'It's quite urgent,' I said, trying to restrain my rising panic.

'No, wait a minute, yes we do.'

She disappeared into a back office and came back a few seconds later.

'What sort of fire is it? Only we've got different extinguishers for different fires.'

'I don't care! Just give me one that squirts something!'

Eventually, a few very long seconds later, she returned with a fire extinguisher.

'There you go,' and she dropped it into my arms.

Now, bearing in mind I'm not much taller or heavier than a standard fire extinguisher, the damn thing nearly flattened me. I half-carried, half-dragged it back into the maelstrom, where we quickly got the flames under control.

'I think that concludes rehearsals,' I said as the foam and smoke settled around us. We quickly marched out under a cloud (literally). The nightclub owners never said a thing.

I once took a booking for a show and wouldn't tell the lads what it was, just that it was somewhere in central London, giving them the address at the last minute. It was only when the music started and they ran onto the stage that they were confronted by a roomful of screaming men in leather and piercings.

'The little git's booked us into a gay club!'

Still, they pulled it off, so to speak, and escaped intact. They planned to kill me as soon as the show was over but I managed to lie low until they'd calmed down.

Finally, after two incredible years, the guys were exhausted, the Velcro had lost its grip and we decided it was time they hung up their G-strings, while they were still at the height of their popularity.

Just as they did so, it was also time for me to dig out my shiny-buckled shoes, re-don my little green hat and speak the immortal line: 'Flee while you can, the future's not good – for no one is safe from a Lep in the 'hood!'

With Peter Burroughs, father-in-law and co-founder of Willow Personal Management as well as *The Half Monty*.

Chapter Seventeen

Guess Who's Back?

Guess who's back? This time for *Lep in the Hood* and *Leprechaun: Back 2 tha Hood*, parts five and six of the unbelievably (in the truest sense of the word) successful franchise.

They were always finding new ways to kill the Leprechaun. On this occasion I was dumped in 'cement' (actually porridge).

Lunch break: Eating Chinese food on the streets of South Central LA while gunfire echoed through the night. Life didn't get any more surreal than that.

Once again, *Leprechaun in Space* had been a great financial success, if not a critical one: 'The best movie I've seen about a leprechaun in space in years,' and 'Do you really need to know any more than the title?'

The producers were determined to make another one but needed to come up with a novel situation in which to put the Leprechaun. They took their job very seriously and formed a focus group to find out who watches the *Leprechaun* films. After much research they concluded that the audience was mainly made up of black Americans.

Needless to say, for *Leprechaun in the Hood: Lep in the 'hood, come to do no good!* I was the only green actor on the set. Every which way I turned there was a rapper. And I had a new set of rules. The iron phobia was gone and now, to my surprise, they expected me to be able to rap.

I kept asking them for the lyrics but the writers just said, 'Don't worry, we'll just write them on the day.' I went to my fellow cast members for advice on how to rap. These included Coolio and Ice-T (his real name's Tracy, I kid you not), among many other rap luminaries. They all thought it was very cool to be in a *Leprechaun* film and they seemed to be having a blast. They were very kind and did their best to teach me how to rap. They even showed me some dance moves and taught me how to fold my arms like a proper gangsta but you just can't become a gangsta rapper overnight, especially when your 'hood, back in the day, was leafy Surrey.

When we eventually did the song I was pretty pleased with it and I thought it might go out as a single. I could see myself performing it on MTV and even today I get requests for the 'Leprechaun Rap' at conventions. I always pretend I've forgotten the lyrics but I must confess that I recall every single word.

Not long after we'd started shooting, Ice-T burst into my trailer in a panic and started uprooting sofa cushions. 'I think, I hope, I left something here,' he said. Ice-T was a cardboard-cut-out version of a rapper; he was always 'in character' and rolled up on set in a massive Merc playing his own music full blast. Eventually, with a sigh of relief, he lifted up the thickest gold chain I'd ever seen. How could you lose something like that? I mean, a ring, fair enough, but a gold chain that weighed more than my daughter?

We filmed the interior scenes for *Lep in the Hood* at Lacy Street Studios – where *Cagney and Lacey* had been filmed. All of the sets were identical, none of them had been changed since the TV series.

Things got a lot more interesting, however, when we moved out into the street. We filmed mainly at night in LA's notorious gangsta 'hood, South Central, which presented a whole different kind of horror.

'Ready Warwick?'

I nodded uncertainly. I was in full Leprechaun costume halfway up a tree in South Central, LA. How ready could I be?

I was supposed to leap onto a young female victim who was walking along the street below and would then be rescued by her boyfriend who happened to pass by on his motorbike while carrying a baseball bat.

'And action!'

Just as I prepared to launch myself, a couple of not-too-distant gunshots from a .357 Magnum[49] echoed through the night.

Suddenly distracted, I lost my footing, missed my cue and landed face down on the pavement below.

'Are you OK, Warwick?'

'Grrrrnfh,' I said, slowly raising my clawed hand to give the thumbs-up.

In order to film there safely we had to pay our respects to the gang that ran the neighbourhood – very smartly dressed young gentlemen who all rode sports bikes. They'd roll up, engines at full revs, and bring everything to a halt, ignoring the fact that this was a 'closed set', and check out anything they wanted, whenever they wanted. Nobody dared stop them.

At first, because I was dressed in green, I worried that I might be wearing the wrong colour. So much of gangland was defined by the colours the people wore, red and blue for the Bloods and Crips respectively, for example. I was very relieved when one of the crew told me that the gangs saw green as a neutral colour.

Amazingly, they seemed to be scared of me; I was always in full costume and I think they actually believed that this was how I looked all the time. Even most of the crew didn't really want to eat with me – except for Gabe, the make-up artist. I suppose only Dr Frankenstein could have lunch with his monster. There's a very surreal photo of me sitting on a wooden crate, alone, in costume in the middle of the road right in the heart of gangland, eating

---

[49] If there's one thing you learn in South Central, it's gun types. When gunshots echo through the night the usual conversation goes something like:

'Smith and Wesson 45.'

'Nah, sounded like a .22 to me.'

I would then say something like: 'Shouldn't we call the police?' which would cause much hilarity among cast and crew.

Chinese food out of a carton.

My fellow rappers, however, were familiar with the films and were thrilled to see my character. And thanks to their involvement there was quite a bit of interest in the film from MTV. I appeared on a few chat shows in New York, including Greg Kinnear, but the best thing I did was a skit for MTV in full costume on their *Beauty and the Beach* show in San Diego.

Gabe and I had a good laugh about this when we rolled into San Diego. 'Who'd have thought it?' Gabe said, 'I can't believe we're five films down the road and about to go on mainstream TV!'

For the San Diego job, Gabe came and made me up as the Leprechaun in a hotel room. This meant a half-mile walk from the hotel to the event – in full costume. I got into the lift and a Hispanic cleaner ran out screaming down the hall. Feeling a bit playful, I decided to chase her and when she ran back into the lift I jumped in behind her just as the doors were closing and laughed like a maniac. She screamed until I thought my eardrums would burst. I dropped the act and tried to reassure her on the way down that I was wearing make-up, that I wasn't 'real', it didn't help; I left the poor woman in a very confused and dazed state, mumbling incoherently in the corner of the lift.

I then strolled down to the beach where hundreds of beautiful college girls and handsome college boys were waiting for me to judge a beauty contest. I kid you not. I was on the panel with one of the guys from *Baywatch* and he didn't know if I was real or not. I decided the best way to play this was to take the judging completely seriously. I tried to do it in the style of Simon Cowell crossed with the Leprechaun and was suitably disparaging to all of the contestants.

Lep in the Hood was a smash hit. 'Actually physically painful to watch,' wrote one reviewer, 'If you need a reason to hate yourself, a reason to want to do yourself bodily harm, or a reason to go completely insane with no hope of recovery, watch *Leprechaun in the Hood*,' and 'I must say, I didn't think that *Leprechaun 4* could be followed. Man, was I wrong.'

As it turned out I was nominated for a Video Premiere Award[50] in the Best Actor category in 2001, which was great because I became part of the VPA Academy and received free DVDs of all nominated movies for life.

It was a tough year; I was up against Jean-Claude Van Damme (*Replicant*), Fred Ward (*Full Disclosure*) and Christopher Lloyd (*When Good Ghouls Go Bad*). We all lost out to Courtney B. Vance who played the lead in *Love and Action in Chicago*, the strapline of which was: 'A hit man rethinks his celibacy'. Like I said, it was a tough year.

Number six, *Back 2 tha Hood*, followed soon after. In that film I smoked a bong that was as big as me. It was filled with herbal tobacco and it made me half-laugh and half-choke, which helped me produce the most evil cackle I've ever done. There are a couple of Laurel and Hardy slapstick moments where after getting stoned I fall over flat on my back – it felt fine at the time but I was in agony the next day.

At one point I get the munchies and attack the fridge but I'm supposed to get stuck inside when somebody knocks the fridge door shut with their butt.

'Couldn't you have bought a bigger fridge?' I asked, not unreasonably, I thought. 'It's tiny.'

'But you're tiny,' the props guy said, trying to force me inside. 'Come on, get your other arm in.'

'I can't,' I protested, shoving a carton of milk and some salami to one side, 'I'm going to come out box-shaped!'

---

[50] In other words, films that went 'straight to video' without a cinema release.

Eventually, with my nose compressed against a tube of Squeezey Cheese, the door was shut and we got the scene.

At the end of this 'episode', the Leprechaun was killed by being pushed into quick-drying cement. The cement was actually edible, a kind of grey porridge. The effects guys stayed up all night making a huge vat of the stuff.

The pressure was really on as we only had one shot at nailing this scene. Once I landed in the 'cement', my costume and prosthetics would be a write-off.

'When you fall in,' the stunt co-ordinator said, 'just lie back and you'll gradually sink.'

When the cry of 'Action!' finally came, I fell back screaming onto the huge vat of porridge. The first thing I noticed was that it was shockingly cold. After a few seconds I realised that I wasn't going to sink – the 'porridge' was too thick.

There were some weights at the bottom, which I was supposed to grab once I'd sunk, so I wouldn't float to the surface too soon, ruining the scene. I pushed my arms down, found one of the weights and pulled myself under. Psychologically, this is a hard thing to do – as the cold, gloopy mess closed around me I took a breath, shut my eyes and stayed below the surface for as long as I could.

Once I resurfaced I looked like . . . like . . . er – well, like a leprechaun that had fallen into an enormous bowl of porridge. I was completely covered and the gloop was really seriously stuck to me. I could hardly open my eyes.

A voice came from the darkness: 'Over here, Warwick!'

I turned, forced an eye open and saw a grinning stagehand holding a hose.

'Oh, kaggernash!'

A freezing-cold jet of water hit me, almost lifting me off my feet. Ah, the glamour of showbiz. As the Leprechaun I'd been killed in a huge variety of innovative ways: I'd been dissolved in a well, impaled with an iron bar, exploded twice (once in space), been annihilated with a flamethrower, and now drowned in the cement foundations of a skyscraper.

The only *Leprechaun* film I didn't die in was *Lep in the Hood*, although some rappers might argue otherwise, as the movie finished with me performing the 'Leprechaun Rap'.

Now to the burning question which millions, ahem, of *Leprechaun* fans have been speculating about for some years now: Will there be another *Leprechaun* film?

Well, a pitch meeting to 'reboot' the franchise has been held with Lions Gate Entertainment. The concept was to do it in 3-D. These films are much better than the days of the red and green glasses. As long as the films don't use 3-D as a gimmick, then I think it's fine. I'd relish the chance to waggle my 3-D shillelagh at movie-going audiences around the world.

My own idea is to make a pirate-themed *Leprechaun*. All the ingredients are there for a perfect *Leprechaun* movie: pirates, chests full of gold, parrots, wooden legs, maidens, eye-patches, sword fights, cannonballs and so on.

I know the *Leprechaun* movie franchise is not to everyone's taste but I had a great time making them and I'm proud of my performances in every one of those crazy films. I'm doubly proud that I had my own horror franchise.

Now, however, I was about to become a small part in an enormous movie franchise, the biggest and most successful the world has ever seen.

It was a story that started with a young would-be wizard . . .

Chapter Eighteen

Pottering About

Another day, another Potter premiere.

Professor Flitwick, he's a great character; rather eccentric, but he possesses a strength that belies his short stature.

B ack in the UK I filmed an episode of the *Murder Rooms*, a series based on the 'real-life' adventures of Sir Arthur Conan Doyle, the creator of Sherlock Holmes. In what was yet another glamorous role, I played a travelling showman with a very sensitive medical problem, namely haemorrhoids.

Of course, I came to Conan Doyle (Charles Edwards) to seek relief. The procedure involved the employment of a device that looked like an enormous pair of metal tongs. The scene was shot from the front, and I pulled appropriately apprehensive expressions as I dropped my britches and bent over a chair. I then looked suitably agonised as the good doctor did his business round the rear.

Between takes, an actress told me that she'd been reading a wonderful book. I asked if there were any short characters in it and she said 'Lots!'

'That's my kind of book.' I looked at the cover: '*Harry Potter and the Philosopher's Stone*. Hmmm. Sounds interesting. I hope they make it into a film.'

Some months later, my agent[51] called, asking me if I'd like to read for the character of Professor Filius Flitwick.

By this time we were three books into what had arguably become the greatest publishing sensation of the twentieth century

---

[51] I had my own agent, independent of Willow Management, and would only audition for roles that he sent me – that way I couldn't be accused of nabbing all the plum roles that came into our office.

so the answer was a resounding 'YES PLEASE!' (as a bonus, I was pleased to see that Flitwick was in all three).

While this was terrific news, I knew it would nonetheless present a tremendous challenge for me. I'd be attempting to play a character already familiar to millions of readers around the world. *Harry Potter* fans all had a certain image in their mind of how the characters looked and behaved, so a great deal rode upon my interpretation.

I spent the night before my audition reading *The Philosopher's Stone*. It's strange really, I've never been a fan of fiction, I tend to prefer non-fiction books like the *Guinness Book of Records*, books about extreme weather, outer space, biographies and so on. But when it comes to films, the more fantastical they are the more I like them.

Having said that, reading *Potter* while trying to imagine the film was wonderful, if a little daunting. How on earth were they going to get all this on screen? Still, this wasn't my problem, I concluded. I just needed to understand my character.

So who was Flitwick? Well, he was described as a gnome-like wizard with a dash of goblin and, from what I could tell from the books, he seemed to be a real trooper, someone who could be totally relied upon, someone who would give his life for his students and Hogwarts. He was kind, trusting and not without a sense of humour. He did not feel the need to intimidate his students, like certain other Hogwarts teachers. Flitwick's small stature belied his physical strength, power and wisdom, contrary to the stereotype of little people.

He was a great character, a testament to Rowling's skill as an author, and the more I learned about Flitwick, the more I wanted to play him.

As I read the books I was reminded more and more of my own

mad professor performance as a child, the one I'd filmed with my sister (when I hit her with my geography textbook). That's just how I imagined a young Professor Flitwick would have been.

Finally, it grew so late that I could read no more. 'Right, that's it!' I said, and closed the book, 'From this moment forth, *I* am Professor Flitwick.'

The next morning I travelled to the audition, which took place at Leavesden Studios. It was full of people besides the director (Chris Columbus of *Home Alone* fame). There were the casting directors, producer David Heyman and several assistants. Although I hadn't worked with Chris before, I was pleased to discover that I knew the casting directors from *Willow*. It's always good to see a friendly face at these things, especially as we'd got on quite well in the past.

Everyone was taking this movie very seriously, it was a huge project and it was important, they said, to get *everything* just right.

'OK,' Chris said, standing up and handing me a script, 'I'll play Harry and the other characters. You ready?'

My heart thumped. 'Yep, whenever you are.'

I was a bit worried, as some directors will read the characters in a deadpan voice. This makes it very hard to produce a lively performance in return and it's only too easy to slip up and deliver your lines a little flatter than you would if you were performing with an actor.

To my delight, Chris read with real gusto and I responded in kind. I *was* Flitwick: kind, dependable, strong but with a soft cheeky glint in my eye. Pretty soon we'd worked our way through the scripted scene and had started improvising. We wound up giggling like a pair of idiots. So was everybody else.

I took this as a pretty good sign, although, as I said to Sam afterwards, 'I hope they were laughing with me rather than at me.'

As anybody who has lived with an actor will probably tell you, we're not that pleasant to be around while we're waiting to hear if we've won a part. Poor Sam had to endure my anxiety as I waited and waited and waited. I went through the casting session with her over and over again, analysing every moment, criticising every aspect of my performance. Sam would try to convince me that I'd done well but that just made me doubt my performance all the more.

I really, really wanted this part. I became very nervous about it and life ground to a halt for a couple of weeks. Normally, if you've won a part you tend to hear back pretty quickly. But if you haven't scored the role you sometimes simply won't get a call to break the bad news: silence speaks volumes.

I'd endured my fair share of silences in my career; these were mainly the result of bad decisions on my part. These days I'm much better at making choices about a role before I go to auditions. This is a key part of being an actor, especially when you can actually afford to turn down roles that you know aren't right for you. But there was a time when I went to every single audition, simply because I *had* to work, I needed the money, and there was really no choice.

I've been to plenty of auditions where I've walked into a room and didn't click with the director or the producer. I've also done plenty of cold reads, when you're given something entirely new to read in character there and then.

Whenever I failed auditions, as unpleasant as that was, I always took something positive from the experience and I never let them knock my confidence. I'm a great believer in what my agent once told me, 'As one door closes another will open.'

Waiting to hear about Flitwick was agony. I jumped every time the phone rang and after three long weeks I'd just about given up all hope when my agent called.

'Yes?!'

'Well, don't get too excited.'

'Oh.'

'You've got the part of Professor Flitwick and –'

'Brilliant! Well, why shouldn't I get too excited?'

'Because, I was about to say, "You need to let me finish", because they want you to play the Goblin bank teller as well. *Now* you can go ahead and get excited.'

'What? Another part? So two roles?' I said, hopping up and down. 'Yes!'

'See, I told you so,' Sam said.

Suddenly I was all sunshine and smiles. Laughter returned to the Davis household once more.

A few weeks later the costume department called me in for measurements. I was delighted to walk in and see that Nick Dudman, one of the finest make-up artists in the world, was running the make-up/effects department. Nick had overseen my very first life cast on the day I got the part in *Jedi* and I still have a diary entry noting the occasion from October 1981: 'Met Patricia Carr and Nick and had my life cast. Let's get on with it.'

After we'd reminisced about the good old days on *Jedi*, *Willow* and *The Phantom Menace* and caught up on each other's news, Nick said, ' Well, I think you know the routine by now, Warwick.'

Having a life cast done is like being inside an isolation tank. Once my head had been covered with the first layer of alginate, I was totally cut off from the world. I was inside a warm womblike environment with a dim orange glow coming through my eyelids and a swooshing sound in my ears as the make-up people rubbed their hands, smoothing the alginate all over my head. I'm sure some people would find the procedure quite claustrophobic but to me it's strangely relaxing.

An exact copy of my head was then turned into a bust for the make-up department, so they could create prosthetics that precisely fitted my face.

Although rumours flew about the studio, I still didn't know who else was going to be in the film. I picked up some clues every time I came in for a fitting at the magical costume department, which was packed full of the most wonderful props, mannequins, materials and clothing. Whenever I got the chance I'd have a nose around and would sometimes spot a famous name pinned to a wall or to a costume. I saw Robbie Coltrane's name first, then Alan Rickman's, then Maggie Smith's. I became more and more excited at the prospect of working with all these great British actors.

The make-up was incredible; it took four hours to put on and an hour to take off. I had to be at the studio for 4 a.m. to be made up and in costume for a 9 a.m. shoot which could last for up to twelve hours. I was quite used to it but some actors really, really struggled.

People tend to think that being made up and wearing prosthetic make-up becomes a lot easier as time goes on, but it doesn't, it's actually the opposite. As the days drag by and you realise that those four torturous hours are inescapable, going to work — just to sit there, while people prod, stick, bend, fold, paint and glue uncomfortable and smelly materials to your face — becomes more and more psychologically challenging.

Imagine hearing your alarm go off at 3.15 every morning, then struggling to get to work for four o'clock only to have to sit in a make-up room and have your face painted with a strong-smelling, freezing-cold glue. Sometimes I felt like punching the glue-painter and I had to grip the armrest of my chair to restrain myself; I often joked that they should just tie me down as soon as I arrived.

Besides, it's very hard to stay combative with half a dozen people working on your face at the same time – especially as they are all so focused on the job in hand that none of them really pays much attention to what you're saying.

Sometimes, despite all the gluing and prodding, I'd fall asleep and then hear occasional instructions such as 'Warwick, can you look up?' and I'd look up and then fall asleep again.

Despite all of the discomfort and mental torture involved in working with prosthetics, I always remind myself that without the likes of Nick Dudman, his brilliant team of make-up artists and his glue I wouldn't be able to play such a diverse range of characters. Prosthetics had even allowed me to play more than one character in the same film.

It was during one such make-up session while we were filming *Harry Potter and the Philosopher's Stone* that Ron Howard called.

'Warwick, I've got a pretty big problem.'

'What is it, Ron, what's up?'

'I'm filming this movie called *The Grinch*, you know the Dr Seuss book. Jim Carrey's playing the Grinch and he's really, really struggling with the make-up.'

'I see.'

'It takes seven hours, every day, we're trying to cut the time down but it's driving the poor guy nuts. I've been made up as the Grinch too, and directed as the Grinch, to try and make him feel better by going through it with him. I've even got an expert in positivity from the Marines trying to help him through it, but it's not working. I want to know how you cope, Warwick.'

'I'm sorry, Ron, there's no real answer. Being made up for one day is quite fun but if you're doing it every day for months, and you're the lead actor, well I think I'd go nuts too.'

Once my first day's make-up was done, I donned my costume. I couldn't believe how amazing it looked; it was just as I imagined, better even. I noticed it had a long, thin inside pocket and I couldn't work out what it was for – until I looked at the wand in my hand. A wand pocket! Fantastic!

If anything this added to the pressure. Make-up and Costume had done such a fantastic job and now, as I walked onto the set, I saw the set designers had as well.

My first scene was filmed at Harrow School, in Winston Churchill's old schoolroom, his signature scored into the dark oak panels a century before. Now it was full of books, parchments and scrolls, jars, hand-carved egg timers, Hogwarts emblems and many other strange and wonderful things – including a box of magical sweets on my desk. Before me were the students I was supposed to be teaching as Professor Flitwick, including young Mr Potter, Mr Weasley and Ms Granger.

When I first saw Dan, Rupert and Emma, I could tell they had all the right qualities. They all knew their lines perfectly; it was immediately clear that they were competent young performers and it was going to be interesting to see how they developed as actors.

But on that first day I was more concerned about my own performance, as this was my first big scene. Every other detail was indeed perfect, as they'd said at the audition. A huge team had put this together, including sculptors, mould-makers, painters, designers, seamstresses, shoemakers, hairdressers and so on. All of these people were there to put me, the actor, on a wonderful stage. If I cocked up my performance then it would reflect badly on them, and their morale and the quality of the movie would suffer.

If, on the other hand, I pulled it off then the entire team might talk about how good I was, and how amazing the film was going to be and so on; they would get excited about it and would go the extra mile to add all those little touches that can turn a good film into a great film.

I also wanted to convince Chris and the producers that I was 'perfect' as well – that they'd made the right choice.

As the cameras rolled I began to teach the class how to levitate feathers and everything just slotted into place. I knew this amazing story inside out, thanks to J. K. Rowling's brilliantly crafted book and thanks to the wonderful script. Now I was in it, really in it. We kept going all day, until Chris was convinced we'd got everything out of the scene that we possibly could.

I returned to the make-up department where Nick was waiting for me. He had a tradition of celebrating at the end of an important day's filming with a single bottle of beer. During *Harry Potter*, he moved on to margaritas, a clear sign of just how enormous his task was.

I'm one of the few actors lucky enough to have appeared in every one of the *Harry Potter* films, so I've been part of the family from beginning to end. Thanks to the production team, who did a fantastic job and left no room for error, the *Harry Potter* films remain the smoothest operation I've ever been fortunate enough to be part of.

Very little went wrong during filming, although I was involved in one small incident during *Goblet of Fire*. It was the scene where we were standing in the Great Hall with the goblet, which is covered by a cloth. Professor Snape (Alan Rickman) reveals the goblet to the pupils by magically whipping the cloth away and into the air.

This special effect was achieved by firing air through a set of pipes behind the goblet, which shot the cloth skywards. The first time we did this it worked perfectly, except that the cloth, on its gentle return to the ground, decided to land perfectly across my face. Everyone tried to finish the scene but we all gradually disintegrated into giggles. Even the usually sombre Snape cracked a slight smile.

Alan and I got on quite well – although, the *Potter* franchise being such a well-oiled machine, we didn't get much time to chat. Very often, the first time I'd meet someone as famous as Alan would be on set. After a quick 'hello' we'd just start acting.

It sounds odd but it worked quite well – as soon as you start acting, you see the person you're acting with through the eyes of your own character, which is just what you want. You don't want to be thinking, 'That's Alan Rickman in front of me; he's been in so many great films,' because before you know it you've forgotten your lines.

Of course, Alan played the wonderful role of Severus Snape, Potions Master, described by J. K. Rowling as 'a gift of a character'. Snape was almost the opposite of Flitwick, bullying his pupils and seeming terribly devious; you'd never know if he was really on your side.

When Alan was made-up and wearing his black robes he looked just as menacing as Snape should, but in between takes the illusion was often shattered by a little pair of white earphones, which snaked out from an iPod secreted somewhere in his costume. I often wondered what he listened to. I imagined a scene in *Potter* where the camera passes Snape's office. His door is slightly ajar and we see Snape inside, dancing merrily, the tinny sound of *Walking on Sunshine* coming from his iPod earphones.

There was one memorable occasion when I got to have a long chat with the older and more established actors. It was during a long night shoot when we had to wait a long time between shots while the special-effects people arranged all their gizmos for a particularly explosive sequence.

We were outside, and I was flattered to see that my chair had been put in a group with Alan Rickman, Maggie Smith (Minerva McGonagall) and Michael Gambon (Albus Dumbledore).

The four of us sat, in full costume, huddled around a tiny heater chatting through the night. Michael was a masterful storyteller and told some incredible tales with fantastic punch lines – most of which I can't remember – and I've been sworn to secrecy for those that I do.

It was sometimes hard for me to follow the conversation because they'd use first names. For example, Michael might ask, 'Have you worked with Robert?' and then you'd realise five minutes later that he was talking about de Niro.

But there was one subject about which we both were experts.

'What do you think of these beards, Warwick?' Michael asked.

'Well, they're a bit of a pain, to be perfectly honest.'

'Yes, they most certainly are, these wisps get absolutely every-where. If I use my arms and wand it always gets entangled and I yank the thing right off my face. And don't get me started on food. Dinner is a total nightmare.'

I nodded in wholehearted agreement.

A couple of days later, we were having lunch in full costume when Michael sat down at the table with a large canvas bag. He tied it around his neck and placed his beard inside and then was able to eat his tagliatelle without having to worry about consuming half of his beard at the same time.

How did the lucky sod get one of those? I wondered, as I battled with forks, pasta and hair.

Michael also loved a joke. After lunch one day, Michael's make-up artist was removing his beard-bag before a shot. As she pulled it away she was amazed to see that Michael had woven a string of prawns, vegetables and other foody assortments into the beard.

'What is it? What's wrong?' the famous actor said innocently.

'Um . . . um,' the flustered make-up artist replied, 'your beard, er . . .'

'Oh these! Well, that's just in case I get a bit peckish, dear girl.'

Harry Potter blasted me into twenty-first century celebdom. Now I'm often asked to give talks at primary schools about fame (as opposed to being short). The great thing about this is that the kids learn there are lots of little people out there and, apart from our size, we're just like everybody else. I also hope I might inspire a physically disadvantaged child by showing them that if they believe in themselves they can achieve anything.

When I'm in the supermarket, kids sometimes can't help but point and blurt out, 'What's that, Mummy?' Mum usually blushes and tries to look busy. If the child persists, they're dragged away and told off, even when I try to intervene. Then they look at me like it's *my* fault – they're turned against little people for life.

I'm passionate about changing these attitudes, and one day I was suddenly presented with an unprecedented opportunity to do so – from a wholly unexpected quarter.

Before that, however, Sam had some rather amazing news.

'You need to sit down, Warwick,' she said as I walked in through the front door.

Chapter Nineteen

Luck of the Irish

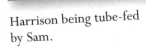
16.11.03
Hi everyone, I'm feeling better.

Sam, Annabelle and poorly Harrison.

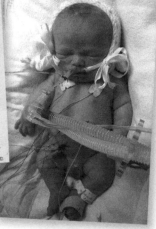

Harrison had an extremely
tough start to life.

Harrison being tube-fed
by Sam.

Harrison in his 'bubble', watching
me watching him.

The doctor gave me the look I didn't want to see. The 'I've-got-some-bad-news-for-you' look.

Nurses, doctors, patients and dogsbodies hurried past us in a blur of white coats, scrubs, clipboards, suits and trolleys.

'Warwick,' he said quietly, 'we're doing everything possible but your son is ill.' He paused and looked down for a moment before meeting my eyes once more. 'He is *very poorly.*'

My heart shattered into a million tiny pieces. I knew only too well what those two dreaded words meant. I couldn't believe it. For a dizzying few seconds, I was at a loss, speechless; I'd been so certain Harrison would make it.

I'd been reluctant to try for another baby after all we'd been through, but Sam was quite adamant. She wanted Annabelle to have a baby brother or sister. 'Just get me pregnant, Warwick, and I'll do the rest,' she said.

'Oh well, that's romantic,' I replied, but I had to admit I liked the idea and I inevitably succumbed to Sam's advances.

The next month she was pregnant.

'Goodness, you just have to look at your wife to get her pregnant, don't you, Mr Davis?' Professor Rodeck said with a grin.

While I turned bright red Professor Rodeck said he would repeat the same amniotic tests that he'd performed for Annabelle. We were pretty worried but the softly spoken Prof was as calm, confident and reassuring as ever. 'We've made even more advances since Annabelle was born. Try not to worry too much.'

Once again we had to wait for two torturous weeks until he called. 'Good news, the achondroplasia gene isn't present!'

Which meant our baby didn't have the lethal double-dominant combination of both of our genes.

Sam sagged with relief. 'Excellent.'

'Would you like to know if it's a boy or a girl? I'm guessing if it were a boy then it would make everything just perfect.'

'I don't want to know!' Sam said, but I think the Prof had blown the surprise in his excitement.

Sam grew steadily and had another wonderful pregnancy, rapidly reaching gigantic proportions, until eventually all she could do was eat and sleep. As her due date approached, she was again scheduled for a Caesarean section, this time performed by Ms Steele, who – like Mr Hackman – wouldn't let me in her theatre.

Sam was knocked out and, after a lightning fast operation, Harrison, who was also little, was whisked away – almost the very moment Ms Steele lifted him out and cut him free.

I watched, still not having seen my son, as the obstetric team scrambled past me with Harrison, headed down the corridor in the direction of the intensive care unit. He wasn't breathing, there was a problem with his lungs. I chased after them with a Polaroid camera, squeezed my way into a gap round the incubator and leaned over the side to take a quick snap.

I stopped. Harrison was *so* tiny, *so* helpless.

But then so was I. There was nothing I could do; my son's future was out of my hands. I came to my senses, took the picture, tried to learn what I could from the doctors and, flapping the photo dry, I rushed back to Sam. I explained that Harrison was alive but very sick.

Sam was in terrible pain and clicked the morphine doser when I showed her the picture.

'He's just like Lloyd,' she said. 'I messed up. It's my fault.'

'Don't be silly,' I told her. 'Look, I'll try and find out more, OK?'

Sam sighed, nodded, and passed out.

And then, five minutes later, there I was, receiving the compassionate doctor's 'we're-doing-all-we-can' speech – the speech with the two words no parent should ever have to hear.

Very poorly.

I forced myself to focus. Harrison was struggling because his lungs were simply too tiny. That meant his blood wasn't being oxygenated and if his oxygen levels fell too low he'd suffer brain damage or die.

My mum, meanwhile, was waiting anxiously outside with five-year-old Annabelle, who was extremely excited about having a little brother and desperately eager to see him.

Unfortunately for Annabelle, with spectacularly bad timing, she'd just developed chickenpox, so wasn't allowed anywhere near the hospital. Luckily, the unit was on the ground floor so, with her nana holding her up to the window and me pointing wildly towards Harrison's incubator, she was able to see her baby brother for the first time.

The joy, love and amazement on her face was overwhelming – and heartbreaking, as I didn't know whether her little brother was here to stay.

Sam, meanwhile, despite being drugged to the eyeballs and almost sawn in half by Ms Steele, was back on her feet only twelve hours after giving birth. Together, we could only watch as Harrison fought through the night, and listen as the doctors explained how they were battling to keep him breathing. He remained danger-ously ill. The doctors thought he was dying. Each time we came back into the unit all they could say was 'He's still here.'

Five days later, he was still hanging in there and they decided to transfer him to another specialist unit in Nottingham. He was unable to drink and so was fed milk by a syringe via a tube that went straight into his stomach.

Gradually, the days went by. Five days became a week, then ten days, then two weeks. As time went on, he was moved from Nottingham to Leicester and then back to Peterborough for different treatments. Harrison showed very slight signs of improvement but progress was agonisingly slow; we were warned that it could all change at any moment. The only way for Sam and me to cope at this time was to try and remain positive. Even-tually, although he remained pretty poorly and needed to stay in hospital, it seemed as though he'd almost managed to fight his way into the world.

Although our lives were pretty much on hold at this time, one or two things inevitably cropped up to demand our time and attention. Once Sam was discharged, they wouldn't let us stay overnight in the hospital, so we returned home to bare cupboards – time for a trip to the supermarket.

We do a lot of online shopping these days but I still visit the supermarket and it's nearly always an adventure for me. Successful shopping requires a large degree of resourcefulness and inno-vation; solutions always need to be found, often at short notice.

Correct trolley selection is vital. I can't use one of the large deep trolleys because I can't get my shopping out once I've put it in and I don't like having a professional bag-packer rooting around in my stuff. I think you're able to judge a person by their shopping and I'm always fascinated by what people have in their trolleys. It sometimes raises intriguing questions. Why does that woman need thirty litres of milk? Why does that man have twenty bottles of bleach, half a dozen bottles of cleaning fluid, ten rolls of clingfilm, foil and a large box of Cook's matches?

It feels like a minor violation to have someone handling my meat and veg, so to avoid this I always make sure I select one of the shallow ones.

One very obvious and unavoidable problem is that some items are beyond my reach. When I was younger, I used to scale the shelves like a ladder but every now and again I'd be halfway up the shelf, one hand on the Corn Flakes, when a voice would come from behind me: 'Can I help you, sir?' I was threatened with banishment on grounds of health and safety so many times that I was eventually forced to abandon that method.

These days I head straight for the household goods aisle and select a mop or broom handle. As long as what I need isn't breakable, I simply poke it off the shelf. It's taken me years of practice but I can now pretty much get anything I want to land the right way up and in the right position in my trolley.

For breakables, I rely upon the direct method, which is to ask people. This is more problematic than it sounds. Whenever I approach someone in this situation, I'm not sure what it is, whether they're flattered, flustered or intrigued, but they very often pass me everything but the item I want, so I end up having to instruct them: It's a bit like playing one of those 'teddy-picker' machines you find in an amusement arcade. 'No, to your right, now left, one shelf up, no, down again . . . no, the red one, yes, that's it! No, now you've gone past it, go back to where you were before.'

It's not just me; Sam has experienced exactly the same thing. Whenever she asks for the jar with the red lid she always ends up with the jar with the green lid and by the time you've got it in your hands it's too late to say, 'Er, actually I wanted the one with the red lid.' Then they look at you as if you're the idiot.

As I whizzed round the store, keen to get back to Sam, I spotted a young mother with a boy of about seven, a good few inches taller than me, at the other end of the aisle. We made eye contact. 'Here we go,' I thought.

He immediately turned to his mum, pointed and loudly blurted out. 'What's that, Mummy?'

Mummy looked up and turned red. She then started studying a tin of beans a bit too closely, ignoring her offspring. Her son grabbed hold of her leg and repeated the question, this time more loudly.

Now, I don't mind curious kids at all. It's quite logical for them to react this way and sometimes I'll end up having a really great chat with both child and parent. What annoys the hell out of me is when the parent's reaction is either to stare like their child and not say anything, or to move away as quickly and as silently as possible.

And that's what happened here – as the child persisted the mother practically dragged the poor boy away and I heard her telling her now tearful son off. 'That's rude!' I heard her hiss, 'you shouldn't point.'

A bit later, when we passed each other in the biscuit aisle, the boy looked at me like the telling-off was my fault. Even if I try to smooth things over, it's already too late; they've been turned against little people for life.

'What a day,' I muttered to myself as I returned to the hospital, parked up and headed for the entrance.

More was yet to come.

I saw them, well, heard them first, a large Irish family, sharing a smoke and a chat right by the front doors. Their conversation tailed off as I walked past. Out of the corner of my eye, I saw that they were staring at me, eyes wide, whispering urgently to one another.

Oh God, not again, I thought.

Thanks to some crazy superstition, some Irish people (a distinct minority but still more than enough for me) have a tendency to want to touch me (well, a 'leprechaun' anyway) for good luck.

I've had similar problems in Japan, and with Japanese tourists in London, who seem to consider little people lucky; they're especially keen on being photographed with us. Going out for a walk on my own in Tokyo is simply impossible.

I picked up speed and jogged for the safety of the hospital lift. Once I found Sam I leaned over and whispered, 'Watch out, there's some, er, *Irish people* downstairs.'

Sam nodded. 'Yes,' she whispered back. 'I know, they've already been after Annabelle.'

The shorter the luckier, it would seem.

Later that day, I had to pop out again. The Irish people were still there. Choosing my moment carefully, I jogged alongside a deliveryman wheeling a trolley full of boxes and escaped. When I finally got outside there was a parking ticket, bang in the middle of my windscreen, impossible to reach – the ultimate insult.

Upon my return, I snuck past the Irish family once more and slipped with relief through the closing doors of the lift. A woman was already inside. 'Oh, hello there!' she exclaimed in an Irish accent.

Trapped in the lift, it was impossible for me to stop her from getting more than her fair share of luck that morning.

Harrison battled his way into the world but remained in hospital for three months before I asked the doctors if we could take him home. They weren't sure at first, but I argued that I knew his condition as well as they did. Harrison still required a fair amount of care, but it wasn't anything Sam and I couldn't provide.

I knew that with the right equipment, Sam and I would be able to watch Harrison twenty-four hours a day at home. Sam and I were delighted when the doctors agreed.

We returned home with our tiny baby son and about five tonnes of equipment, including a dozen oxygen tanks, an oxygen maker and a SAT monitor. Suddenly, our home looked like a mini-hospital. It was only after I got all the gear set up and switched on that we discovered the thing was as noisy as a milk-bottle factory and made the whole house rattle. It was as if a never-ending goods train was rumbling past. Sam and I had to yell at each other to make ourselves heard whenever it was on. People could hear us from the street and thought we were having an almighty row, when all we were doing was discussing what to have for dinner.

Once we were free of the doctors and nurses, the responsibility really hit home. It was just us and Harrison, now. We couldn't just turn around and ask for help, we were on our own.

Having said that, we were delighted to have our son home and once again our house was full of laughter.

One day, not long after we'd brought Harrison home, the doorbell rang.

'Avon call– . . . oh!'

'Yes?' I said. A middle-aged woman stood before me, cradling a basket of perfumes and other toiletries in her arms.

'Um. Yes.'

I sighed. This always happened. Whenever a door-to-door sales-person called they were usually so surprised by our appearance that they instantly forgot what it was they were supposed to be selling.

'You rang my doorbell, did you not?'

'Um. Yeeeas,' the woman said uncertainly in a strong Welsh accent.

'Well?'

'Oh right, yes, sorry. I'm in the area recruiting Avon Ladies, I wonder if this would be something that your wife would enjoy doing?' Thank goodness it was me who answered the door. If it had been Sam, we would have ended up with a house full of Avon supplies.

'No thanks, she wouldn't be able to reach the doorbells.' I shut the door, leaving her dumbfounded.

Sam had been hiding in the hallway. She looked at me in disbelief and mortification. 'What on earth did you say that for?'

'Well, it's true though, isn't it?' She couldn't argue with that and we both collapsed into fits of giggles.

When I look back at photos of Harrison now, I'm amazed we were allowed to take him home when we did. I can truly understand our doctor's reluctance. It's given me a real jolt to see just how sick our son looked. I genuinely didn't realise the amount of responsibility Sam and I were taking on.

Poor Annabelle. She'd been so excited to have her baby brother home at last and now suddenly found herself a bit left out, as everything revolved around us constantly checking Harrison's blood saturation levels. The ideal is around 98 per cent, but Harrison's sometimes fell to the low seventies.

Feeding was a job and a half; I used a tiny syringe to very slowly push formula milk down a tube that went into his stomach. Harrison hated it; he got into the almost reflexive habit of tearing the tube out, which meant another trip to the hospital to have it reinserted.

Once he'd yanked the tube out for the third day in a row, I decided enough was enough – and that I'd replace it myself. Putting aside the thought that this was supposed to be a medical procedure wasn't easy, but I'd studied the doctors doing it so often and had received lots of practical advice from a specialist nurse, so I knew I could manage it.

Getting this right was all about speed and precision. I disinfected my hands and unpacked a fresh tube, took a very deep breath and threaded it through his nose, felt it reach his oesophagus; right on cue Harrison coughed and swallowed, I pushed it down and it was in.

I now had to use a syringe to draw out a little fluid via the tube – this was to check the tube was in his stomach and hadn't gone down into his lungs. I dripped a little of the fluid onto litmus paper and it turned pink – it was acidic, so it could only have come from the stomach.

Although it was nerve-wracking at first, I was soon able to perform the whole procedure before Harrison even knew what had hit him.

Feeding was difficult for Harrison. He'd simply refuse food if we tried to feed him without using the tube. One day Sam said in complete frustration, 'Harrison, if you don't start eating then I don't know what I'm going to do!' Incredibly, just at that moment, Harrison decided to eat every last morsel.

Once things were a bit more settled at home, the hospital called and asked Sam and me whether we'd talk to some tall parents who had just been told their unborn baby had achondroplasia. They wanted us to explain to the parents about our lives and our kids and how we lead a 'normal' existence – well, as normal as any family can!

We readily agreed and have done this a few times now. We're always more than happy to talk to parents expecting a baby with dwarfism. Some are still put up for adoption, just because they're born small. Many people still see it as a disaster and think that it will lead to a life of solitude and difficulty – which is quite depressing really. Of course, life isn't like this at all, and I've made it one of my missions to overturn misconceptions concerning 'littleness'.

Tall people who talk to parents expecting a little person tend to be too politically correct, and go on about how little people are 'normal people who bear the burden of a physical difference'. They then spend the next hour describing exactly how little people *aren't* like ordinary people.

Of course, physically speaking there is a significant difference. What you look like is an important element of who you are and how others look at you. So rather than pretend a little person is just like a short tall person, it's much better to talk about the practicalities of everyday life, how certain difficulties are overcome and how being small shouldn't hold you back from doing anything you want to do. OK, being a professional basketball player might be tricky[52] but there are little people who are set designers, psychologists, priests, professional card players, casino managers, motorcycle mechanics, molecular biologists, production co-ordinators, chefs, PE teachers, gynaecologists, veterinarians, etc., etc.

Sometimes parents find it difficult to accept the diagnosis and ask for second and third opinions, hoping to hear something different from a new doctor. Their disbelief might be followed by anger, guilt, denial, helplessness or avoidance.

My advice for parents expecting a little child is to relax. I know it's easy for me to say – but little people pretty much take care of the little side of life themselves. They deal with being small just

---

[52] Having said that, Tony Cox at three-foot-six was a professional basketball player and once took on the Harlem Globetrotters. He could score from the halfway line with an underarm throw and was unstoppable when dribbling – he went through everyone's legs and kept the ball so low his giant opponents didn't have a hope.

fine. As long as there's love, fun and security then everything else will follow. Despite the occasional awkward moment, public attitudes to little people are generally pretty good.

Poor Harrison had to wait until he was three until he was well enough to have a proper birthday party. We got the final all-clear after a few visits to Great Ormond Street where the doctors ran some pretty scary tests, including a sleep study and a vacuum chamber which measured his lung pressure that eventually confirmed he was now perfectly healthy. We were able to get rid of the oxygen tanks and the milk-bottle factory and threw him a cracking birthday party. Ever since then Harrison has been just like your typical child: wild, obnoxious, eats anything, and so on and – like Annabelle – is living life to the full (as I can most sincerely attest).

I'd pretty much stopped working around the time we had Harrison but as he started to get stronger, I did a couple of commercials just to keep things ticking along. They're usually hard work, but take up relatively little time and the pay's not bad.

The first big commercial I ever did was for British Telecom when I played ET, who, unsurprisingly, trotted out his famous 'phone home' quote. Spielberg was very protective of ET and BT had to pay a fortune for the rights and that was only as long as they fulfilled several strict conditions. One of these was that ET was not allowed to speak unless it was with his trademark voice. So I was instructed not to say a word while wearing the suit. This made sure that the illusion was not spoiled for the young actors on set.

We filmed the scene at a children's party. The costume was extremely heavy and ET has very long arms, so my fingers didn't reach to the end, although I was able to operate ET's hands with a kind of lever system from his elbow.

It was all going well – until the kids were released. I was standing in a pit of coloured balls in one of those little adventure play-grounds. When the director shouted 'Action!' a screaming horde of overexcited children who'd been pumped full of hyperactivity-inducing sweets by the production staff stampeded towards me, all of them determined to be the first to hug ET.

My eyes widened in alarm and I waved ET's long arms in panic, remembering not to shout anything like 'Help!' or 'Stop them!' as per the contract. They steamed into me and I flew back, disappearing under a screaming heap of laughing children and plastic balls.

An anxious production assistant pulled them off while I lay there in a daze.

'ET needs to take a break,' she told them. 'He's feeling a bit tired now.'

I don't know about that, but I was definitely seeing stars (or was it balls?).

I also leapt back into costume for 'Get Rid of Your Gremlins,' a long-running adult literacy campaign for the Central Office of Information where I tormented people who couldn't read or add up. One of the commercials received lots of complaints – people said I'd scared them. It's a performance I remain proud of to this day.

I even played a garden gnome for Top-Up TV. We were filming in a launderette in the East End. A day or two afterwards, someone showed me a copy of the *Star* newspaper. Inside was an article that said we'd had to stop shooting because there was a knocking shop upstairs and the moaning and groaning meant we couldn't film. I hadn't noticed myself but it was in the *Star* so it must have been true . . .

As I folded the paper the phone rang. It was my agent.

'There's no audition,' he said excitedly, 'they want you! You'll be shooting with Jamie Foxx and you leave for New Orleans next week!'

That's my life for you. One week a garden gnome under a knocking shop in Canning Town, the next in New Orleans hanging out with Jamie Foxx in the world's coolest jazz club.

Chapter Twenty

For the Love of Cheese

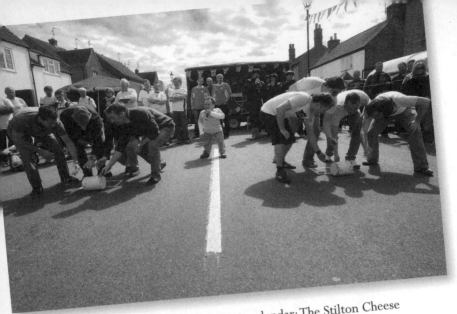

The premier event in the Warwick Davis calendar: The Stilton Cheese Rolling Championship.

Robbie Coltrane couldn't wait to get involved in some Stilton rolling action.

Courtesy of Paul Biggins.

Taylor Hackford, the Oscar®-winning director, had offered me the part of Oberon in the movie biopic *Unchain my Heart*. The film's name was changed to *Ray* after Ray Charles died, as it seemed to be more appropriate and an affectionate tribute.

Before I travelled to the USA for two weeks of filming Taylor invited me to his large East London home, which sat right on the edge of the Thames, to talk about the movie.

I was already sitting in the lounge when an attractive lady appeared in the doorway. Taylor introduced her as Helen.

She smiled and asked me in a regal voice if I'd like a cup of tea.

'No thank you.'

'Sure? It's no trouble.'

'No, really, I'm fine,' I said, and she left.

Goodness, I thought to myself, these film directors do all right for themselves, employing housekeepers like that.

It was a good job I didn't say as much because I'd just mistaken Taylor's wife for the housekeeper. On top of that she was Dame Helen Mirren, so it wasn't as if her face wasn't well known.

I must confess that even after meeting Taylor I was still a little in the dark as to what he wanted Oberon to be like. Although this movie was based on the life of Ray Charles, Oberon, who was a master of ceremonies in a jazz club, was semi-fictional. He was supposed to be an amalgamation of several real-life characters of the day.

There was a brief craze in the 1950s to have little people as nightclub announcers. Taylor sent me a load of CDs where you could hear them introducing some of the biggest acts of the day and I listened to them all with great interest as I prepared for the role, but I did wonder how on earth I was supposed to waltz on to a set in New Orleans and become this super-confident American compere who would introduce Ray Charles to millions of cinema-goers.

But then inspiration hit. Of course! I had extensive experience as a master of ceremonies.

The premier event in the Warwick Davis calendar is, of course, the Stilton Cheese Rolling Championships. You may recall that I am a huge cheese fan (although my favourite cheesy nibble is, of course, Cheddar) so when the organisers of the Stilton Cheese Rolling Championships, which took place in Stilton[53], just up the road from where I lived, asked me if I'd like to compere the event, I was only too delighted to accept. This was an unpaid role, although the organisers were prepared to make a generous donation to Peterborough's Special Care Baby Unit in return.

There is something so delightfully English about a cheese-rolling festival that takes place in a village where they don't actually make the cheese, even though the village *is* called Stilton.

In fact – I'm letting you into a secret here – neither do they roll real cheese. Well, you didn't think they'd be so silly as to roll real Stilton down their high street, did you? The cheese is actually sawn-up sections of telegraph poles painted to look like cheese.

I'd love to be able to claim that the origins of cheese rolling are lost in the mists of time, but the enterprising landlord of the Bell Inn (where the finish line used to be[54]) created the sport in 1959

---

[53] Who'd've thought, eh?
[54] It's known as the Bell End.

when his passing trade dried up, thanks to the completion of the A1 bypass. He started rolling a cheese up and down the street outside the Bell and claimed he was 'reviving an ancient tradition'. Of course, he was doing no such thing but it wasn't long before other 'cheese rollers' turned up from all over the UK to join him, and each May Day bank holiday the event now attracts thousands of visitors to the village of Stilton.

It's a knockout competition in which two teams of four men or women, wearing fancy dress (of course!), attempt to roll the cheese, using their hands, in a race from the Bell Inn to the cross-roads just fifty yards away. Each team member has to touch the cheese at least once during its roll and they must stay on their side of the road throughout – if their cheese crosses the centre line then they have to stop and restart from wherever it crossed the line.

This seems straightforward enough, but, with the landlord's enthusiastic encouragement, competitors are encouraged to drink copious amounts of booze throughout the day. By the time the two teams of finalists meet, they barely know where they are, let alone have the ability to keep their cheese under control.

I once watched as four burly young men dressed as French onion sellers lost control of their cheese and hurtled through the crash barriers and into the crowd. It's surprisingly hard to stop yourself when you're running in a crouch. One of them actually continued through the pub door and vanished, handing victory to a group of yellow-haired Vikings in tights.

At the end of the course is a large wooden board (yes, the Cheese Board) and you have to whack the cheese into that board to finish. There are several referees to make sure everything is done correctly, although they mainly shout insults at the contestants to try and put them off.

There is much cheese punnery and, as the host, I have to provide most of it. The teams tend to come up with weird and wonderful names in a blatant attempt to make me say something rude; one such team is the Four Skins of Edam.[55]

An important part of the cheese festival are the Pig Dyke Molly Dancers but why, I have no idea. These are extremely strange people who dress in black and white and dance around waving broomsticks (a bit like Morris dancing but without the bells). It's a very odd world around the fens.

Anyway, I realised my MC-ing at Stilton stood me in good stead for *Ray*. Indeed, with a little bit of Americanisation (and a reduction in cheese), there was barely any difference between:

'I got a special treat for all you satin dolls and I'm not talking about Oberon's big thunder. No, that's for another show. We got some new blood for ya. Fresh off the bus from Florida I give you Ray "Don't Call Me Sugar" Robinson.'

And:

'Now I know you all want me to roll my Babybel along the course and, don't worry ladies and gentlemen, that will come later. For now though, *Beaufort* things get out of hand, I'm here to introduce you all to our two finalists. First, all the way from Lincolnshire, give it up for . . . Cheese Whizz! And taking the right side of the street, all the way from Israel, please put your hands together for Cheeses of Nazareth![56]

---

[55] 2009 was an extra special year as it was the fiftieth anniversary and my fifth year as MC. The Golden Balls took home the Bell Trophy while the Fromage Fairies won the Women's Institute Cup. The winners are rewarded with a whole Stilton cheese for their efforts (and some booze).

[56] OK, I made that one up. They were from Wales and were called 'Caerphilly Does It'.

Needless to say, playing Oberon was a doddle after that.

I had a few scenes with Jamie Foxx, who would go on to win the Best Actor Oscar® for his performance as the legendary singer. Neither of us really knew how much of a smash this movie was going to be, but we certainly had a great time together.

He told me Ray Charles himself had given him a great confidence boost when he was preparing for the role. Taylor arranged for Jamie to meet the legendary performer and they sat at two pianos (Jamie is a classically trained pianist) where they played together for two hours. Eventually, Ray Charles stood up, hugged Foxx, and said, 'He's the one . . . he can do it.'

Jamie Foxx was quite the method actor. Instead of simply shutting his eyes to pretend to be blind, he had them covered with prosthetic eyelids that were glued on so he really couldn't see all day long and wasn't suddenly able to get his sight back when things got a bit difficult.

Jamie would tinker away on a portable keyboard between takes, making up his own songs. You could give him any subject and he'd sing a song about it, straight away, right off the top of his head.

As usual, although I was in New Orleans, a city famous for its extraordinary and exciting food (crocodile gumbo, anyone?), all I wanted was a nice bit of Cheddar. They had a multitude of cheeses there but no Cheddar. Just bright-orange overprocessed stuff packed full of colours and chemicals.

I couldn't believe it when I spotted one that was called *Cheeze Whizz*.

'Well, I'll be edamed!'

Chapter Twenty-One
Paranoid Android

The prototype Marvin suit.

I look like a mini Robocop.

With director Garth Jennings, quite possibly the nicest, most delightful and enthusiastic director in showbiz. He put me through living hell.

Warwick Davis as "Marvin"
The Hitchhiker's Guide to the Galaxy

I may have been smiling here but I was falling to bits thanks to what was one of my most physically and mentally demanding performances.

'Son, one day you're going to grow up to be just like me.'

Apart from cheese festivals, I also attend many charity auctions. I'm not a massive fan of these but people must think I love them because I'm asked to do them all the time. I find it very hard to say no because they're always for such good causes. The problem is that they can sometimes be pretty gruelling affairs – and especially toe-curling for me.

Now and again, film studios will donate some amazing items for me to auction off for local charities, which makes the whole experience a delight. One example, courtesy of Warner Brothers, was the original handwritten letter from Dumbledore to Harry Potter as seen in *Harry Potter and the Philosopher's Stone*. It was inside a wax-sealed envelope with the Hogwarts crest on it and was addressed to 'Harry Potter, The Cupboard Under the Stairs'. It came with a photocopy of the letter so you could see what was inside without having to break the seal. It sold for £800.

I also auctioned a Quidditch World Cup programme, signed by Daniel Radcliffe. Warner Brothers' amazing art department produced these perfect programmes with team listings, form guides and notes about the day's events for every match featured in the films. It went for a healthy £2,000.

Those sorts of things are quite fun to auction off, as collectors are desperate to have them and they are works of art in themselves, so there's no shortage of enthusiasm and excitement.

It isn't always like that, though.

Once, Sam said 'yes' on my behalf. 'OK then,' I grumbled after she broke the news that I'd sacrificed my forthcoming Saturday night. 'What's it in aid of?'

'I've forgotten.'

'What? Are you sure they need *me*?'

'Well, you have to go now, I've said yes. They've promised a good dinner.'

Sam dragged me moaning and groaning all the way. I'd brought a few signed photos of me to auction off; it was all I had at short notice. I hate auctioning 'me' as it looks bad either way – if I sell them for ten pounds each it looks like I'm not worth much, but if I keep pushing for higher bids it seems as if I'm flogging a dead horse and think I'm worth more.

On this occasion the dinner was very nice; Sam decided to have a few wines and was quite merry, while I stayed professionally sober. Eventually, the organiser, Pauline Miley, called me to the stage, while the 200-strong crowd looked on.

The first item, an old portrait of some bigwig, went well enough.

'Sold!' I exclaimed, 'to the gentleman at the back.'

A gruff voice said, 'I'm not a man.'

One of the many hazards auctioneers face.

'Sorry, it's rather dark back there. Um . . . moving on.'

The next item was a weekend for eight in a caravan in Norfolk.

Aw, no, I thought to myself, here we go.

I loved caravans, but even I knew that you'd have to be extraordinarily optimistic to think we were going to shift this, especially as we were already in Norfolk.

The bidding started at £140. I didn't try to oversell it, as I didn't think it was that amazing. Unsurprisingly there were no takers.

I suddenly felt a prodding in my shoulder.

'Tell them it's got air-conditioning,' she said.

I did. No takers.

'And heating.'

I did. Still no takers.

'And a power shower.'

It was then that I realised it was her caravan and that she was determined to find a buyer – and that meant I'd be flogging it all night. The pressure was on.

Suddenly, Sam's hand shot up.

My mouth fell open in surprise. What on earth was she up to? I pretended not to see it. This evening was suddenly about to get very expensive. I'd be damned if I was going to come here, lose my quiet Saturday night in, make small talk with perfect strangers for two hours *and* fork out £140 for a caravan holiday I most certainly neither needed nor wanted.

Pauline elbowed me in the shoulder. 'She's bidding!' she hissed urgently. 'Can't you see? Over there. Take it, take it!'

'Are you sure? Yes, you are. Right, um, yes, well, indeed we do have a bid, ladies and gentlemen. Anyone else? Anyone else for this beautiful van with all mod cons?'

I dragged it on . . . and on . . . and on.

'Going . . . Anybody, an amazing bargain here, it sleeps eight . . . eight people! Isn't that amazing?'

'Going . . . A weekend in Norfolk with your whole family, come on, what's not to love?'

I scanned the audience looking for the slightest twitch. Everybody stayed perfectly rigid, petrified in fact, like a spaceship full of people in suspended animation. They knew what I was up to. None of them dared move.

Pauline, meanwhile, was staring at me as if I were totally insane.

I saw a hand move at the back of the crowd, right on the edge of my vision. With lightning reflexes I slammed the gavel on the table.

BANG!

'Sold for one hundred and fifty pounds! To that gentle– . . . lady at the back.'

I wasn't sure if she meant to bid or not but it was good enough for me.

I grinned with relief at Pauline who was looking at me incredulously. 'See? Good job I held out there.'

Afterwards I asked Sam what she was up to. 'I thought it'd be fun for me and some friends.'

'But we own a caravan in Norfolk already!'

'It doesn't sleep eight, though.'

All arguments about caravans were forgotten the next morning when I had a very interesting call from Jim Henson's Creature Shop. They wanted Willow Management to find an actor who could play a robot in a movie that had just been green-lit.

And this wasn't just any film. This was for the decades-long-awaited film adaptation of the funniest, most philosophically fascinating and all-round amazing book in the universe: *The Hitchhiker's Guide to the Galaxy* by Douglas Adams.

They needed someone to play Marvin the Paranoid Android, arguably the *Guide*'s most famous and cherished character, which is somewhat surprising considering that Marvin was afflicted with severe depression and boredom. He even had his own fan club, the short-lived Marvin Depreciation Society.[57]

In the book, Marvin was built as a prototype of the Sirius Cybernetics Corporation's GPP (Genuine People Personalities) technology. They had the extremely irritating idea that machines should be given 'personalities'. They manufactured doors that took great

---

[57] No one could be bothered in the end.

delight in telling you how much of a pleasure it had been opening and closing for you and robots that were so depressed they would turn Disney chipmunks into lemmings. Marvin's morose nature seemed to stem from the fact that he had a 'brain the size of a planet', which he was seldom able to put to good use.

Peter and I met with Jamie Coutier, the Creature Shop's creative supervisor. He showed us a CGI model of Marvin on his Mac. He was a short white robot with an enormous head and he looked as if Apple may have influenced his design.

Jamie and I talked a bit about the costume; I wondered how we were going to find anyone short enough for the role, as I imagined that the actor's head would have to be below Marvin's to make the costume work. Then there was the question of how an actor would cope with the weight of the enormous head on their shoulders.

Jamie said, 'Don't worry, we'll make all that work. Look, I'll show you how. Do you mind if I take a picture of you, Warwick?'

'Not at all.'

He snapped a pic of me with his mobile phone and uploaded it onto his laptop. He overlaid my image with Marvin's. 'That's interesting. You fit the prototype precisely,' he said.

'Do I?'

He showed me. I had to admit it did seem that way; in fact it was like Cinderella and her glass slipper.

'Warwick, how would you feel about doing it?'

'Blimey, well . . . I don't know.'

As I've already mentioned, I didn't take roles that came via Willow Management, so I hesitated. Jamie, however, was already certain. He was totally convinced that I was the right size and, moreover, the only person with enough experience to take on what would be one of the most physically and mentally demanding roles a short actor had ever attempted.

'Wow . . . er, can I let you know?'

On the drive home I told Peter about my reservations about taking the role. I'd gone to the meeting on behalf of the actors we represented, not for my own personal gain. It didn't seem ethical to me. Then Peter reminded me that it was Jamie who'd come up with the idea of using me. I half wondered if he'd planned it all along.

I called Jamie back to accept.

Two Henson artists, Paul and Nicola, built Marvin. They assembled flexible plastic foam pieces to form a prototype suit for me and when I tried them, without the head, I looked like a mini Stormtrooper.

I was very impressed. 'Gosh, it looks a lot heavier than it actually is,' I said. The final version, made of fibreglass, would be a lot heavier.

I then met Garth Jennings, the director, a very bubbly effervescent man who was incredibly enthusiastic about . . . well . . . well, about life, the universe and everything!

'It's brilliant! Can we make the head bigger?' he asked.

Once Garth had given his approval, construction of the fibreglass suit began. It steadily became heavier and heavier. Eventually, when it was finished, Paul and Nicola did a show and tell session in front of Garth.

'It's great, but the head's still too small.'

Paul and Nicola went back to the drawing board. They were worried about the weight of the head – how much would my neck be able to take? It would get even heavier because several special gizmos had yet to go inside.

They eventually constructed a metal body brace where two rods came up from my shoulders. These would support the fibreglass head, taking the weight away from my neck. The head would then rotate on a gimbal, which I would control by moving my head.

I felt a bit like I was wearing a Formula One racing car, as Paul and Nicola played with the design, trying to shave off a few grams of weight here and there.

The first time I tried the finished costume on it was about twice as heavy as the prototype we'd started out with.

'Just the head to go, Warwick,' Paul said.

'They're not paying me enough for this,' I muttered as the head clicked into place and the world turned dark. With the head, the costume weighed about four stone, not much less than me.

Then the lights came on.

'Wow, now *this* is cool.' In front of me were two TV screens. One was linked to a pin-hole camera in between Marvin's eyes, so I could see in front. The other screen was linked to a remote camera that provided me with a director's-eye-view of the scene so I could see what was going on around me.

I wore a headset and microphone so I could communicate with my support crew. When we started rolling, my voice was broadcast through speakers placed around the set so the other actors could hear my dialogue.

Above me, a small fan whirred away, in an effort to cool the giant cranium that was nonetheless heating up pretty quickly.

It felt like I was inside the Millennium Dome, there was this enormous space above me.

'Hey,' I said, testing the microphone, 'I could tape my lines to the inside of Marvin's head!'

Marvin looked amazing. He was painted the exact same white that BMW use on their snazziest models.

'Just be careful, Warwick,' Paul told me. 'Marvin scratches very easily and if you fall over he'll crack. We've got one set of spare body parts but that's all, he's just too expensive.'

Once again, I was under tremendous pressure not to let an

enormous team down during filming. If I fell, it didn't bear thinking about. Marvin's fibreglass body (which cost a lot more than a brand-new BMW) would shatter into a hundred pieces – not to mention what might happen to me.

While the suit was fairly easy to get into, I found it much harder to get into Marvin's character. I'd never experienced depression and extended boredom. I'd been through my fair share of tragedies and had my heart broken but that wasn't Marvin. Marvin was bored and depressed by the futility of his own existence and he didn't mind letting everyone else know about it.

Besides, once I was in the costume all my strength and concentration was taken up by moving this massive, incredibly heavy costume – as well as keeping it upright. I wasn't able to act and move at the same time, it was simply impossible.

I had a chat about this with Garth.

'Why don't you speak to Peter Elliott?' he suggested. 'He's an expert at that sort of thing and we've hired him as the Vogon co-ordinator. I'm sure he'd be able to help.'

Peter was a movement director; we'd met briefly when I was filming *Jedi*. He'd been on a nearby stage in the same studio, playing the silverback gorilla in *Greystoke: The Legend of Tarzan, Lord of the Apes*.

Peter is the world's primary primate performer. You'd never know that any gorilla he's played wasn't real and he's helped hundreds of actors behave un-humanly – as animals, aliens and androids.

The actors who played the Vogons (the bureaucratic aliens that demolished the Earth to make way for a hyperspace bypass) were having a very hard time of it. They looked like a cross between a giant slug and a turtle without its shell. The costumes were extraordinarily huge, wobbly and had poor visibility. I watched as the actors rebounded off each other, teetered and then tripped, arms a-flailing as they tried to find something to stop their plunge to earth.

I sighed nostalgically. 'Reminds me of my days as an Ewok,' I told Peter.

After the rehearsal was over, I explained my problem.

Peter nodded enthusiastically. 'You've been approaching it from entirely the wrong angle,' he said. 'You're trying to work as a puppeteer rather than treat this as a proper acting job. Get into character first, then worry about the puppeteer part, that will come naturally if you're thinking like Marvin.'

I liked Peter straight away. He was straight-talking, short (for a tall person) and packed full of positive energy. He then demonstrated how it was possible to drain all that positive energy when we went to his studio and got into character.

'Think like Marvin,' he said. 'Come on, what would he say if he were here now?'

I stared at a vacuum cleaner. 'Such a primitive device,' I said morosely.

'That's it!' Peter said. 'Come on, keep going.'

Maintaining my glum, suicidal tone, I continued. 'Do you come here often?' Obviously, the vacuum cleaner failed to respond. 'OK, be like that then. See if I care. Brain the size of a planet and they've got me talking to the likes of you.'

'Keep going!'

'And you,' I said, dragging myself towards Peter. 'You're so happy it makes me sick. You could fit my capacity for happiness into a matchbox without removing the matches first. Do you want me to fall apart now, or should I just sit here and rust away?'

'Hold that thought,' Peter said. 'Not another word until you've got the costume on.'

Once I was in costume, Peter recorded the scene. I mooched around the studio saying things like: 'Life. Don't talk to me about life. Just when you think it can't possibly get any worse it suddenly does.'

Peter started interacting, quoting lines at me. 'Haven't you got any ideas as to how we get out of this?'

'I have a million ideas. They all point to certain death.'

When we watched the playback, Peter said, 'Now we can see what you're thinking.'

He was dead right. The walk I'd given Marvin was now so different. I didn't even think about technique. Sure, it was still incredibly tough to move in there, but if anything that only helped me to bring out Marvin's character. Every movement was an effort and so that came out in his character.

Peter also taught me how the robot would turn its head depending on what it was saying and how other people were responding, something he called 'the continuity of movement'.

He was absolutely brilliant, he had taught me so much in no time at all and he helped me bring a lot more to my performance than I would have done otherwise.

The *Heart of Gold* spaceship, where a great deal of the action takes place, was constructed on the George Lucas Stage at Elstree Studios. The *Heart of Gold* was supposed to be the most amazing spaceship ever constructed and the builders had done an exquisite job. The set was a fully realised, three-dimensional space with a bathroom, kitchen, bedrooms, connecting corridors, cargo hold and a central crew area.

The only catch was that lighting it took 10,000 light bulbs. Within seconds, despite the fan, I felt like I was in one of those little machines that once appeared on *Dragon's Den*, you know, the one that supposedly boils an egg perfectly without water.

They'd leave switching the lights on until the last possible moment because it would get extremely hot in no time at all. The terrible thing was that the motor that powered the fan in Marvin's head was too loud so it had to be switched off whenever we were about to start a scene. I'd hear it whirr to a halt with no little dread.

At the end of a day trying to walk around in costume I'd go home in agony. Every joint, muscle and nerve-ending in my body would scream at me not to get up in the morning. Each day was harder than the last. And then things got truly unbearable.

We went to shoot on location in Wales – in the QUARRY OF DOOM. I found myself in the same nightmarish place that Tom Baker and all the other Doctor Whos know only too well.

When we arrived it appeared the Quarry of Doom was actually stuck in a parallel universe. While the rest of the UK basked in what was turning out to be a pleasant summer, the clouds that hung permanently over the quarry dropped freezing sleet upon us every single day. They clearly belonged in January, not July.

'Aha!' I hear you say. 'Surely now your wonderful superheated suit would have come into its own?'

Oh, you poor naive fools. Have you learned nothing?

With the cold came ferocious winds, which threatened to blow me over, thanks to my terrifically un-aerodynamic, enormously round head (thank you very much, Sirius Cybernetics Corporation!).

On top of this, there were loads of gaps in the costume, at Marvin's limb joints (all the black bits were just Neoprene), so the wind just whistled its way straight in, turning Marvin into an icebox. And inside, all I was dressed in was a thin Lycra bodysuit.

In between takes everyone else was able to dive into their trailers to hide from the cold weather, but I had to stay put and freeze. This was what happened to Marvin in the film; he kept getting left behind for millions of years while everyone else had lots of jolly time-travelling adventures.

The first time I was left standing there, shivering, the rain pattering on my white head, I heard an ominous click, followed by a whirr. The fan had started up to 'cool me down'.

'Oh, how thoughtful.'

As a chill ran down my spine I was suddenly struck by how familiar this all felt. 'Ah, yes, that's it,' I said to myself, 'it's just like our old Monza caravan.'

I was finding it easier and easier to get into Marvin's character.

Paul and Nicola, bless them, stayed out there with me and threw their coats over me in an effort to keep some of the wind off.

'Yeah, cheers, thanks for that.'

It didn't help.

To add insult to injury, everyone else was in comfy clothes. Martin Freeman (Arthur Dent) even got to wear a dressing gown for most of the movie. And thanks to my inaccessible costume, I didn't really get to 'see' and hang out with my fellow actors. But I liked Martin and I also liked Sam Rockwell (Zaphod Beeblebrox) who was about as mad as a hundred frogs in a pond spiked with LSD. He had a habit of drumming on my head between takes, which would create a donging echo louder than Big Ben.

Life? Don't talk to me about life.

Throughout the shoot I cursed, raged and fumed, red-faced inside my overheated dome. I wanted to tell Garth that he was killing me, that he was an insane megalomaniac who took delight in torturing his actors, that he should be banned from directing another movie ever again.

But then I'd see Garth lolloping towards me like a lanky two-legged Bambi to ask how I was doing. He was so childishly enthusiastic in such a sweet and charming way that all my Marvin tendencies evaporated. I just couldn't bring myself to disappoint him. Garth is quite possibly the most delightful man on the planet, who should be allowed to direct as many movies as he could possibly wish.

'No, everything's great,' I'd tell him.

'Not too hot?'

'Nope.'

'Cold?'

'Nope, I'm fine.'

'Fantastic! I thought you looked quite uncomfortable. Just another six or seven takes and we should have it.'

'Great!'

And he'd run back to his wonderfully warm trailer and slam the door.

'Git!'

My only cinematic tantrum to date remains the wobbly I threw at Ron Howard when I faced certain death from drowning during *Willow*. That's how far you have to push me. However, if they were to announce a sequel to *Hitchhiker's* (the books are the galaxy's first six-part trilogy) and they wanted to bring Marvin back in that same costume I would have to think about it *very* seriously. With all my other characters (apart from Petchet in *Prince Valiant*), I'd jump at the chance to leap into their costumes again, but Marvin, well . . .

I was thrilled with the end result in that people who saw the film didn't realise that Marvin was actually someone in a suit. I took this as a compliment; he is supposed to be a robot, after all.

At the time I thought I would do the voice as well but Garth managed to get Alan Rickman. Alan called me up and checked that I was OK with him doing it. Of course, I would have preferred to do it but, well, Alan Rickman is *Alan Rickman* – and he has that incredible voice that defines the word 'sardonic'.

As it was, I was flattered that he had asked for my blessing. Marvin really was a huge team effort; so many people had brought him to life. But we did get something wrong, and fans of the film may be interested to re-watch it with this little fact in mind.

As they were using Alan Rickman to re-record my dialogue, someone decided they would give Marvin a few more lines. This would have been fine except for one thing: the new dialogue didn't match Marvin's body language.

When I saw the film for the first time I cringed whenever Marvin spoke a new line, as it failed to match the movement. As far as I was concerned, much of Marvin's wonderful character had been lost. This may just be because I was so close to the part but I did observe that the lines that still matched Marvin's movements were also the ones that got the biggest laughs from the audience.

It's easy to say this with hindsight, but it would have been better to have the actor on set reading the lines live, as the performance was being recorded. This technique was used on *Harry Potter* where Toby Jones was on set to record the voice of Dobby, and, however subtly, I think you can see and hear the difference.

I mainly kept going as Marvin for Peter's sake. He'd taught me so much and I really wanted to show him it had worked. So I was delighted when I got the chance to work with him again when I was offered the part of a baby gorilla in a movie called *Vanilla Gorilla*, with former James Bond Pierce Brosnan pencilled in to take the lead role.

The plot of the movie went thus: 'A New York girl befriends Gogo, the world's only living albino gorilla. Through sign language they communicate and bond, and their ensuing trans-African quest to return Gogo to the wild puts ruthless poachers, determined CNN reporters, and one very concerned parent on their tail.'

I spent an amazing two weeks with Peter, who was going to play the albino gorilla, learning how to behave like a primate. Peter had played gorillas in dozens of movies, including *Gorillas in the*

Mist, and it was a real treat to see a true artist at work. It was really tough, but Peter was so enthusiastic that I found myself pushing myself harder and harder to get the performance that he wanted. Peter transformed his studio into a zoo and had placed tyres, tree branches and fruit all over the place.

'Gorillas don't think about what they're going to do, they just act on their impulses,' Peter told me, handing me a pair of arm extensions. Gorillas have much longer arms than humans and we needed to get used to using them.

It was incredibly difficult trying to maintain a gorilla's stream of consciousness while waving a pair of metal arm extensions, but eventually I did it without thinking and by the time I left the studio I'd almost forgotten I was a person. It was a wonder I didn't swing my way across Hampstead Heath to the train station.

There's a good reason why you haven't heard of *Vanilla Gorilla*. Although the film was green-lit, all the bits of paper that had to be pushed about between agents, producers, actors and financiers failed to get signed and the project died. This was a real shame because I was keen to act alongside Pierce, but such is life.

It was a far from wasted experience however. Peter had taught me so much and just how much was brought home to me not very long afterwards.

Chapter Twenty-Two

A Little Extra

FOLLOWING two substandard episodes, this series of Extras didn't so much hit its stride on Thursday as sprint down the road marked "comedy classic".

In an episode awash with moments to rank up there with Del Boy falling over in the pub, we had Daniel "Harry Potter" Radcliffe saying: "I've done it with a girl, intercoursewise."

There was also a priceless Richard and Judy appearance by Stephen Merchant as Andy's manager, asking for a line-up of children to see if it's possible to spot the one with Down's Syndrome from the back.

But, best of all, the following exchange between Andy and Maggie, after observing small actor Warwick Davis with his large girlfriend.

Andy: "Makes me sick. Those showbiz dwarfs who use their fame to get women out of their league."

Maggie: "Who, Warwick?"

Andy: "No. Paul Daniels."

Appearing on *Extras* proved to be a life-changing experience.

With Ricky Gervais and Stephen Merchant, hamming it up as Wayne Rooney before the big England v Portugal World Cup match in 2006. *Courtesy of the BBC.*

My phone rang. 'I've had Saatchi and Saatchi on the phone,' my agent said, 'they've asked if you'll do an ad for them.'

'Head and Shoulders, is it?'

'Yes, that's right, how did you know?'

'We've already sent about half a dozen actors from Willow Management and they've all been rejected.'

'Will you do it?'

'Sure, I'll give it a try.'

When I tried the costume on I wondered how on earth nobody else had managed to get this job. I was supposed to play a character called Hair, and if you've ever seen *The Addams Family* and recall Cousin Itt, then you will know exactly what my character looked like. Essentially, I was covered in an umbrella of hair that stretched all the way down to my feet.

I put it on, imagined myself as Hair, walked up and down and got the part. I didn't understand. Why did it have to be me? Why didn't they give the job to one of the other actors we'd sent from Willow Management?

The advert was a love story between a man and his hair, with the strapline: 'Don't lose your hair'. We filmed in West Yorkshire, at Keighley train station, a beautiful part of the world. Filming started at 3 a.m. in temperatures of minus four.

As I stood on the platform in a skin-tight leotard underneath the hair suit, I had one of those moments where I looked down on myself from above and asked, 'Why am I doing this?'

And as I stood there in the dawn light, shivering, waiting for my cue, I worked through the answer (it took my mind off the cold).

I never consider myself too good for any role and firmly believe that my last job really could be just that – my last. So I have to be up for anything and whatever part I'm playing, no matter how silly, I give it my all.

Sometimes it would be easy to say 'No' when a physically and mentally challenging role like Marvin comes along. But if I feel excited about it, I'll go for it. A lot of people might think that's a bit odd, but that's the kind of person I am. As a result, I think I've played one of the widest ranges of characters in British acting history.

It was then I realised why I got the Hair job. It's because I can bring this thing to life. Somehow, I'm able to convey emotion from beneath all that hair. I could make it look sad, happy, in love, broken-hearted. Much of that skill had come from all my creature acting, but I also had to thank Peter for making me realise how your body can say so much – even when you can't even see it properly.

'I'm good at this,' I thought to myself as I stood by the train, 'this is what I do – this is who I am.' I thought about all I'd done, from Wicket to the Leprechaun, from Flitwick to Willow, and I felt a rising tide of excitement; there was still so much I hoped to pack into my life.

It was quite a revelatory moment and, as if right on cue, the train suddenly hissed warm steam, which rose up beneath my dome of hair. Lovely. But as soon as the train left, the steam condensed and started to freeze. As soon as the next break came I staggered over to the only warm place on the station, the waiting room.

Inside were four extras dressed as train guards, all aged about seventy, all talking about their prostate troubles. I nodded 'Hello', and lay down on a bench for a nap. I sat up when the food trolley appeared. Normally I'd never eat a hot dog, but when you're on a film set at 3 a.m. you sometimes do strange and irrational things to pass the time.

As I was about to take a bite out of the end of the sausage, one of the men turned to his companion and said, 'Fred, have you ever had that little camera stuck up the end of your old man?'

Yep, this is the life, right enough.

I was in my kitchen when the phone rang. It would be another in an already long line of life-changing calls.

'Hiya,' a voice said, 'it's Ricky Gervais.'

Now, most actors upon hearing those four words would have said something along the lines of: 'Hello, Mr Gervais, I'm a big fan of your work,' while praying the phone call wasn't a dream.

I, on the other hand, responded with an extremely sceptical-sounding: 'Oh yeah?'

I had a friend, Paul Zerdin, who was pretty good at impressions and who liked to wind me up by pretending to be Ron Howard saying he wanted me to star in *Willow II* or the Director of BBC Drama telling me they wanted me to be the new Doctor Who, so I had good reason to be cautious. I mean, Ricky Gervais calling up out of the blue? How ridiculous was that?

This was followed by a very distinctive laugh, a unique giggly screech that could only come from one person.

Oh no!

'It is you, isn't it?'

'It is. You are Warwick Davis, aren't you?'

'Err . . . Yes.'

'I'm making a show called *Extras* with Stephen Merchant and we're planning the series at the moment. There's one episode which we'd like you to be in.'

'Great!' This was when *The Office* – a show I adored – was at its height.

'Well, hang on a moment,' he said. 'Before you say yes, I'm calling to check whether you'd be OK with what we're thinking. Essentially, the episode finishes with me kicking you in the face.'

I didn't hesitate. 'Ricky,' I said, 'it would be an honour to be kicked in the face by you.'

They said they'd be in touch and that was all I heard for a few months, until the BBC announced they'd finished filming the series. I was gutted but then Ricky called back to say they were making a second series. 'Do you still want to be in it?' By then the show was a huge hit and famous actors were queuing up for the chance to be on it.

I met Ricky and Stephen for a quick read-through in London before we shot the episode at Pinewood. They were terrific to work with, really down-to-earth. At the time I was producing a *Star Wars* show for Disney World and I asked if Ricky and Stephen would mind contributing a few questions as part of a celebrity-led quiz. They got into it straight away and quickly improvised a whole overly nerdy *Star Wars* routine while reading out the questions.

Ricky may have been a brilliant improviser but when he was shooting *Extras* his approach was painstaking. Ricky and Stephen were tireless; they couldn't move on unless they were completely satisfied that the scene was as funny as it possibly could be and they had tried every single thing they could think of. At the same time, they worked at high speed and would shoot scenes faster than anyone else I'd worked with before.

Filming took place between 8 a.m. and 4 p.m. 'I'm always funniest between these hours,' Ricky told me. It was a smart move and was typical of their ability to rewrite the rule book and do things their way. Like most actors, I was used to working on films and programmes that started shooting before dawn and didn't wrap up until 9 p.m., and I'd seen many actors and crew become so tired that they started to lose morale.

On *Extras*, everyone was full of energy and intensely focused. We'd come back from lunch knowing we just had a couple of hours to go. Ricky would get us all fired up and would say, 'Right! Let's rattle through this and go home!' and we'd always manage. That way we all left Pinewood Studios at a reasonable hour and saw our families, so morale remained high throughout the shoot.

In the episode I was in, Andy Millman (Ricky) was appearing in a new fantasy film starring Daniel Radcliffe. Andy accidentally offends the mother of a Down's syndrome teenager while eating in a restaurant, leading to a typically overwrought reaction from the British press, who take the comments out of context.

Andy manages to deal with this but then gets into a fight with me over remarks he privately made to his best friend Maggie (Ashley Jensen) – which she later repeats to my fiancée. I then physically attack Andy who accidentally knocks me unconscious, although everyone else thinks he does so deliberately.

In the run-up to this last scene, I'd been listening to Ricky's podcasts with Stephen and Karl 'head-like-an-effing-orange' Pilkington on the radio station XFM and had been tickled by the fact that Stephen had poked fun at Ricky's tubbiness.

My verbal attack on Ricky as I started to punch him was ad-libbed: 'You git,' and then, scrabbling to add something else, 'You fat git!' Afterwards Ricky looked at me, grinning. It was pretty funny, I guess, especially coming from me, with my rather more obvious physical dissimilarity.

'Sorry, Ricky, I don't know why I said that.'

He took it in his stride.

We did this scene over and over again. I was supposed to punch Ricky in the stomach and as he was wearing padding (which added to his tubbiness) I could hit him as hard as I liked. During one take I really let fly and really caught him a beauty. He yelled at me to stop. He'd forgotten to put on the padding and I'd caught him perfectly in the solar plexus.

I didn't have any padding in the scene where Ricky knocked me unconscious by accidentally kneeing me in the face. Once his knee had 'connected' with my chin, I was supposed to throw myself backwards to the floor. Thanks to Laurel and Hardy and almost three decades of playing characters who fell over a lot (often accidentally), I was able to do this pretty well. Nonetheless, we practised over and over again with a stunt co-ordinator. Ricky tried all sorts of lines after I'd fallen to the floor until he finally settled on the one he wanted.

Once the cameras started to roll, adrenaline took over and I said I was happy to bounce off the floor for as many takes as it took. Twenty-three takes later, we were done.

The next morning, I opened my eyes.

'OOOAAARGH!'

I was in excruciating pain.

'Oh my God, I am *never* going to do that again.'

My body was covered in bruises, my muscles were twisted and my joints were swollen. It took me an hour to get to the edge of the bed. Now I understood why they say that comedy is all about pain.

While we were filming *Extras*, the England football squad were about to play Portugal in the World Cup. Ricky, Steve and I made an appearance on BBC1 just before the match. Ricky appeared as himself, pretending he was in Germany, and introduced Steve, who was wearing the England kit, as Peter Crouch (at six-foot-seven, Peter and Steve are the same height). I was waiting off camera, ready for Ricky to introduce me – as Wayne Rooney.

Ricky then says that we're not the best choice for playing up front because of the height difference. Steve and I explain that we've devised a new system.

When Ricky kicks over the ball, Steve lifts me up so I'm able to head it into the back of the net. Steve imitates Peter Crouch's signature robotic dance and asks me for a high five. I can't reach so get into a bit of a strop and throw my boots at him.

When the cameras cut back to the studio, Gary Lineker was sitting with former Arsenal and England star Ian Wright. Ian was laughing uncontrollably and blurted out, 'I don't know what it is about little people like that, I just love 'em man, I love 'em.'

Steve later complained: 'Out of all the stuff I've ever done, *The Office*, *Extras*, the radio shows, my mum thinks that *this* is my best work – a dodgy impression of Peter Crouch.'

I was chuffed to bits when I saw the finished version of *Extras*. I was delighted with my performance and that we had highlighted some of the unnecessarily awkward interactions between little and normal-sized people. Although Darren Lamb's reaction 'Oh. Midget!' was grossly exaggerated and played brilliantly by Steve, it contained echoes of what I sometimes encounter in my everyday life.

And then a little seed, one that had been planted some time ago, suddenly took root.

I'd had a meeting with a documentary maker several months before. He'd wanted to do a Louis Theroux style documentary where he and a cameraman would live with me and my family and film our day-to-day lives. I liked the guy and said it was intriguing but that I couldn't do it. Whenever we go out as a family, our size always becomes a significant part of our day, whether we go to the shops, a museum, a restaurant and so on. Our home is the one place where we can really be ourselves and not worry about anything else.[58] That space and privacy are just too precious for me to give up.

Besides, we live in an ordinary house in a small village near Peterborough, it's very nice but nothing is gold-plated. I certainly don't have a driver or custom-made designer-label clothing – unless you count Next Kids or Mothercare. I put out my own rubbish and take my kids to school; it's incredibly ordinary and if I had agreed to a TV documentary it would have been yawn-inducing.

'But hang on,' I thought, 'wouldn't it be amazing to make a mockumentary that I could fully control? Wouldn't it be fun to play with people's misconceptions of me as a little person and actor?' I started to get excited. I could really go overboard and give my character an enormous ego, a huge car with a chauffeur, an insufferable personality . . . I'd get as far away from my own reality as I could.

This idea really took hold. I started working it out, taking scenes from my everyday life and putting a very conceited, obnoxious and bigheaded version of my own character into them. Inspired by shows such as *Curb Your Enthusiasm* and *Alan Partridge*, I created a monster, someone who thought he was more famous than he actually was, who pushed his terrible ideas for films down people's throats and who tried to steal the limelight whenever he could. I was surprised to find myself laughing uncontrollably as I wrote. I showed the scenes to a few friends and got some genuinely good feedback.

---

[58] No, we don't live in a little house. I've had bits of the kitchen customised but that's all!

I decided to do a little bit of filming, and found a gifted TV producer, Jago Lee, who was prepared to help me out. Once I'd edited a few scenes and put them on a DVD, I decided that I'd send a copy to Mr Gervais to get some feedback, as it was in his area of expertise and was in part inspired by *Extras* and *The Office*. If Ricky told me I was on the right track then that would give me all the encouragement I needed to keep going.

I sent him a text and he replied telling me to send it for the attention of Stephen at their office. I popped it in the post in August and then forgot about it.

Life went on, and work kept me really busy. After *Extras*, I began panto season in Manchester. While there I was asked to audition for the part of Nikabrik in *The Chronicles of Narnia: Prince Caspian*.

'They've seen you in *Leprechaun*,' my agent told me.

'Oh dear,' I thought, 'that doesn't bode well.' As it turned out, my *Leprechaun* experience proved to be instrumental in my getting the part, as it showed I could act my socks off while covered in prosthetics.

In *Prince Caspian*, my character had a long beard (it was incredibly itchy and caught on everything – swords, tree branches, other actors, etc.), a false nose and full-face gelatine make-up, which was used to age me. This was pretty interesting, if slightly spooky as I saw myself steadily transformed into how I'd look in about forty years' time.

Oscar-winning Howard Berger designed the make-up. I used to think of him as the sensible version of Gabe, my crazed *Leprechaun* make-up artist – until early one morning when I entered the make up trailer to find Howard and make-up assistant Sarah Rubano dancing like nutters to the 'Ewok Celebration' song from the soundtrack to *Return to the Jedi*. He had also declared his love for Ewoks by scrawling bizarre messages to that effect on the mirror in black eyeliner. As the Roman philosopher, Seneca once said: 'There is no great genius without a touch of madness'. I rest my case.

Although *Prince Caspian* was part of the Narnia film franchise, I wouldn't be around for long. Poor Nikabrik is stabbed in the back and killed by Trumpkin, his supposed friend (played by Peter Dinklage). Still, Nikabrik was a great character and I always relished the chance to die on screen.

As it turned out, I overdid it slightly and died like a shot cowboy in an old western. As I was 'stabbed' in the back I opened my eyes wide in horror before falling to my knees, pausing and then falling forward with a heavy thud. It was edited for length in the final cut.

This multimillion-dollar production was quite different from the BBC version I'd acted in years before – everything was so much bigger. Aslan's stone table (Aslan is the Great Lion, the central character in Narnia) had been about the size of the average dining table in the BBC production. In the Hollywood version it was as big as a house.

A large part of filming took place in Prague. I stayed in a fabulous apartment in town and the studio was nearby. We then moved out into the Czech countryside, to the former industrial town of Ústi, to film some of the battle scenes. I was really looking forward to this until I discovered that I was going to need an injection.

'An injection? What on earth for?' I asked when I found out. We were in Europe after all. As I've already mentioned, I never travel anywhere that required injections if I can help it. It's quite ironic really; I live in mortal fear of all things small and poisonous – insects, snakes and lizards – you name it, I'm afraid of it.

It turned out that the area was full of ticks that could give you Lyme disease – also known as tick-borne meningoencephalitis, a potentially fatal illness (1 per cent of cases result in death with 10 to 20 per cent of cases suffering permanent neurological damage).

As it turned out I wasn't on set when the nurse turned up to inoculate everybody. By the time I found out and tracked her down it was too late – the immunity took several days to kick in.

So I travelled to Oostie without being inoculated. 'Just keep off the grass,' the nurse told me, 'that's where they live. Avoid fields and bushes and you'll be fine.'

The scene we were filming involved us returning from battle, wounded and exhausted, to Aslan's How (a full-scale set of which had actually been constructed). I made sure I stuck to the dirt and stone path leading to the How, which was surrounded by fields.

Then, to my horror, director Andrew Adamson decided he needed us all to take a step back onto the grass so he could get a nice shot of us approaching from a distance.

'Oh no,' I thought. As far as I was concerned those fields were shark-infested waters. I tucked my trousers into my socks and waited until the last possible minute before stepping gingerly onto the grass on tiptoe. My eyes roamed the fields looking for any sign of advancing ticks but I saw nothing.

After a successful day's filming I returned to the hotel room and got in the shower. I was soaping away when my hand ran over a lump on my bottom. After climbing on a chair and twisting around in front of a mirror I saw with horror that a massive black tick had clamped itself firmly to my posterior.

'Aaaaaaaaaaaargh!'

I paced up and down the room. 'What do I do? What do I do?' After making a few frantic phone calls I was put through to the unit nurse.

She had an extraordinarily thick Eastern European accent.

'Votever you do, do not touch it! I'll be right over.'

Her urgent tone both impressed and terrified me. She took forever to arrive and I paced up and down the room, wearing out the carpet (I could hardly sit down, after all).

Finally, the nurse arrived and I immediately bared my bum at her without so much as a 'How do you do?'

'Oooooh,' she said, obviously impressed, 'zat's a big vone.'

'Thank you,' I replied, 'but what about the tick?'

She extracted a pair of tweezers from her bag.

'Ve must not let ze head stay inzide your behind.'

She crouched over me and I could feel the tugging as the tick resisted the pull of the tweezers. I felt terribly queasy.

Suddenly there was a soft 'pop'.

'Got it!' she exclaimed triumphantly.

She was right. It *was* massive. I even took a photo of it. I was given a course of antibiotics and had to wait for a worrying few weeks to be certain I didn't have any symptoms of Lyme disease.

From that day forth I was known on set as Tickabrik.

In December I was suddenly struck down with a horrendous flu. I was also waiting to hear whether I'd got the part in the sixth *Harry Potter* film, so I was in a lousy mood. Mindful of this, I still kept one feverish eye on my iPhone.

I awoke from an agitated sleep and staggered, iPhone in hand, to the toilet. As I sat down I saw I had a voicemail from an unknown number.

Could that be the studio? I fumbled with the screen and pressed play.

'Hi, it's Ricky Gervais here. With me Stephen Merchant.'

I'd just been listening to one of their podcasts, so I assumed I'd accidentally pressed play on the iPod. Then I thought I was hallucinating.

'Warwick, we've watched your thing, and we loved it. I loved the conceit, I thought it was tremendous. There were proper laugh-out-loud moments. What are you doing with it? Give me a call. Anything you want to add, Stephen?'

'Yes, thanks Ricky, we thought it was great, loved it. We were only sorry it was so short . . . Oops, no offence.'

Both of them started giggling.

I couldn't believe it. Here were comedy heroes of mine telling me I'd made them laugh.

Suddenly, thanks to Ricky, a project that had been not much more than a pipe dream was at the top of everyone's to-do list. I couldn't help but grin – one of the greatest accolades of my career had come while I was sitting on the toilet.

'I always felt we'd underused you in *Extras*,' Ricky told me when I called him back. 'Look,' he continued, 'I want to executive produce this, OK?'

A couple of weeks later I was standing at reception in BBC Television Centre with Ricky Gervais and Stephen Merchant (we really stood out from the crowd), waiting to see Mark Freeland, Head of Comedy. I had another one of those out of body experiences. I looked down on myself and asked, 'How on earth did this happen?'

We were shown into Mark's office. All four of us use Apple Macs and we all had the usual chat about how marvellous these machines are as I pulled my MacBook Pro out of my bag.

Of course, just at that moment, the DVD refused to play. I ejected it and reinserted it a couple of times. Nothing. I restarted the thing, all the while apologising, bright red and sweating profusely.

Why me? Why at this moment in my life? I felt as if I were making them all look like idiots for singing the praises of Apple and now here I was, demonstrating the exact opposite. Finally, just as I was about to surrender once and for all, it started playing.

I'd been so traumatised by the whole event that I hardly noticed that the three of them had started laughing.

Surely, I thought, they're just being nice? Laughing out of politeness. Surely it's not that funny?

Then Ricky turned to Mark and said, 'This is BAFTA-winning stuff.'

Holy cow.

We left the office with a development commission, which meant we could develop the script into a full episode and do some casting. My head span. I hardly knew what to say or what to do next. Suddenly I was on the verge of having my very own TV series.

After a comedy master-class from Ricky and Stephen, I began to refine the idea. The show (called *Life's Too Short*) stars me playing a different version of myself – who has just divorced his average-sized wife. Essentially, it's about me struggling to rebuild my life and career as well as dealing with the day-to-day issues that being short throws up.

To say this was a subject close to my heart would be a massive understatement. This, to me, was really powerful comedy, the best kind there is as far as I'm concerned.

Right now, Ricky, Stephen and I are writing a pilot episode which they will direct, I hope it will be commissioned as a series by the BBC.

It's not as if I'm short of material.

'Does my nose look big in this?'

The Great Tick of Usti. It was bigger than it looks in this photo.

Chapter Twenty-Three
My Wonderful World

My nifty 'scissor' work!

Celebrity Scissorhands: Despite all the training, I still managed to shave one of my own eyebrows off in a bizarre accident.

Harrison gives a thumbs-up. He obviously didn't have his hair cut by Steve Strange.

Annabelle, aka 'Tweeny Todd'.

I was back in Peterborough, fresh from the commissioning meeting at the BBC and I was full of the joys of spring. Life couldn't be better.

I'd just popped into a newsagent for a pint of milk and a paper and was on my way back to the car, whistling as I walked. I was approaching a white van when a bag half-full of chips came flying out of the passenger window and landed at my feet.

I've got a big 'thing' about littering. If I could, I'd make it a custodial offence. And this litterer would receive the maximum penalty. As it was I was powerless. I fumed, insensible at this outrage. This was intolerable!

With no thought for the consequences, I scooped up the chip-wrapper and lobbed it back towards the van. As soon as it had left my hand I knew that it was about the best possible throw I could have made – but I was already regretting it, like lobbing a rock-hard snowball across a crowded playground straight towards a distant target which then turns out to be the school bully, who (obviously) gets it full on the nose.

As it approached the van the chip packet opened up and I saw a flash of ketchup just as a round, fat head appeared at the window. The chips hit him on the nose and the packet exploded inside the van, depositing sauce-covered chips all over the seats.

A string of four-letter words erupted from the now furious fathead. He looked left, then right.

Then down.

'There's a bin just there! Use it!' I said firmly.

Fathead looked at me, outrage giving way to confusion. What were the rules about beating up little people? Could he get away with it?

I took off down the road, praying that he wasn't a psychopath, before diving gratefully into the safety of my car and leaving him to wipe the sauce off his face.

This may seem strange, but I've come pretty close to having a punch-up on more than one occasion. Size need not be a barrier to anything, and that includes violence.

Not long after the chip bag incident, I was at a Keane concert at the Manchester Arena. My taste in music is either very mainstream (Keane) or very weird (John Hopkins). I love anything out of the ordinary and a bit bizarre, especially if it doesn't sound like music at all. Keane was a band that Sam, Annabelle, Harrison and I enjoyed together and so I'd booked seats. Problem was, the bloke sat in front of us decided to stand for the entire show.

I wouldn't have minded, but there was a standing area at the front for those who wanted to dance and run around. We'd been to see Coldplay at the O2 and everything there had been great, people had pretty much stayed sitting and we'd been able to see no problem.

The guy in front of us, however, was determined to dance and 'sing' along (I use that term extremely loosely) to every tune, and to drink himself senseless. Now, this would be all well and good in a field at Glastonbury or down at the front in the standing area, but not here. As he danced and drank during Keane's set I was presented with alternate views of his head and bottom.

'Right, that's it,' I said, 'I give up. Let's go.'

Sam agreed. But, as we were about to leave, I couldn't help myself. I leaned over and tapped Dancing Boy on the shoulder. He turned and looked for the source of the tapping.

'Down here!'

He looked down, clearly perplexed.

'Next time,' I told him, 'book your ticket for the standing area, then we'll be able to see the show. I might as well have sat at home looking at a picture of your arse while listening to my Keane album.'

His mouth fell open in disbelief. I could see I was obviously not going to get a response, so I shrugged and left.

I felt him make a grab for my shoulder as I turned away but decided to ignore him.

I caught up with Sam and the kids in the deserted foyer when someone shouted 'Oi!'

I turned and was surprised to see that Dancing Boy had chased after us. I told him again that we couldn't see, and that he'd ruined it for us.

He then surprised me by getting down on his knees. A wave of alcohol-tainted breath washed over me.

'Your sort,' he said, prodding me drunkenly in the shoulder with his finger, 'shouldn't come to the conshert.'

Now it was my turn to display an open mouth of disbelief. Was he picking a fight with me?

'Everything all right here?' a steward said, walking rapidly towards us.

I was about to say everything was fine and we were off when the drunk bloke said, 'Thish man ashaulted me.'

I looked at the steward, who was already trying not to grin.

'Come on,' I said, 'what do you think really happened?'

The steward let us go and helped the gentleman back to his sheat.

Fortunately, incidents like this are few and far between. I have a wonderful life. I've been so lucky. I actually believe I have a *height advantage* over everyone else. Being short has helped me achieve so much and has brought me much joy.

Many people can't help but trip over their tongues when they meet me – the words 'big' and 'little' are two of the most common words in the English language and we have, according to my dictionary, over seventy words that also mean big and little. Lots of people start talking to me because they kind of know that I'm an actor. They know they've seen me somewhere which, more often than not, leads them to ask *the* question:

'Weren't you in *Time Bandits?*'[59]

For the most part people are wonderful and we usually have a great chat. I was in a London café just after visiting the publisher of this book when a man in a very smart business suit came up to have a chat about the Stilton Cheese Rolling Championship and we whiled away a very pleasant few minutes sharing cheese-related anecdotes over a Cheddar toastie.

I think today people are far more aware of little people, thanks in part to the work of organisations like the Little People of America (LPA)[60] as well as television and film, not to mention the Internet, so usually it's not too much of a shock for people when they see me rolling down the street on my Razor (this makes it easier for me to keep up with tall people and to get from A to B once I've parked my car). I also have a Segway (one of those two-wheeled, self-balancing electric vehicles), although mine is especially adapted so the steering column is shorter, meaning the 'S' is missing – making it an 'Egway'.

I'm proud to say my own kids are also adventurous individuals whose experience of being little is proving at least as wonderful as

---

[59] I don't know why, but the Internet Movie Database lists me as an extra. I wish I'd been in it but really, honestly, I promise you I wasn't.
[60] There is an equivalent UK version called the Restricted Growth Association.

my own. To have brought them into this world is by far the greatest privilege that Sam and I could have asked for – something I have to remind myself of after I've discovered Harrison's dismantled my iPhone or while Annabelle's screaming the house down with her friends.

The LPA, founded by legendary little actor Billy Barty (who coined the phrase 'little people' and who played High Aldwin, the village wizard in *Willow*) is a brilliant non-profit organisation that provides support and information to little people under four-foot-ten and their families. There are more than 6,000 members worldwide and their annual convention, which can attract up to 3,000 people, is quite a sight to behold. They've gone from strength to strength in recent years and in 2009 I attended the LPA annual convention in New York to take part in an actor's workshop.

It was being held in a huge Brooklyn hotel where for once the average-sized guests were in the minority. The staff there had very kindly provided some great little touches like steps to use at reception, so we didn't have to stand back from the desk to be seen. Neither did we have to yell to get attention. It was a real pleasure to be able to lean on the desk, have a pleasant chat with the concierge and just check in without having to stare at all the many years' accumulation of chewing gum stuck to the underside of the desk like I usually do.

They also added some steps to the breakfast buffets so we could see what we were choosing, which made a change from playing 'buffet roulette' or having to get the server to list everything (which in New York can stretch to more than sixty items and includes numerous baffling delicacies such as muffulettas, pastry mistas and zucchini bread).

While I was checking in, I turned back and looked across the lobby, which was packed full of little people. Just as I did so an airline pilot (I don't think there are any little ones, not that I know of anyway) and three stewardesses walked in. They were still in full uniform. For them, this must have been a surreal moment. They clearly weren't expecting to see a couple of hundred little people staring back at them.

As they walked uncertainly up to the desk, the captain turned to one of the stewardesses and said, completely deadpan: 'This jet lag's worse than I thought.' LPA members tend to be very enthusiastic people and the LPA itself is very forward-thinking. They make sure that some of the world's foremost medical experts on little people are always on hand, so if you don't yet know what variety you are, then there's a good chance someone there will be able to tell you – as well as help treat some of the little physical aches and pains that are sometimes part of being little. I, for example, have to take good care of my joints as they wear a lot quicker than normal. This provided me with a great excuse to build my very own customised indoor pool and hot tub at home.

I love going to the LPA conference because it provides a rare chance for me to mix with people who share the same perspective; it's a great place to swap stories. It also works as a great match-making event; many, many little couples have found romance at the LPA dinner and dance.

The LPA are all about encouraging little people to make the most of the world. 'It's your planet too,' they say, 'so get out there, enjoy it, embrace all it has to offer!' One evening, staying true to that motto, I went out for a stroll around the local neighbourhood. The hotel itself was wonderful and the street immediately outside was clean and sparkled in the neon lights of posh stores, bars and restaurants. Once I was a couple of blocks further west into Brooklyn, however, I found myself in a nightmarish ghetto where I saw drug deals, cardboard cities and the sort of people who made the gangsters I'd seen in LA look like the Chuckle Brothers. If I'd had my Leprechaun costume on, then I would have fitted right in, but as it was I was attracting no little attention.

As I hurried past one zombie-like individual he whispered, 'Look at the midget, man, look at the midget!' to his friend. I looped back round at the next corner and zipped back to the hotel as fast as I could, wishing I'd brought my Egway.

I'm not bothered by the many different words used to describe little people, although many little people find 'midget' an incredibly offensive word. I want very much to do my 'bit' to raise awareness about little people, to try and reduce the number of startled and awkward reactions people sometimes have when they bump into a little person. It was this that made me say 'Yes' when *BBC Children in Need* asked me to sign up for the reality show *Celebrity Scissorhands*, in which celebrities take over a hairdressing salon and attempt to cut people's hair to raise money for charity.

I had no ambition to be a barber, but I thought if I did this then it might inspire people to try something which they might once have thought was too difficult, or which other people had told them was impossible, or beyond their reach.

Cutting people's hair actually proved to be quite tricky, and not just because of my height. The only practice I had was with my daughter's Play-Doh Mop Top Hair Shop play set and the first time I picked up the scissors they shook in my hands, not the most reassuring of sights for my first vict— . . . er, customer.

Steve Strange, the former Visage front man, had already shaved two people's heads by the time I got going, which was a simple but courageous cut. Customers soon stopped telling Steve to do what he wanted as that meant he would simply give them a number one.

Nothing could have prepared me for the cold-blooded terror I felt when I cut someone's hair for the first time. After a long three weeks, I started to get a bit better but I was never comfortable doing it; my last haircut was just as difficult as my first. One guy who came in worked with problem teenagers and I sent the poor man home looking like he had more than a few problems of his own. I even added insult to injury by cutting out the shape of a pair of scissors on the side of his bonce.

One of the 'famous' clients who came along for a chop was celebrity 'medium' Derek Acorah. I had no idea who he was at the time and so I guessed he had something to do with football and started talking about that. It then seemed as if I was the one with psychic abilities as he'd been a professional football player as a young man.

Derek's hair was pretty neat already and didn't need much cutting, so I stayed around the back. All of my best work was done at the back because no one was able to see what I was doing. When I was round the front I could see their eyes widen in terror at the sight of my shaking scissors and this made it very hard to concentrate. In the end, I trimmed Derek's eyebrows while he started to talk about ghosts and spirits.

'You should talk to Steve Strange,' I suggested, 'I think he's had quite a few paranormal experiences.'

Chris Moyles came along to watch the live final show, as his producer Aled was taking part. I also had the honour of waxing Moyles's sidekick Comedy Dave's backside and I couldn't help but collapse into giggles as he screamed in agony. I signed the wax strip, now resplendent with a thick coating of his bottom hair: 'From a short arse to a hairy arse', and he kept it as a souvenir. I was excused from doing any more 'intimate' waxes, in particular the back, sack and crack, as my face was so close to the action, so to speak, that the BBC wasn't able to show any of it. Thank God for that.

The event was a light-hearted competition. We were judged by Toni and Guy of the well-known hairdressing company and a hairdresser whose name I can't remember (I recall he was *very* tanned with far too many highlights but that doesn't really narrow it down). To my surprise, I finished third out of nine.

I went back as a client the following year and my daughter Annabelle had a go at cutting my hair while Harrison had his chopped by Jessica-Jane Clement from *The Real Hustle*. A look of panic crossed his face about halfway through but he was happy in the end.

The whole *Celebrity Scissorhands* experience was great. I learned loads while I was there – although I haven't touched a pair of scissors since.

Once the show was finished, I treated myself to a nice pair of battery operated hair clippers. I was in the shower when I decided to see if I could use them to trim my own eyebrows, just like I'd done in the salon. I did it without a mirror and it was with no little horror that I looked down and saw, after doing the first eyebrow, that I'd put the clippers on zero, which meant I was now practically missing one eyebrow.

'Kaggernash!'

I had no choice but to do exactly the same thing to the other one so they'd match. This time it was much more difficult as I was now knowingly shaving my other eyebrow off.

Sam stopped what she was doing as I came downstairs and looked at me curiously. 'Have you got an acting job on today?'

'No,' I said, 'why?'

'There's something different about you.'

'Really?'

'Yeah. You look like you've got makeup on.'

'Oh, good grief.'

Sam was paying close attention to my movements at this time because she needed to pull the wool over my eyes for a very special surprise event. On the day in question, Sam had told me we had to be home at a certain time because we were having an important home assessment by someone from the school board. When I say this now it sounds ridiculous, but Harrison was in fact about to start school and so I bought Sam's tall story hook, line and sinker. I even obeyed her orders to spruce myself up, remembering that my dad had done the same thing for me when he successfully got me into Little Chint, my primary school. I don't smarten up for anyone in my own home; in fact it's rare to find me with my trousers on at all.

I noticed there was a bit of a commotion coming from the back garden and saw someone with lots of wild bleached hair and wearing a large brown duffel coat marching towards the house.

'Mr Warwick Davis, you lovely man.'

The crazy hair turned out to belong to comedian and broadcaster *extraordinaire* Justin Lee Collins.

Justin was making *Bring Back . . .* for Channel 4, a show in which he tries to locate people from cult music, TV or film backgrounds to reunite them for a one-off performance or get-together. He was after me for *Bring Back . . . Star Wars*.

When Justin saw my hot tub he immediately suggested we do the interview in there.

'Erm, OK,' I said hesitantly, 'but I don't think you'll get into my spare swimming trunks.'

'That's all right, I'll keep my pants on.' And, thank goodness, he did. I swear he wasn't naked, even though he said so during the programme.

So, despite Sam's best efforts, my trousers were on the floor just five minutes after Justin arrived and we spent the next ninety minutes being poached by the hot tub. By the time we climbed out, our skin was so shrivelled we looked like a pair of Dressillians.[61]

Justin was lovely, full of infectious childlike enthusiasm. When I told him about *Return of the Ewok* I thought he was going to pop with excitement and we watched it together, sipping lots of fruit juice to try and rehydrate. It was the first time I'd seen it in years and the memories came flooding back. That was where it had all started, thanks to good old Nan.[62]

As I saw my eleven-year-old self clowning about with Mark, Harrison, Carrie and so on, I wondered what would have happened if I hadn't made it into *Return of the Jedi*. I'm pretty certain I would have ended up acting one way or another, but life could have been very different. I'm extremely grateful for the way things turned out, which is thanks – in no small part – to my parents, who gave me the best possible start in life.

Justin stayed all day, and seemed to be really enjoying himself, and the fun and games continued long after Annabelle and Harrison returned from school. We stayed in touch after the programme was finished.[63] I liked Justin, he was a charming chap with a king-size heart and I had a brilliant experience going down memory lane with him. Good times!

And I've had a wonderful time going down memory lane here. So much has happened in my life already and I'm barely halfway through. Like so many people I meet, I'm full of hope for the

---

[61] One for the geeks.

[62] She's now haunting her old house, no doubt giving the new owners the willies.

[63] The climax of *Bring Back Star Wars* came when Justin, myself, Kenny Baker (R2-D2), Jeremy Bulloch (Boba Fett) and David Prowse (Darth Vader) met for a reunion in a London nightclub. Carrie Fisher appeared via hologram as Princess Leia. It was all very civilised.

future and, although I'm in no hurry, I'm looking forward to writing part two of my story in another forty years' time.

Just before *Willow* came out, George Lucas took me to one side. He looked me in the eye and said: 'Warwick, when this film comes out, your life is going to change.' He stared me dead in the eye and said, 'If you remember nothing else, just don't let the fame get the better of you. Stay true to yourself.'

George was completely right. Lots of other people have given me all sorts of advice but this is the only thing that has stuck in my mind and is still there twenty-one years later, and it's something I've found surprisingly easy to live by. (Although there has been the odd slip-up – once when some movie fans ran up to me in a London street and bowed down in front of me chanting, 'We're not worthy!' and I agreed with them.)

I still don't believe the hype and remain, despite all my weird and wonderful adventures, my tragedies, failures and successes – much like Willow – firmly me: a son, father, husband and friend.

A case in point occurred a few years ago. I was in London with Sam, Annabelle and Harrison and we were just on our way home to Peterborough when the iPhone rang.

'Warwick!' an American voice yelled excitedly, 'it's Val! I'm in London doing a play, where are you?'

'Wow! Val, hi! Well, I'm in London but we're on our way home, the kids are just about asleep.'

Val insisted we come to his apartment. 'It's my birthday, come on! Just five minutes!'

I looked at Sam. She shrugged. 'OK then, five minutes.'

'Great!'

He gave me the address, which was right on the banks of the Thames near Battersea. I was pretty excited and curious to see him again, it had been some years since we'd last met. He was in

London starring in a West End play, *The Postman Always Rings Twice*.

He was in a huge and extraordinarily beautiful modern apartment, the likes us mere mortals never get to see, let alone live in. He grabbed me as I arrived. 'Where's your family?' he asked.

He insisted I bring them up and wouldn't take no for an answer, so I did. The party was amazing, it was full of famous folk; Kevin Spacey was at the piano singing a jazzy number. It was utterly surreal to see Harrison in his Babygros in Val's huge arms. 'Remind you of anything, peck?' he joked.

'Hey, don't call me peck!' I laughed.

'Peck, peck, peck, peck!'

We stayed for five minutes and then I insisted we had to go since it was a school night. Val almost blocked the door so we couldn't leave and said, 'Wait just a second, I've got to give you something,' and vanished. He ran upstairs and returned a minute later with his entire uncut birthday cake and a picture he'd painted.

'Here, these are for you.'

'I couldn't . . .'

'Seriously, take them!'

'It's been amazing to see you again,' I said, staggering under the weight of the Battenberg and Val's artwork as we left.

'Likewise, kid.'

As we headed back down in the lift after our very sudden and surreal glimpse of Hollywood in London, and as Kevin Spacey sang 'Fly me to the Moon' to a room full of A-list stars and champagne-drinking artists and multimillionaires, I looked at Sam over Val's giant birthday cake, which I was struggling to hold.

'I don't know about you,' I said with a sigh, 'but I could murder a cuppa and a chocolate digestive.'

Justin Lee Collins invaded the Davis household for *Bring Back Star Wars*. The kids loved him – and so did I. You lovely man!

Annabelle at Jedi training school.

The Davis family at a *Star Wars Weekends* in Walt Disney World.

Of all the places I've been in the world, my favourite place for a family holiday has to be the Lake District.

Sam and I treasure
every moment
with Annabelle
and Harrison.

Harrison attended his first
premiere in 2009. It was for
*Harry Potter and the Half-Blood
Prince* in New York.

Epilogue
The Moral of the Story

Some time ago, we had a decorator working in our house. He whistled incessantly while he painted, which irritated me no end. It was one of those random up-and-down, this-tune-is-going-nowhere whistles. He'd done several jobs for us before and we'd got on quite well. This time, however, he seemed to be a bit standoffish.

Eventually, I couldn't let it lie any longer and asked him straight out: 'Is something the matter?'

'Well,' he said hesitantly in a strong Welsh accent. 'I had a run-in with one of you lot the other day.'

'A run-in?' I repeated. 'With –'

'One of you lot, yeah.'

I let the term 'you lot' go – for now.

'What happened?'

'Well, I was doing some work down near the public swimming pool and had just parked when this little guy came out of nowhere and drove straight into the back of my van.'

'I was there, I saw it,' said Sam, 'that was the day of the swimming championships for the World Dwarf Games.'

I know, I'd never even heard of them either and couldn't quite believe it when I did. I'm not a massive sports fan and so they had somewhat passed me by, but I was delighted to learn that my home town was playing host to 200 competitors from around the world, in what was essentially the Olympics for little people.

It turned out that one of the competitors had been about to

drive off when the bolts that fastened the adapter pedals for the accelerator, brake and clutch in their car came loose and they fell off, landing on the accelerator. The car took off across the car park, the driver helpless to do anything but grip the wheel in terror and to bravely stop his vehicle by crashing into the first thing he could – which happened to be our whistling decorator's van.

'Well, you needn't tar us all with the same brush,' I told him sternly. 'If there's one thing I've learned in life, it's always make sure my nuts are tight.'

The final word
goes to my aged Aunt Jan

A SMALL TRIBUTE

You accepted the hand that life dealt you
And stayed well ahead of the game
With tenacity, humour and courage
And with your endeavours found fame.

Although being vertically challenged,
In the eyes of the world you walk tall
With a very remarkable talent,
There's so much you've achieved being small.

Metaphorically you have climbed mountains,
Though sometimes the going was hard,
By resolve, and your great perseverance,
You deservedly hold the trump card.

Aha! So I did take my head off after all! I found this
photo just as the book was going to press (see page 74).

Acknowledgements

First off, I must acknowledge Sam Harrison at Aurum for his unique and passionate vision for *Size Matters Not* and for turning it into his obsession – as he recently said: 'I've watched *Labyrinth* far more times than is healthy.'

Similarly, I'd like to express my gratitude to Kris Hollington for his editorial wizardry and to his photographer wife Nina for shooting me, metaphorically of course. Surely they are the Han Solo and Princess Leia of the publishing world.

My literary agent Andrew Lownie provided me with much effective Yoda-like counsel, delivered at light speed.

I'd also like to show my appreciation to all the young Jedis who used the Force to hunt through archives all across the galaxy, supplying me with photos which have delighted, amazed and embarrassed: Chris Holm and Tina Mills from Lucasfilm, Tracy Ames, Chela Johnson and Lindsey Boccia from Lionsgate, Julie Heath from Warner Brothers, Margaret Adamic from Disney and my Mum from Sussex.

Much gratitude to Melissa Smith at Aurum, David Welch of SS Graphics and Rob Brown at Saxon Graphics for all their work in assembling and laying out the book's dozens and dozens of pictures, not to mention Clare Stacey at Head Design for her work on the jacket. Many thanks also to Gilvanio Bragagnolo and WAES for providing the studios for the photo shoot – and for returning my lightsaber after I left it there (though it did need a new set of batteries when I got it back).

Many other people have generously provided me with their time and input during the writing of this book, especially: George Lucas, Ron Howard, Ricky Gervais, Kenny Baker, Mark Hamill, David Heyman, Lynne Hale, David Baron, Vanessa Davies, David Iskra, Derek Maki, Daniel Balaam (even though he's an idiot), Nicky Melina, Kristen Waidalowsk, Oliver Moore, Lisa Blackman, Deidre and David Milner.

Thank you all for toiling long and hard to bring my little autobiography to fruition. You have passed the Hogwarts 'Nastily Exhausting Wizarding Tests' with flying colours, and your certificates are in the post.